Contemporary East Asian Visual Cultures, Societies and Politics

This series brings together diverse perspectives on present-day relationships between East Asian visual cultures, societies and politics. Its scope extends to visual cultures produced, disseminated and received/consumed in East Asia – comprising North and South Korea, Mongolia, Japan, mainland China, Hong Kong, Macau, and Taiwan – as well as related diasporas world-wide, and to all aspects of culture expressed through visual images, including across perceived boundaries between high and popular culture and the use of traditional and contemporary media. Taken into critical account are cultural, social and political ecologies currently shaped by geopolitical borders across the East Asia region in addition to their varied intersections with an increasingly trans-cultural world. The series emphasizes the importance of visual cultures in the critical investigation of contemporary socio-political issues relating to, for example, identity, social inequality, decoloniality and the environment. The editors welcome contributions from early career and established researchers.

More information about this series at
https://link.springer.com/bookseries/16532

Sophia Kidd

Culture Paves The New Silk Roads

palgrave
macmillan

Sophia Kidd
Sichuan University
Chengdu, China

ISSN 2662-7701 ISSN 2662-771X (electronic)
Contemporary East Asian Visual Cultures, Societies and Politics
ISBN 978-981-16-8573-6 ISBN 978-981-16-8574-3 (eBook)
https://doi.org/10.1007/978-981-16-8574-3

Cover credit: Xia Yuan

This Palgrave Macmillan imprint is published by the registered company Springer Nature Singapore Pte Ltd.
The registered company address is: 152 Beach Road, #21-01/04 Gateway East, Singapore 189721, Singapore

To my father, who reminded me of more things on heaven and earth than are dreamt of in my philosophy

Preface

I

Oh, the Five Talents work in concert
and of the Five, Water's virtue is greatest
the Yangzi flows from its source at Mt. Min
a cupful to begin with
it flows through the Luo and Mei
merging myriad streams in Ba and Liang
crossing Wu Gorge at mad speed
rising at the river ford beginning to swell
when churning full as the sea
leading both Han and Si
converging Huai and Xiang
swallowing Yuan and Li
drawing out the Ju and Zhang
the source splits into Ju and Lai
diverging nine ways at Xunyang
pummeling Mt. Chi'an
submerging Chaisang in waves.

II

Teeming flow enmeshed
overtaking brooks and ditches
it shows its divinity, converges at Jiangdu
merges with many others headed East for the sea

filling up Five Lakes with its limitless self
irrigating Lake Taihu with the sound of a roar
flowing long and hard through the Six Provinces
commanding even these lands so far South
hewing a boundary between Chinese and outsider
emboldening distance between Heaven and Earth.
—River *Fu*[1]

1700 years earlier than Chinese president Xi Jinping, Chinese scholar and writer Guo Pu (276–324 CE) presented a grand narrative for the Chinese empire in which he described a Community of Common Destiny. Guo Pu's ontology was made not of countries, banks and global forces, but rather a river source and its terminus. In describing the flow of the Yangzi River, Guo Pu enlisted material, spiritual, and cosmic elements pulled from both popular and elite maps available at the time. He mapped out these landmarks and elements in the well-known *fu* prose-poem, the 'River *Fu*'. This *fu* describes a Chinese spiritual legacy flowing from one end of the Chinese empire to the other. The poet used an extremely erudite language of an archaic Han dynasty style, to express how the Yangzi River incorporated other rivers and flowed through major cities, placing special emphasis upon what the river nurtured, articulating the spirit and realm of the Chinese people. Today, Chinese President Xi Jinping's remarks on nurturing a Community of Common Destiny, although spoken originally about Asia; refer not to a closed system within Asia but to the world at large. Xi's grand narrative and signature project is the Belt and Road Initiative, originally known by its literal translation, One Belt One Road (*Yidai yilu* 一带一路), and more popularly referred to as the New Silk Roads. The New Silk Roads have grown into a world-idea which ties all the civilizations together in a Community of Common Destiny. The Chinese have historically named this world-idea '*Tianxia* 天下' (all under heaven).

Guo Pu's *fu* reflects a political economy of Chinese culture that is still in practice today, and which we will talk about at length in this book.

[1] This and subsequent translations in this text are by the author, unless otherwise specified. This translation is a rough colloquial translation which leaves out the careful studies and commentary made by David R. Knechtges in his own translation of Guo Pu's 'River Fu.' Cf: Tong Xiao, *Wen Xuan: Or Selections of Refined Literature*, trans. David Knechtges, Princeton Library of Asian Translations (Princeton University Press; Taipei: SMC Publishing, 1990), 320–350.

The 'River Fu' is a cultural product; a prose-poem written by a court official commissioned with the work of legitimizing the refugee Jin court. Prior to the presentation of this prose-poem to Emperor Sima Rui at the Eastern Jin court in 316 CE, the Jin had suffered the humiliation of being dethroned and purged from the northern capitals of first Luoyang and then Chang'an (present day Xi'an). They had been pushed out of the Central Plains of China, out of all lands north of the Yangzi River by the Xiongnu and the Xianbei peoples who then ruled the north for the next four centuries in a period known as the 16 Northern Kingdoms. The newly established Eastern Jin court poised itself anew to rule *Tianxia*, this time from the newly named southeastern seaboard capital city of Jiankang (present day Nanjing). In other *fu* by Guo Pu, such as the "Suburban Ritual *Fu*," the poet describes emissaries from foreign cultures coming to pay tribute, standing in their allotted space for the ritual, wearing their exotic costumes. The political economy of culture in China today is much the same as it was in Guo Pu's own times, with tastes dictating that art and literature serve the state, and thus the people. We will be discussing this in much greater detail in Chapters Three through Five of this book.

There are similarities between the China back in 316 CE, when the River *Fu* was written; and 2015, when Xi gave a speech in Baoa, in which he highlighted a Community of Common Destiny.[2] China today is rebuilding itself, much as it was back then. After the 'Century of Humiliation,' and massive internal restructuring, China has recovered politically and economically after the Great Divergence marked by the Opium Wars, when the country lost its geoeconomic, geopolitical, and geocultural supremacy.[3] Guo Pu spent a good deal of his life watching his Western Jin empire crumble, and spent years on the road as a refugee, along with the entire Jin court and population of the people. Xiongnu tribes from the north had overrun all lands around the Yellow River, and the Western Jin court fell, fleeing to the doorsteps of ruling classes nearer to the Yangzi River, in the South. They set up a new Eastern Jin court there in a capital

[2] "Full Text of Chinese President's Speech at Boao Forum for Asia—Xinhua: English.News.Cn," accessed October 4, 2021, http://www.xinhuanet.com//english/2015-03/29/c_134106145.htm.

[3] See: Kenneth Pomeranz, *The Great Divergence: China, Europe, and the Making of the Modern World Economy*, The Princeton Economic History of the Western World (Princeton, NJ: Princeton University Press, 2000).

they renamed Jiankang, known today as Nanjing. With a whole new physical map of China, there was pushback from ruling aristocratic families of the region, who were skeptical of the new Eastern Jin emperor Sima Rui's claim to power.

Thus, Guo Pu's 'River *Fu*' was written as a cultural narrative meant to legitimize Eastern Jin rule throughout marginal regions of Southwestern, Central and Southeastern China. These regions had their own intellectual, philosophical, local historical, and religious histories. Guo Pu painted a picture with words that illustrated the dimensions in which these histories and traditions all revolved around one thing, the Yangzi River. Thus, Guo Pu grafted the northern mythos with its material and non-tangible cultures, which revolved around the northern Yellow River; onto a new cultural 'map' or narrative about China's culture. It worked well, and the Eastern Jin went on to rule for over a hundred years.

Segueing back once again to today; we see that China's cultural authority has yet to be recognized outside of Asia. Xi's new narrative of a Common Destiny which revolves around the New Silk Roads, tracing back to the ancient Silk Road, is a modern-day prose-poem, a cultural imaginary articulated in political language, swapping out rhyme and meter for rhetoric and talking points. There is no single river long enough to nurture lands as far away from China as Duisburg, Germany, Djibouti in Africa, or San Paulo in Brazil. However, there is a network of global trading routes, the cultural imaginary of which embraces all these lands and more, and it is known as One Belt One Road, Belt and Road Initiative, or the New Silk Roads.

There are mixed messages about what Chinese culture is, and much of this has to do with the high degree of interaction between politics and culture in China, which in turn has to do with the high interaction of politics and economy in China. China works in gestalts, in wholes which are larger than the sum of their parts. Therefore, anytime one tries to look separately at either the politics, economics, or culture of China, the real picture slips out of view, because the real picture is systemic and *relational*. This book is written from within China, and its point of reference is that of one on the ground, interacting with the cultural and fine arts sectors of China daily throughout the past decade. While reading Chinese cultural messaging as it appears outside of China, I notice a huge disconnect between China and its many audiences. If culture is a performance, then China's acts of *parole* are often being misinterpreted.[4]

With so many schisms and fractures in China's cultural identity; the binding agent missing is geocultural power; the ability to win the hearts and minds of people throughout Asia and the rest of the world; without relying primarily on, political, military or even economic force.[5] When Guo Pu wrote the 'River *Fu*' seventeen centuries ago, he succeeded in creating a literary map which embedded not only the refugee Han Chinese of the north, but also the hosting Han Chinese of the South into its mythopoetic of a new China. At this moment in today's world, Xi Jinping does not have a singular writer who will legitimate his claim as the architect of a global Community of Common Destiny. He has, however, an entire cultural industry which the Chinese Communist Party has control of, at regional, national and international levels. This industry is tasked with the job of winning the hearts and minds of people all over the world. China's cultural and creative industries operate through public and private spheres, and when they operate through the latter, they serve as a kind of private-sector cultural diplomacy. Both public and private sector cultural diplomacy are crucial elements in China's attempt to construct a *Tianxia* narrative which spans both time and space in such a way that it embraces the global imagination. The New Silk Roads constitute this narrative, and it needs both public and private sector cultural diplomacy to lay down its tracks. If culture is not given its due, then tracks, shipping lane, dry port, shipping port, mine, gas pipeline, and road may prove unsustainable and risk prone. The populations, not just the governments, of over one hundred and forty collaborating New Silk Road nations must understand and accept the overall narrative of this massive project. This book explores the role that culture does and will continue to play in the construction of not just the New Silk Roads, but also a Community of Common Destiny.

[4] See: J. L. Austin, *How to Do Things with Words (Second Edition)* (Oxford: Clarendon Press, 1962).

[5] See: Tim Winter, *Geocultural Power: China's Quest to Revive the Silk Roads for the Twenty-First Century* (Chicago: University of Chicago Press, 2019), https://doi.org/10.7208/chicago/9780226658490.001.0001.

Contents

Abbreviations

AIIB	Asian Infrastructure Investment Bank
APEC	Asia-Pacific Economic Cooperation
ASEAN	Association of Southeast Asian Nations
BCIM	Bangladesh-China-India-Myanmar Corridor
BRF	Belt and Road Forum
BRI	Belt and Road Initiative
BRICS	Brazil, Russia, India, China, and South Africa
CADGAT	Central Asia Data-Gathering and Analysis Team
CASS	Chinese Academy of Social Sciences
CCECC	China Civil Engineering Construction Corporation
CCP	Chinese Communist Party
CCTV	China Central Television
CEE	Central and Eastern Europe
CGG	China Goes Global
CGTN	China Global Television Network
CITIC	China International Trust Investment Corporation
CLEC	Center for Language Education and Cooperation
CNOOC	China National Offshore Oil Corporation
CNPC	China National Petroleum Corporation
COSCO	China Ocean Shipping Company, Limited
COVID-19	Corona Virus Disease of 2019
CPEC	China-Pakistan Economic Corridor
CSCEC	China State Construction Engineering Corporation
DCI	Development Cooperation Instrument
DIFTZ	Djibouti International Free Trade Zone
ETIM	East Turkestan Islamic Movement

EU	European Union
FIFA	Federal Internationale de Football Association
FOMO	Fear of Missing Out
ICRC	International Committee of the Red Cross
IMF	International Monetary Fund
ISSAD	Institute of South-South Cooperation and Development
NDB	New Development Bank
NDRC	National Development and Reform Commission
OBOR	One Belt One Road
OGCI	Oil and Gas Methane Alliance
OSCE	Organization for Security and Co-operation
RCEP	Regional Comprehensive Economic Partnership
SCO	Shanghai Cooperation Organization
SEO	State-Owned Enterprise
SICAS	Study in China Application Services
SME	Small and Medium-Sized Enterprises
SMG	State Mobilized Globalization
SRCBI	Silk Road Community Building Initiative
SREB	Silk Road Economic Belt
TCM	Traditional Chinese Medicine
UNCTAD	United Nations Conference on Trade and Development
UNDP	United Nations Development Programme
UNESCO	United Nations Education, Science and Cultural Organization
UNICEF	United National International Children's Emergency Fund
USAFRICOM	US-Africa Command
WDP	Western Development Program
WHO	World Health Organization
WTO	World Trade Organization

List of Figures

List of Tables

CHAPTER 1

Introduction

> To build a community of common destiny, we need to seek win-win cooperation and common development. Our friends in Southeast Asia say that the lotus flowers grow taller as the water rises. Our friends in Africa say that if you want to go fast, walk alone; and if you want to go far, walk together. Our friends in Europe say that a single tree cannot block the chilly wind. And Chinese people say that when big rivers have water, the small ones are filled; and when small rivers have water, the big ones are filled. All these sayings speak to one same truth, that is, only through win-win cooperation can we make big and sustainable achievements that are beneficial to all. The old mindset of zero-sum game should give way to a new approach of win-win and all-win cooperation.
>
> *Xi Jinping, March 28, 2015*
>
> *"Towards a Community of Common Destiny and a New Future for Asia."*[1]

Two years after Chinese President Xi Jinping officially announced the Belt and Road Initiative in Astana, Kazakhstan and Indonesia, he gave this speech at the Boao Forum for Asia, an annual meeting of government, business, and academic leaders of nations all over the world. The theme of

[1] "Full Text of Chinese President's Speech at Boao Forum for Asia—Xinhua | English.News.Cn."

S. Kidd, *Culture Paves The New Silk Roads*, Contemporary East Asian Visual Cultures, Societies and Politics, https://doi.org/10.1007/978-981-16-8574-3_1

that year's Boao conference was, "Asia's New Future: Toward a Community of Common Destiny (CCD), and sixteen countries were represented, including Armenia, Australia, Austria, China, Indonesia, Kazakhstan, Malaysia, Nepal, the Netherlands, Qatar, Russia, Sri Lanka, Sweden, Thailand, Uganda, and Zambia. Fast forward to 2021, again in Boao, a speech delivered by video focused on global governance, a seemingly appropriate developmental focus for Xi's global vision for a Community of Common Destiny.[2] More than sixty countries were present for the Boao Forum, with keynote speeches given by important figures from the global governance community, including Jin Liqun, president of the Asian Infrastructure Investment Bank (AIIB), Liu Zhenmin, UN undersecretary-general for economic and social affairs, Vladimir Norov, secretary general of the Shanghai Cooperation Organization (SCO), and Marcos Troyjo, New Development Bank President. The phrase "Community of Common Destiny" was coined publicly for the first time in 2007 by Hu Jintao at the 17th National Party Congress report in referring to cross-strait relations between mainland China and Taiwan.[3] President Xi has taken this message of a Community of Common Destiny as the narrative rudder for his flagship project, the Belt and Road Initiative. Indeed, in May of 2017, we see Xi using this narrative, which we earlier saw at the Boao Forum in 2015, now reinforced at the inaugural Belt and Road Forum for International Cooperation, a forum of 29 countries hosted by China in the nation's capital of Beijing.[4]

The crux of the CCD project is to stress what in Chinese is known as *he er bu tong* 和而不同, which translates literally as 'harmonious but different,' and bears some similarities as well as differences in comparison to 'E pluribus unum,' ('Out of many, one'), the traditional motto of the United States. *He er bu tong* derives from the Confucian Analects, a book of sayings by Confucius 孔子 (551–479 BCE) compiled in the

[2] "Boao Forum for Asia Annual Conference 2021 Holds Opening Ceremony—Xinhua | English.News.Cn," accessed October 6, 2021, http://www.xinhuanet.com/english/2021-04/20/c_139893192.htm.

[3] "Can China Build a Community of Common Destiny?—The Diplomat," accessed October 6, 2021, https://thediplomat.com/2013/11/can-china-build-a-community-of-common-destiny/.

[4] Denghua Zhang, "The Concept of 'Community of Common Destiny' in China's Diplomacy: Meaning, Motives and Implications: Concept of Community of Common Destiny," *Asia & the Pacific Policy Studies* 5, no. 2 (May 2018): 196–207, https://doi.org/10.1002/app5.231.

Spring and Autumn period by the philosopher's students. In a gloss by late Eastern Han (25–220 CE) dynasty and early Cao Wei (220–266 CE) period philosopher and politician He Yan 何宴 (196–249 CE), we find an interpretation of this statement by Confucius that refers to the ability of a *junzi* 君子 (gentleman, or cultivated person) to maintain composure whilst acknowledging difference. Another hundred years on, during the Western Jin (265–316 CE) dynasty, poet and writer Xia Houzhan 夏侯湛 (c. 243–c. 291 CE) spoke of *he er bu tong* in terms of the *chaoyin* 朝隐, or court hermit. The court hermit was unique to the period of of the Wei and Jin period, as well as of the Six Dynasties period, both periods after the fall of the illustrious Han empire in the early third century. This period of disunity continued for nearly four hundred years, consisting of the Three Kingdoms period, then the 6 Southern Dynasties and 16 Northern Kingdoms. It wasn't until 581 CE that the Sui Dynasty unified China for the first time since the Eastern Han fell apart in 220 CE. Throughout these hundreds of years, political leaders and poets alike had a hard time keeping their head on their shoulders, as with the rapid shifts in political climate and going ideology of the day, beheadings and other uncomfortable tortures befell many. Thus, the court hermit practised dissent whilst toeing the line. *He er bu tong* refers to one's ability to command respect and abide harmoniously with others with whom you may not agree. In his 2015 Boao Forum speech which we cite at the opening of this chapter, Xi quoted Mencius (c. 372–c. 289 CE), a Confucian philosopher living two hundred years after Confucius as saying, "Things are born to be different." Xi then went on to say:

> Civilizations are only unique, and no one is superior to the other. There needs to be more exchange and dialogue among civilizations and development models, so that each could draw on the strength of the other and all could thrive and prosper by way of mutual learning and common development. Let us promote inter-civilization exchanges to build bridges of friendship for our people, drive human development and safeguard peace of the world.[5]

President Xi's call for regional and global cooperation is the master narrative for the Belt and Road Initiative. What we have seen unfold from

[5] "Full Text of Chinese President's Speech at Boao Forum for Asia—Xinhua | English.News.Cn."

this narrative over the past 8 years may tell a different story, as antagonistic narratives are being superimposed upon it, spinning its trajectory, and complicating its plot. One focus of this book is to examine the ways in which a Community of Common Destiny is being cultivated, both as narrative and praxis. Cultivation requires practise and study. Mistakes will be made, indeed mistakes are being made, as China meddles in the affairs of over one hundred and thirty nations thus far, building infrastructure, commandeering resources, changing finance structure, and building surveillance systems in the sky, under the earth, and beneath the sea. These actions are creating a stir amongst the peoples whose lives they effect, and these people are giving their feedback, either violently in public protest, or peacefully in their local, regional, and national media. China's ability to field this feedback, to study it, and make alterations to its course will anticipate further issues before they arise as conflagrations. All of this will determine the success and future of China's Belt and Road Initiative. This book examines the role cultural activities, exchanges and diplomacy all play in conjunction with policy, infrastructure, trade, and finance along the New Silk Roads. Without culture smoothing out rough surfaces and laying down high quality slurry seal, if you'll allow me the crude metaphor, roads that are built will be washed away in the tsunami of Western media. Cries of China-threat and Asian hate are as old as yellow-peril ideologies from the olden days of US railroad construction, and early industrial and colonialist journalism. Dragon-slaying rhetoric as an ideology is only too happy to point out the mistakes and ills of China's new bid to change the world order. Countries in power now will not give over power easily, and will make great effort to stop China from bringing the other half of the human race into the fold of global governance, from providing the Global South with public goods they have never had access to, and from forming a Community of Common Destiny.

This book uses an integrated culture-based approach to studying Chinese domestic and international political economies of culture in New Silk Road (NSR) regions. This approach reconceptualizes People-to-People bonds as not mere rhetorical flourish, but rather at the core of NSR policy implementation. People-to-People bonds are the alpha and omega of this global initiative, as the *raison d'etre* and historical exegesis of this global initiative will have first and foremost to do with people. In this approach to culture and geo-political economies, the author positions herself within the contemporary arts and culture sectors of China, with training in Classical Chinese literature and history. With the Chinese

Classical canon being as rich in history as it is, and the Chinese historical method being so geographically based; this book is concerned with space, and with flows that connect spaces between China and Europe, Africa, Latin America, the Middle East, Southern Asia, Southeastern Asia, as well as East Asia.

Chapters 2 through 5 are research based, balancing Chinese and Western points of view in discussing the Belt and Road Initiative's People-to-People (P2P) pillar. Chapter 2 researches the basic framework, geography and financing of the initiative, and most research explores primary sources such as speeches, manuscripts, research articles, official and trade reports, case studies, dissertations, news reports, and online sources including video documentaries. This overview of the New Silk Roads ends with a discussion of its financing structures, and this is where we begin to focus on the relationship between power and discourse in the context of geopolitical, geoeconomic, and geocultural power. This discussion of geocultural power is strongly informed by Tim Winter's important book *Geocultural Power*, which is a fascinating study of the role of cultural heritage and other cultural exchange and diplomacy projects in the building of the New Silk Roads.[6] While Winter does a thorough job of discussing the role of cultural heritage in China's geocultural power-forming, he does not spend as much connecting this with NSR's fifth pillar objectives. Nor does he explore to the extent that this book does the role of cultural and creative industries outside of the public sector, especially in the contemporary fine arts sector. Chapter 2 ends with a discussion of how geopolitical and geoeconomic power work in a way of 'mutual arising' with geocultural power, pointing out China's need to bootstrap a more positive image onto the world arena.

Chapter 3 focuses on a typology of P2P connections, and it is here that we begin to create space for discussing grassroots policy influence, private sector investment, and alternative cultural narratives such as found in avant-garde creative sectors. Once this seed has been sewn, Chapter 4 then presents a very brief survey of political economies of culture, balancing the discussion between Euro-American and Chinese political economic histories. The main point here is to emphasize the appropriation of culture as a sub-category of political economy in China; and the severing of not only culture from political economy, but also

[6] Tim Winter, *Geocultural Power*.

politics from economics in the Euro-American tradition. While Chapter 4 focuses on the mechanism of cultural export as a tool of soft power, or as a generator of geocultural power, as the very crux of P2P connections; in Chapter 5 we observe how culture behaves or performs internationally when directed by the Chinese state. A comparison is drawn to avant-garde cultural product, which is one of the relatively few Chinese cultural exports retaining and even adding value outside of China. This discussion draws upon some of the ideas surrounding the ideas of translation-appropriation and cultural parallax as developed in Paul Gladston's book, *Contemporary Chinese Art, Aesthetic Modernity and Zhang Peili: Towards a Critical Contemporaneity*. Looking at the appropriation-translation of culture as a sub-category of political economy in China, we see that "persistent translations-appropriations of artistic thinking and practice between 'China' and West' have resulted in an open-ended series of refractions (diffraction) of meaning suspending the categorical presences of both."[7] We look at how these diffractions of meaning play out in international art markets, and how these plays inform China's branding of the New Silk Roads as a cultural matrix reshaping the world's values and markets. In Chapter 6, we look more closely at the exception of avant-garde Chinese art as a very successful cultural export, and explore how artists and museum directors in Southwest China are both helped and hurt by New Silk Roads arts infrastructure being built in the region. This last chapter of Part I in the book is based upon field research conducted in Chengdu and Chongqing, China in 2017. These findings were presented at the British Museum later that same year. This last chapter as well as all other discussion of contemporary art in this book also draw from a decade of experience spent in the region researching, curating, and writing about contemporary art.

Chapters 2 through 5 analyse and draw discussion from both primary sources, such as white papers, transcriptions of speeches, lectures, and news reporting; as well as secondary sources which engage such sources with discussion and analysis of their own. Chapter 6 draws mainly upon field research consisting in interviews, the research residency mentioned, as well as the surveys and symposium transcripts which arose out of that residency. All of these sources, from the interviews to the survey and symposium, were conducted or written in the Chinese language. Even in

[7] Paul Gladston, *Contemporary Chinese Art, Aesthetic Modernity and Zhang Peili: Towards a Critical Contemporaneity* (Bloomsbury Methuen Drama, 2019), 38.

cases where the interviewee could speak English with me, we decided that my level of Chinese language proficiency would expedite communication more so than if we spoke in English. My goal was for the interviewee to communicate as comfortably as possible, and thus interviews were always held in a time and place of the interviewee's choosing. The symposium did require all participants to travel to the Luxehills Museum, and thus participants were removed from their work environments, but they did so at their own choosing. In all cases, I made my best effort to not only speak in the interviewee's language, but to adopt my interviewee's frame of cultural reference in contextualising my questions as well as their answers. Having lived in China for nearly two decades, one realises how much is lost in translation, and in order to arrive at better mutual understanding with my subject, much can be done to regain what is lost through logical, rhetorical, and cultural reframing.

Chapters 7 through 10 are primarily desk-research-based, using primary sources such as government publications, public records, historical and statistical documents, business documents, and technical and trade journals, as well as a good deal of literature and theory in these fields. Information on the actual workings of People-to-People programs in New Silk Regions outside of China is sparse, and while the Chinese news sources releasing official Chinese news on this subject are informative, they tend to characterise top-down government organised and implemented programming. Information on private sector and public–private partnerships in places like Syria and Tehran are not readily available, and can only be pieced together through extensive research into the creative and cultural internet spheres of these localities. It is in this sense that this book is mainly suggesting a research trajectory. We have mapped out a trajectory and looked for tendencies along these trajectories, hoping that other scholars will look further into this, to further explore People-to-People programs arising in an entrepreneurial and enterprising manner to benefit both China and its collaborating regions along the New Silk Road.

Chapter 7 explores New Silk Road cities, discussing how China's political, economic, and cultural influences evoke a rhizomatic geography of New Silk Road nodes. After diving deep into the local arts ecology of China's Southwestern New Silk Region in Chapter 6, we pull back out for a long shot of sixteen NSR urban cultural centers, fifteen of which are outside of China. This chapter will attempt to fill a void created by overemphasis in the world media as well as in scholarship upon the first four pillars of China's New Silk Roads, namely the pillars of policy, infrastructure, trade, and finance. We will do this by tracking China's fifth pillar People-to-People development in major urban cultural centers along the New Silk Roads, including: Beijing, China, Islamabad, Pakistan, Ankara and Istanbul, Turkey, Riyadh, Saudi Arabia, Damuscus, Syria, Jerusalem, Astana, Kazakhstan, Moscow, Russia, Bishkek, Kyrgyzstan, Dubai, United Arab Emirates, Kuala Lumpur, Malaysia, Djibouti, Djibouti, and Duisburg, Germany.

Chapter 8, then, continues building out the space created in Chapter 3; wherein private sector and public–private partnerships are operating on grassroots levels to foster indigenous voices and creative practices. This happens in some cases because of and in others, despite arts and cultural infrastructure put in place by New Silk Road P2P policy. We revisit the notion of the 'spatial fix,' as set forth in Chapter 4 as an ideal conceptual framework for understanding the New Silk Roads, and discuss the cultural components of this spatial fix. With an emphasis upon private-sector creative and cultural industry development as a set of best practises, especially when working in conjunction with public sector cultural programming, we turn our attention towards the younger generations of China's population. This chapter relies, as with other chapters in this book, upon desk research and analysis of secondary sources. However, we also work with primary data again in this chapter, bringing forth research I have done teaching a course on the role of culture in the New Silk Roads to large groups of Chinese university undergraduates in Chengdu, China. Presentations by students on Chinese soft power, cultural production, as well as on language service and dissemination as parts of fifth pillar development are highlighted in this chapter.

Chapter 9 discusses how New Silk Road futures can be optimised. Given the amount of development that has already been achieved across the five pillars of the New Silk Roads, we determine that the future of the world is one with the New Silk Roads in it. Five years ago, first world nations and the leaders that speak on their behalf could have made moves to counteract China's bid for global governance. However, with the isolationism in this period on the part of the US and UK until quite recently, and with the trend of Western media not taking the New Silk Roads quite seriously enough, this massive international infrastructural rerouting of world supply chains has crept up on the Global North, quite unawares. While the US-Biden administration is scrambling to unite allies in counteracting the effects of the Belt and Road Initiative, and the G7 have proposed an allegedly greener more sustainable plan of its own with the Build Back Better World (B3W) program, these efforts will have to be expedited with great care and coordination in order to make a dent in China's New Silk Roads.

In the meantime, the number one dent that can be made in the New Silk Roads is the same dent China has been banging out since its Century of Humiliation ended after World War II—the dent of 'China-threat' and Asian-hate. This last chapter of our book outlines key nodal areas of the 21st Century Maritime Silk Road and strategic areas of the overland Silk Road Economic Belt to be developed culturally by China through fifth pillar People-to-People development. Through geocultural development stemming in these nodal and strategic areas, China may be able to illuminate its aims and objectives, readjust to public feedback, and explain more clearly on its own discursive terms what it means by a Community of Common Destiny, and what role the New Silk Roads play in this destiny. We also examine how each of the types of P2P described in earlier chapters compare in effectiveness, looking at top-down versus bottom-up grassroots People-to-People programming, and at two types of the latter, namely supplementary and complementary P2P. Chapter 10, then, is our concluding chapter in which we review our main points, arguments, and discoveries. As New Silk Road studies cover so much ground, and work across so many disciplines, with new articles and books appearing daily to reflect rapidly changing conditions, climates, and perspectives, this book can only serve as a brief introduction for each area of research it presents. From cultural diplomacy and international affairs, to cultural political economics and contemporary Chinese art, this study of how culture creates inroads for infrastructure and trade is but a cursory one. I look forward to others delving more deeply into areas I have only been able to touch upon, and to experts doing a thorough job where I have performed mere sketches.

CHAPTER 2

An Overview of the New Silk Roads

Buttressed against two dates; September and October of 2013 at Nazarbayev University in Astana and at Indonesian parliament, respectively; Chinese President Xi Jinping announced first the overland Silk Road Economic Belt and later the Twenty-first Century Maritime Silk Road. These New Silk Roads are an expanded iteration of a network of trade routes conceived separately by China and its competitors in the region, Japan, India, and Australia. These competitors have been in talks with the US to build an alternative to the Belt and Road Initiative, an Indo-Pacific strategy which would deepen cooperation amongst regional democracies in a bid to contain China's own developments in the Asia–Pacific region.[1] The most developed of these Indo-Pacific strategies at present sees the US engaged with India in building a 'New Silk Road' to counter China's move for consolidating power. As of 2019, India had withdrawn any commitment to the Bangladesh-China-India-Myanmar (BCIM) branch of China's BRI's Overland Economic Belt, leading to BCIM not being included as one of 35 planned corridors announced at the April, 2019 2nd Belt and Road Forum (BRF). Later that year, however, agreements were made between the four participating

[1] "Australia, U.S., India and Japan in Talks to Establish Belt and Road Alternative: Report," *Reuters*, February 18, 2018, sec. Business News, https://www.reuters.com/article/us-china-beltandroad-quad-idUSKCN1G20WG.

S. Kidd, *Culture Paves The New Silk Roads*,
Contemporary East Asian Visual Cultures, Societies and Politics,
https://doi.org/10.1007/978-981-16-8574-3_2

nations to continue building this network, only not under the name of BRI.[2]

Former Secretary of State Hillary Clinton made a speech in 2011 at Chennai in India in which she discussed the project in conjunction with an Indo-Pacific Economic Corridor between South and Southeast Asia. Secretary Clinton had spoken of how Turkmenistan could provide gas for Pakistan and India, and Tajikistan could provide cotton for Indian textiles. Agricultural and manufactured goods from Afghanistan, such as fruit and furniture, could flow north to Kazakhstan and south to India.[3] In 2017, there was talk that President Donald Trump would be reviving this initiative and corridor as a public–private initiative, with the US state department making room in its budget for these plans to link Afghanistan with south and south-eastward neighbouring regions. These shifts from military engagement in Central Asia towards an array of investment projects and regional trade networks were meant to bring about stability in Central Asia. While these plans failed to come to any significant fruition, it is seen that the US-Biden administration has been developing these networks, as the US seeks to develop strategic managed partnerships with allies in all the regions in which China's Belt and Road Initiative, also known as the One Belt One Road Initiative or the New Silk Roads, has already reached various stages of development.

Japan and South Korea, potential US allies in the Silk Road regions, have also been active in the Central Asian region since the Soviet Union pulled out. Prior to the Asian Economic Crisis of 2008, Japan seemed poised to successfully integrate its agenda, with Prime Minister Koisumi visiting Uzbekistan and Kazakhstan in 2006. Japanese efforts resemble China's in that they are top-down and state mobilized, so much so that corporate and public engagement tends to be lacking.[4] South Korea has

[2] "Kunming Meet Revives BCIM Link Plan—The Economic Times," accessed October 7, 2021, https://economictimes.indiatimes.com/news/politics-and-nation/kunming-meet-revives-bcim-link-plan/articleshow/69921135.cms.

[3] "US, India To Revive 'New Silk Road' Seen As Counter To China's Belt And Road Project," accessed October 7, 2021, https://www.ndtv.com/india-news/us-india-to-revive-new-silk-road-to-counter-chinas-belt-and-road-obor-project-1697632.

[4] "Craving Jobs? Revisiting Labor and Educational Migration from Uzbekistan to Japan and South Korea -Acta Via Serica | Korea Science," accessed October 7, 2021, https://www.koreascience.or.kr/article/JAKO202005054962763.page.

done better in this regard, focusing on corporate involvement and industrial development. South Korea has generated a number of programs in Central Asia, including the Comprehensive Central Asian Initiative (2006), the Korea + Central Asia forum institutionalised into the Korea-Central Asia Cooperation Forum in 2017.[5] Both Japan and Korea focus on the People-to-People component of involvement in Central Asia, establishing cultural centers in the region, training local Uzbek populations in Japanese and Korean, as well as in other vocational skills. Also, and very importantly, there have been labor migration agreements made, especially in the case of South Korea. South Korea's engagements in Eurasia include New Asia Diplomacy and New Silk Road Policy (2008–2012). South Korea's New Northern Policy (2018-present) focuses on 9 nine channels of development: gas, railways, ports, power generation, Arctic Shipping Route, shipbuilding, agriculture, fisheries and industry.

BRI/NSR Evolving from Western Development Project & China Goes Global

China's own New Silk Roads (NSR) are best understood through the lens of state-mobilized globalization (SMG), most similar to Japan's own state-centered market development abroad. In this way, NSR can be seen as a continuation of China's earlier Western Development Program (WDP) and the China Goes Global Policy (CGG).[6] These national strategies have been in play for over two decades and operate in tandem with China's NSR, each rhetorically open and nebulous in praxis, "precipitating globalization and market expansion inside China." Chinese strategies in Central Asia, as in other New Silk Road regions, have picked up tools used by other nations, such as India, Japan, and South Korea. Tools in China's kit include market, state, as well as cultural integration, and it's this last element of the New Silk Roads, 'People-to-People Connectivity,' that we focus on. Min Ye states all this in a practical way, pointing out that;

[5] "13th Korea-Central Asia Cooperation Forum Takes Place View|Press Releases Ministry of Foreign Affairs, Republic of Korea," accessed October 7, 2021, https://www.mofa.go.kr/eng/brd/m_5676/view.do?seq=321408.

[6] See: Min Ye, *The Belt Road and Beyond State-Mobilized Globalization in China 1998–2018* (Cambridge: Cambridge University Press, 2020).

> "foreign" strategies such as the CGG and BRI have lasting effects inside China. They help local governments and market actors promote their preferred economic and business plans. Since local governments are important elements in the tri-block state system, Chinese foreign policy's external effects are also deeply shaped by domestic and local players, with whom foreign observers typically are least familiar.[7]

This interaction of local government with market actors, say, in the cultural and creative sphere, as we'll be discussing in later chapters of this book, allow for diverse cultural voices to express themselves, and as well for different types of cultural messages to be disseminated throughout regions both domestic and international along the New Silk Roads. The diversity of both messages and modes of dissemination when it comes to culture, enhances both the potential of cultural implementation of centralized cultural policy, as well as the potential for regional cultures to accept integration and to support other development objectives from policy to infrastructure, and from trade to finance.

Five Pillars of NSR

In Chinese discourse there are five pillars (*wu tong* 五通) holding up the New Silk Roads. These are Policy Coordination (*Zhengce goutong* 政策沟通), Facilities Connectivity (*Sheshi liantong* 设施联通), Unimpeded Trade (*Maoyi changtong* 贸易畅通), Financial Integration (*Zijin tongrong* 资金通融), and People-to-People Connectivity *(Minxin xiangtong* 民心相通). 'Five pillars,' however, like much translation, loses the original Chinese sense of *wu tong*, which translates literally as 'five channels' or 'five connections.' *Tong* is a component character in all five of the pillars: *goutong* 沟通 (coordination), *liantong* 联通 (connectivity), *changtong* 畅通 (flow), *tongrong* 通融 (integration), and *xiangtong* 相通 (connectivity). This book proposes that rather than 'pillars' holding up the roof of an overarching structure; these five *tongs* configure as a hub of People-to-People Connectivity; around which four main spokes of policy, infrastructure, trade, and finance revolve.

All five of the English translation terms: coordination, linking, flow, integration, and connectivity refer to continuity and connection, just

[7] Min Ye, *The Belt Road and Beyond State-Mobilized Globalization in China 1998–2018*, 174.

as their original Chinese terms do. Yet the subtle differences between them are worth noting. *Goutong* is an old word, appearing in the *Luo Commentary to the Spring and Autumn Annals* as the act of digging out ditches in order to bring two bodies of water into confluence with one another. Thus, Policy Coordination takes on this sense of altering the topography of the land, in order to bring about confluence, such as one would do to bring two or more rivers into mutual flow with one another. *Liantong* is a relatively new word, with no classical precedent, not appearing until contemporary Chinese times. This linking is verb-oriented, an activity of connecting segments of trade and supply chains. Facility connectivity is being built with thousands of infrastructure projects already breaking ground. *Changtong* is an adjective describing, indeed, an unimpeded movement, either through a space, or of speech and diction. Its use was popularized in the late Qing, by early Republican intellectuals such as Guo Moruo (1892–1978), writer, communist party intellectual and cultural apparatchik, as well as Cao Jinghua (1897–1987), professor at Peking University and essayist as well as translator from Russian. Unimpeded Trade (*maoyi changtong*) requires the recalibration of obstacles into regulated channels, such as visa restrictions for tourists as well as workers. *Tongrong*, of Financial Integration belongs properly to the financial vocabulary of China today, used to denote the lending of a short-term loan. However, it also refers to flexibility, accommodating, and stretching to get around regulations, in order to make something happen. '*Rongtong*' would have seen all five terms as symmetrical and rhyming evenly, which is common in Chinese rhetoric and speech. *Rongtong* is indeed a word of integration, an integration born of circulation, flow, intermingling, merging and being assimilated into something larger. It's curious why the term '*tongrong*' was chosen instead. Perhaps it was because of its currency within the financial lexicon of today. There may have been intentional avoidance of imperial or tributary connotations attached to '*rongtong*' in China's branding of the initiative's 'Financial Integration.' Lastly, *xiangtong* has to do with People-to-People Connectivity. It is as old as any of the other five words, occurring in the *Records of the Historian* by Sima Qian (145–86 BCE). It does indeed mean to interlink, connect, and more importantly to communicate, but by the Song dynasty, it was used by a major proponent of the Neo-Confucian school of *lixue* 理学 (School of Principles), Zhu Xi (1130–1200) to connote 'mutual burden' as well as 'mutual benefit.' The significance of *xiangtong* leans into an awareness that everyone shares not only in the effort of bringing something into being; but that everyone also bends their own original shape or trajectory to find mutual workarounds for otherwise unworkable mutual challenges. Thus People-to-People Connectivity works to cultivate a global Community of Common Destiny, wherein mutual sacrifices will lead to mutual benefit, all brought about through interlinking and connecting the hearts and minds of people who have a stake in the projects at hand.

While the fifth pillar of People-to-People Connectivity seems on the surface to address only the human and cultural element of the New Silk Roads, we see that by looking just a little closer at the language; all five pillars involve connecting and interlinking aspects of people-centric projects. For example, Policy Coordination involves, in the past more than post-COVID, peoples of a nation's government travelling to meet and communicate with one another. The service and media industries that are attendant to the pomp, circumstance and logistics of policy-coordination are also important categories of People-to-People Connectivity. In the case of the media reporting on meetings and summits, these people have a great deal of influence over not only populations ruled by policy makers, but also upon the policy makers, themselves, who are also consumers of broadcast information. Facilities Connectivity involves a great deal of infrastructure building, and generally China imports a varying portion of labor into the regions where infrastructure is being built. While this portion was larger in the past, labor disputes in some of these regions have encouraged China to rethink this practice, or to ameliorate it, bringing in only those managerial workers who can impart skills to native populations, thus more seamlessly handing off control and operation of dams, roads, and container shipping ports. Whether in the former case, where all or most labor is imported from China, or in latter cases where only enough labor is exported to constitute vocational training and to guarantee outcomes, infrastructure on a scale as large as the New Silk Roads sees large-scale human migration. Populations of Chinese people develop connections with large and small populations of various regions throughout the world in developing the infrastructure for Facilities Connectivity. It goes without saying that trade, whether impeded or unimpeded, constitutes a category of People-to-People Connectivity. The old Silk Roads, with trade routes through Eurasia, saw the rise of a mercantile class that was responsible for a great portion of cultural flow in these regions; and this as a byproduct of the People-to-People nature of trade and commerce. War, famine and natural disasters caused other large portions of these shifts in cultural and human geography; but trade and commerce are largely responsible for the flow of material culture from region to region. In this flow of materiality, technological knowledge also transfers from region to region, affecting how we think about ourselves and the world. Lastly, Financial Integration is also a category of People-to-People Connectivity, if we understand economics as integral to politics, and politics as the management of a political body made up out of people. In financially integrating regions, there are financial values which fluctuate according to cultural values (Figs. 2.1 and 2.2).

Geography of NSR

Before we look at the geography of the New Silk Roads; let us look at cartographic and literary geographic representations of the ancient Silk Roads. These maps and representations are as diverse as are the myriad cultures that separate China from the Mediterranean and South Indian Sea shores. A study of the development of Silk Road geography and cartography is a study of how ideas, themselves, move through plural spaces. Some would see three separate trajectories of development; such as that of a Buddhist Road, a Mongol Road and a Mediterranean Road. Such a narrative would see Buddhist monks and scholars travelling, from the second to the eleventh centuries, through the Pamir mountain passes, suffering natural elements along the route spotted with oases in the Takla-makan as well as Gobi deserts. During the Eastern Han dynasty, one period in which the Silk Road saw favorable conditions for development and maintenance was from 90–130 CE. The Han controlled what is known today as Eastern China, with garrisons posted throughout Western regions, in what is known today as Xinjiang. The Buddhist Kushan empire contained regions from today's Xinjiang to Afghanistan. The Parthians (modern day Iran) controlled a large part of the Central Asian region; and the Roman Empire controlled areas based along the Mediterranean. The route began, as today's Silk Road Economic Belt does, in the Chinese city of Xi'an (then known as Chang'an), and continued westward toward the Yumen Pass, the famous exit point through which the renowned Laozi 老子 (c. sixth-fourth century) went when he had retired from his official post as court librarian in the Zhou dynasty. The border crossing guard allegedly would not allow him to leave China until he had written down his wisdom. What resulted from this interaction is the book we know today as the *Daodejing* 道德经 [Classic of the Way and Virtue], a text of

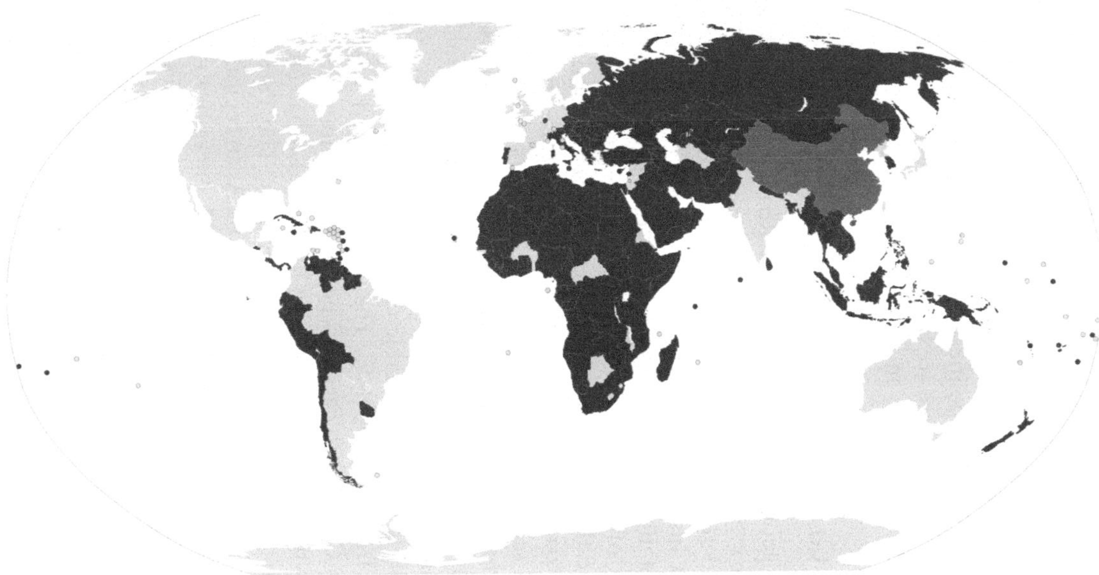

Fig. 2.1 [8]Red: China Blue: Countries which signed cooperation documents related to China's Belt and Road Initiative

[8] Owennson, English: This Is the Map of the Countries Which Signed the Belt and Road Initiative Cooperation Documents 中文: 這是簽署一帶一路相關合作文件國家的地圖, April 27, 2019, April 27, 2019, Own work, https://commons.wikimedia.org/wiki/File: Belt_and_Road_Initiative_participant_map.svg.

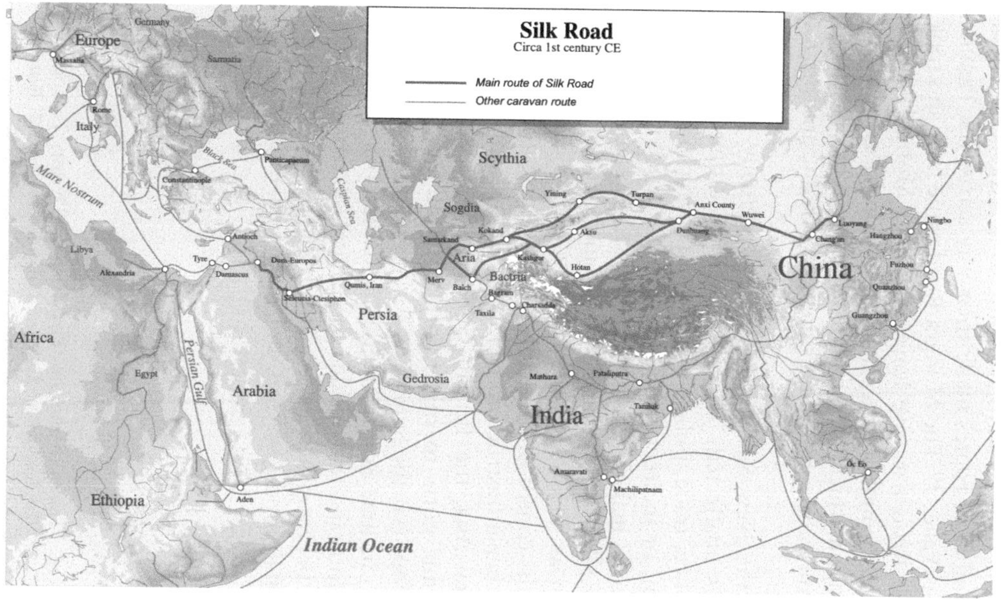

Fig. 2.2 [9]The Ancient Silk Road (First century CE)

[9] Kaidor, Русский: Великий Шёлковый Путь и Другие Караванные Маршруты Евразии в I Веке н.э., October 27, 2016, October 27, 2016, Own work based on File:Transasia trade routes 1stC CE gr2.png Map: Natural Earth (public domain) and SRTM3 V2 data (public domain) edited with Mapthematics Geocart and vectorized with Inkscape. Albers equal-area conic projection. Scale 1:50,000,000 (1 cm = 500 km). Projection center = 0°N 68°E. Latitude of origin = 0°. Standard parallels: 29°30′N and 45°30′N., https://commons.wikimedia.org/wiki/File:Silk_Road_in_the_I_century_AD_-_ru.svg.

over 5000 characters in 81 chapters, divided into two main parts; one to explain the meaning of Dao, or way, and the other to explain the machinations of De, or virtue. From the Yumen Pass, the ancient Silk Road branched off into a northern and a southern route, which then converged at Kashgar. Then a number of routes made their way across the Pamirs, to Fergana, or the Indus Valley.[10] The Mongol Road came later and took up where the Buddhist Road narrative leaves off, with Mongol leaders extending their influence throughout the Islamic region as far as meets the Mediterranean Road, upon which Islamic and Christian scholars, clergy, adherents, merchants, migrants, and soldiers met up with one another for an array of reasons.[11]

When it comes to the New Silk Roads, there is virtually no region on this earth that goes unaffected. The effect may be a direct one, as with infrastructure, policy, trade, policy, or cultural programming taking place in a given region; or indirect, with geopolitical, geoeconomic, or geocultural reverberations making themselves known in a region. The geography of the New Silk Roads is divided into land and water routes. The former are known as 'belts,' and the later are known (confusedly) as maritime 'roads.' Belts consist of overland roads, bridges, tunnels, railroads, pipelines and other infrastructure elements. These connect China with South and Central Asia, the Persian Gulf, and Europe. Maritime roads link Eastern China ports to other ports throughout the Indian Ocean, Africa, and Europe (via the Suez Canal). This geography has been extending, however, to include South America, and the polar regions of the earth. It's also important to consider the digital silk roads; which we'll talk more about below, which leave virtually no part of the world unconnected with digital goods, services and ideas that travel the New Silk Roads.[12]

[10] Phillipe Nicolas Zufferey, "Traces of the Silk Road in Han-Dynasty Iconography: Questions and Hypotheses," in *The Journey of Maps and Images on the Silk Road*, ed. Philippe Foret and Andreas Kaplony (Leiden: Brill, 2008), 11.

[11] Phillipe Foret and Andreas Kaplony, "Introduction," in *The Journey of Maps and Images on the Silk Road* (Leiden: Brill, 2008), 2.

[12] Sarwar Kashmeri, *China's Grand Strategy: Weaving a New Silk Road to Global Primacy* (Praeger, 2019), 11–12.

Silk Road Economic Belt

Today's Silk Road Economic Belt begins in Xi'an, as did the Silk Road in ancient times. However, rather than mythologically in some accounts reaching only as far as Rome, this time the Silk Road reaches as far as Duisburg, Germany. This Belt winds north from Lanzhou along the former route girding north of the Turpan Basin of modern day Xinjiang, passing through Urumqi in Xinjiang. It touches the south-eastern border Kazakhstan shares with China, at the Chinese city of Korgos. It then winds through Almaty, Kazakhstan's largest metropolis before moving through Bishkek, Kyrgyzstan; Samarkand, Uzbekistan; and Dushanbe, capital of Tajikistan. It then swathes across the northern territory, passing through Tehran, Iran, and then onto Istanbul, Turkey. It then crooks northward through Eastern Europe making a stop in Moscow, then sweeping westward through northern East and Central Europe. The Belt then arrives at its terminus in Duisburg, Germany. Another part of the Silk Road Economic Belt is a route connecting the 21st Maritime Silk Road terminus of Venice with Rotterdam via a northwest-southeast route through Italy, France and the Netherlands.

Twenty-first Century Maritime Silk Road

China's expertise in port management developed alongside its building and cultivation within China of seven of the world's ten largest ports. These seven ports are in Shanghai (#1), Shenzhen (#3), Ningbo-Zhoushan (#4), Guangzhou Harbor (#5), Hong Kong S.A.R. (#7), Qingdao (#8), and Tianjin (#9).[13] As if none of these record-breaking ports were big enough; China is building the new mega-sized Luoyu Port in Putian City, in the southeast of Fujian Province. It's important to note how these ports serve as hubs for sea-land-air transport networks making up the overland Belt and maritime Road. China News Service reported in 2019 that Fujian had opened sixteen shipping routes with foreign ports and had seen 175 cargo trains along 127 international container lines transporting goods via Fujian between Taiwan and Europe. Fujian is also poised as a hub for China's proposed and already partially implemented Digital Silk Roads, branded by Chinese authorities as an information

[13] "Top 50 Ports," World Shipping Council, accessed October 7, 2021, https://www.worldshipping.org/top-50-ports.

corridor between the Association of Southeast Asian Nations (ASEAN); involving Indonesia, Thailand, Malaysia, Singapore, Philippines, Vietnam, Brunei, Myanmar, Cambodia, and Laos. The information corridor will "provide solutions in the fields of telecommunication and remote sensing and navigation"[14] with a Maritime Silk Road satellite data service center facilitating, "data products, value-added products and a satellite remote sensing application system."

After departing from Fujian, the Twenty-first Century Maritime Silk Road will pass along Hainan Island and Zhenjiang, Guangdong before heading to Guangxi. The connection with Guangxi is important for the services and logistics opportunities it will provide to the Southwest of China, which as we will see throughout this book, is an essential part of the New Silk Roads, as China pivots to move westward across its own borders. The Maritime route then swings south to meet with Hanoi, Vietnam before moving further south to pass through the Strait of Malacca. This main shipping channel between the Pacific and Indian Oceans passes between Malaysia and the Indonesian island of Sumatra. The route then splits, with one arm going on a relatively short jaunt to its terminus in Jakarta, Indonesia's capital city; and the other arm heading on to Colombo, the largest city and commercial center of Sri Lanka; before skipping northeast to what was going to be India, but is now the Pakistani port of Gwadar, and then crossing the Indian Ocean straight to its next stop in Nairobi, Kenya. The route then wraps around the Horn of Africa and through the Red Sea en route to the Mediterranean, where it meets with Chinese-owned Piraeus Port in Athens, Greece; then meeting up with its own land-based Silk Road Economic Belt at the Maritime Silk Road terminus point in Venice, Italy[15] (Fig. 2.3).

14 "Fujian to Speed up Building of Core Area of 21st-Century Maritime Silk Road—People's Daily Online," accessed October 7, 2021, http://en.people.cn/business/n3/2019/0122/c90778-9540213.html.

15 "A new Silk Road for the 21st Century," Global Affairs and Strategic Studies, accessed October 7, 2021, https://www.unav.edu/web/global-affairs/detalle/-/blogs/a-new-silk-road-for-the-21st-century.

Six Economic Corridors

Originally there were six Economic Corridors announced as planned to connect the Silk Road Economic Belt and the Twenty-first Century Maritime Silk Roads. These corridors constitute infrastructure clusters throughout countries participating in the New Silk Roads which are projected to cumulatively cost somewhere between four and eight billion US dollars. These include: the New Eurasian Land Bridge, the China-Mongolia-Russia Corridor, the China-Central Asia-West Asia Corridor, the China-Indochina Peninsula Corridor, the China-Pakistan Economic Corridor (CPEC), and the problematic Bangladesh-China-India-Myanmar Corridor (BCIM). This last one was originally planned to run from the Southwestern Chinese city of Kunming in Yunnan Province through Mandalay, Myanmar and Dhaka, Bangladesh into Kolkata, India; but was dropped after the 2019 Second Belt and Road Forum in Beijing, at least partly due to India's unwillingness to participate in the Belt and Road Initiative, manifest in India not sending a representative to the forum meeting. This was attributed to India's reaction to another one of the Economic Corridors—the China-Pakistan Economic Corridor (CPEC)—passing through Kashmir, a territory over which India and China skirmish.[16] Some news sources announced that, just prior to the summit, plans for the BCIM corridor were resumed, just not under the aegis of Belt and Road Initiative.[17] India's primary concerns include national, energy, and trade security, fearing that China's Belt and Road will shift regional power too strongly towards China. India has its own vision for Indo-Pacific connectivity, and recent meetings between India and China's leaders see a battle over narratives, each party wishing the other would enter into its own version of the ancient Silk Roads. While China leans towards connecting with Kolkata, India is proposing a Chennai-China connect; insisting upon a set of better practices which are rules-based, with greater transparency.[18] It is useful to look at the

[16] Darshana M. Baruah, "India's Answer to the Belt and Road: A Road Map for South Asia," Carnegie India, accessed October 9, 2021, https://carnegieindia.org/2018/08/21/india-s-answer-to-belt-and-road-road-map-for-south-asia-pub-77071.

[17] "Kunming Meet Revives BCIM Link Plan—The Economic Times".

[18] "PM Modi Offered Xi Indo-Pacific Connect in Response to BRI Offer—The Economic Times," accessed October 9, 2021, https://economictimes.indiatimes.com/news/politics-and-nation/pm-modi-offered-xi-indo-pacific-connect-in-response-to-bri-offer/articleshow/71608439.cms.

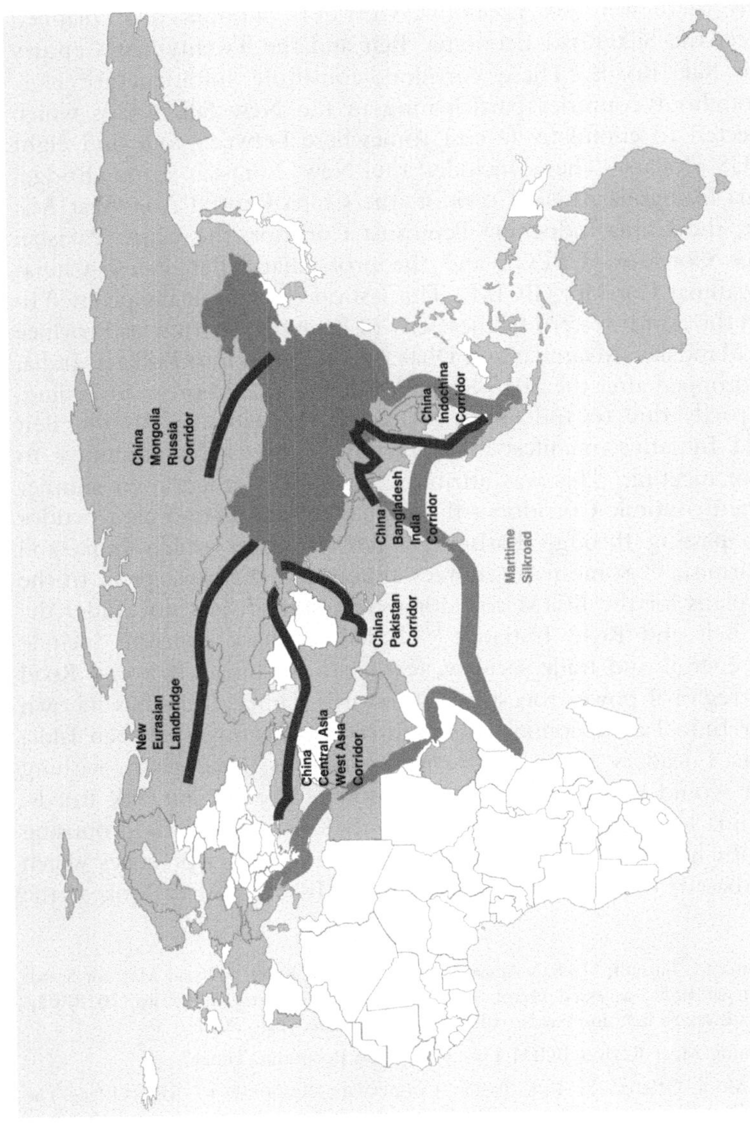
China Mongolia Russia Corridor
New Eurasian Landbridge
China Central Asia West Asia Corridor
China Pakistan Corridor
China Bangladesh India Corridor
China Indochina Corridor
Maritime Silkroad

◀**Fig. 2.3** [19]Proposed Six Corridors of Overland Silk Road Economic Belt (Black) and the proposed 21st Maritime Silk Road (Blue). (Orange) Signifies member countries of the Asian Infrastructure Investment Bank

BCIM Corridor, as with the other corridors, as a loosely modelled matrix around which actual implementations will organize themselves in time. There are some instances in which plans are cancelled, and others where plans remain practically the same while assuming another name. Still other instances see plans cancelled in favor of development in other areas of the same region, or in other regions all together.

The New Eurasian Land Bridge goes from Western China through Kazakhstan to Western Russia, moving onward to Belarus, Poland and Germany. The China-Mongolia-Russia Corridor originates in North-eastern China towards the far eastern regions of Russia; while the China-Central Asia-West Asia Corridor provides service from Western China to Turkey. The China-Indochina Peninsula Corridor originates in China and runs through to Singapore; and the China-Pakistan Economic Corridor sees a number of routes crossing from northern to southern Pakistan, gravitating towards the terminus of Pakistan's Gwadar Port, where shipments can then be sent onward to Africa and Western Asia. There are also additional corridors being planned and implemented, such as the Second Eurasian Bridge, which as of 2017 began development on an as-the-crow-flies straight shot from Xi'an, China to Moscow in Russia.

New Expansions Since 2018

Polar/Ice Silk Roads

When in 2013, a COSCO ship successfully made the voyage from China's Dalian port all the way to Rotterdam, Netherlands via the Arctic Ocean;

[19] Lommes, English: China in Red, the Members of the Asian Infrastructure Investment Bank in Orange. The Proposed Corridors (Https://Www.Merics.Org/En/Merics-Analysis/Infographicchina-Mapping/China-Mapping/ and Http://Www.Cbbc.Org/Cbbc/Media/Cbbc_media/One-Belt-One-Road-Main-Body.Pdf) in Black (Land Silk Road), and Blue (Maritime Silk Road).Português: Mapa Com a China Em Vermelho, Membros Do Banco Asiático de Investimento Em Infraestrutura Em Laranja, as Rotas Físicas Em Preto e Azul.Русский: Транспортные Коридоры Проекта "Один Пояс - Один Путь"., May 14, 2017, May 14, 2017, Own work, https://commons.wikimedia.org/wiki/File:One-belt-one-road.svg.

China's Twenty-first Century Maritime Silk Roads took on a new additional direction. Rather than concentrating all its attention on developing the South China Seas and Southeastern China land, air and seaports; China now grew interested in the fact that shipping from Dalian to Rotterdam took a third of the time the southern route would take. In June of 2017, China's National Development and Reform Commission (NDRC) and the State Oceanic Administration (SOA) released a policy paper specifically addressing the role that this arctic role could play in future shipping, particularly in BRI shipping. However, it was not just about shipping; the paper also addressed gas and oil exploration in the arctic regions, upon which China sought Iceland, Norway and Russia's cooperation. There were also mining projects mentioned, involving rare earth elements and zinc, having to do with Greenland. Then in October of 2017, a principal proponent of Arctic development, Wang Yang, was promoted from Chinese State Council Vice-Premier to Politburo Standing Committee (PSC). Later that same year, President Xi met with Russian Prime Minister Medvedev, the two agreeing on the efficacy of developing an Ice Silk Road, on the ice in the North Polar Sea. The narrative engines have been churning since, and in early 2018, a Chinese State Council white paper titled "China's Arctic Policy" outlined China's history in the Arctic region since 1925, connecting this historical arc with present trajectories.[20] In a slightly uncomfortable (to read) yet opportunistic reading of the data, the newly proposed shipping route would be able for the time being to enjoy unfrozen waters for six months out of the year; but by sometime between 2035 and 2050, this restriction would be lifted, as ice would remain unfrozen full-time.

Pacific Maritime Silk Road

China's plan for the Pacific Maritime Silk Road establishes historical roots in the Sixteenth century, when the Silk Road allegedly linked Fujian Province with Mexico via the Philippines. Goods such as Chinese silk, porcelain and spices were traded for agricultural products from the New Americas such as corn, potato, and pepper. The Pacific Maritime Silk

[20] "BRI-Economic-Corridors-and-Key-Operational-Investments__SIIS.Pdf," accessed October 9, 2021, http://www.chinainvestmentresearch.org/wp-content/uploads/2018/07/BRI-Economic-Corridors-and-Key-Operational-Investments__SIIS.pdf.

Road of today is organized by the Forum of China and the Community of Latin America and Caribbean States (LAC), established in 2015. In January of 2018, Foreign Minister Wang Yi delivered a letter from Xi Jinping prioritizing further development of the cooperation framework of the China-LAC Cooperation Plan 2015–2019. These coordination priorities emphasize trade, investment and finance in the fields of energy, resources, infrastructure, construction, agriculture, manufacturing, scientific and tech development, and especially information technology.

Digital Silk Road

If one looks at the classical Greek notion of *techne*, as the art of a skill, involving and expressing not only principles, but methods for the attainment or creation of something, one can see that the New Silk Roads are, indeed, an array of new technologies. Many of these technologies are digital. When Julian Assange warns of surveillance capitalism; and Slavoj Zizek speaks of capitalism's growing indifference to democracy and its principles; we are prone to begrudgingly think about China's strength in the technology and information sector. Fear of China's Huawei, for example, dominates Western media representations of New Silk Roads, and especially digital roads.[21]

The Digital Silk Road involves six main areas: physical infrastructure, advanced technologies, satellite navigation systems, AI, quantum computing, and digital commerce.[22] When China scholars warn that the New Silk Roads are not just a foreign policy initiative; but also China asserting itself as a dominant world state; the verb could be not 'assert,' but 're-assert.' China's Ming dynasty (1368–1644) was the world's most powerful nation, and continued to be until the time of the Great Divergence, when European *episteme* and *techne* overcame that of China. Information on the role of Digital Silk Roads is slowly emerging, but we already know enough to realize that China's strength in digital technologies will contribute strongly to China's global ascendancy. Quantum computing is emerging as an advanced technology in which China prioritizes investment funds. These funds support organizations such as the

[21] Eurasia Group, "Digital Silk Road Expanding China Digital Footprint" 2020.

[22] See: Richard Ghiasy and Rajeshwari Krishnamurthy, "China's Digital Silk Road," *Institute of Peach and Conflict Studies, Leiden Asia Center*, 2020, 26.

National Laboratory for Quantum Information Science, which spearheads efforts to supersize potential military and intelligence capabilities. The goal is not only to accumulate the most data and find applications for that data; but to shield one's own data and operations from other nation's quantum computers. China's capabilities are growing in both arenas, contributing to the reassertion of China's status as the world's leading power.

Health Silk Road

The Health Silk Road (*Jiankang sichou zhi lu* 健康丝绸之路) has always been a part of the fifth pillar of New Silk Road development, serving as a major component of People-to-People Connectivity. Previous to COVID-19 this largely took the form of promoting awareness and practice of Traditional Chinese Medical modalities, such as acupuncture, moxibustion, and Chinese herbs. It also correlated with the academic exchange component of People-to-People, with many students arriving in China from other parts of Asia to study Western and Chinese health modalities. With China's medical and technological advancement growing in recent decades, these skills are seen as valuable to regions outside of China which otherwise do not have this medical and technological knowledge.

The Health Silk Road has taken on a whole new and much more important dimension post-COVID, however, adapting the New Silk Roads to a world in the grip of an ongoing pandemic.[23]Initially, the Health Silk Road kicked into high gear to provide Personal Protection Equipment (PPE) to health care workers throughout NSR regions. Once China had developed its two vaccines, Sinopharm and Sinovac, the Health Silk Road was strengthened and expanded to provide NSR partner nations as well as non-partner nations with vaccines they otherwise could not obtain. The US-Biden administration's own scramble and shifting of focus away from vaccinating its own US citizens in order to establish its own vaccine diplomacy abroad illustrates how effective China's Health Silk Road has been in strengthening ties with other nations. The shift of power in the Indo-Pacific region towards China due to Health Silk Road flows of People-to-People Connectivity has proven too significant to ignore.

[23] "Snapshot," accessed October 9, 2021, https://merics.org/en/short-analysis/chinas-health-silk-road-adapting-bri-pandemic-era-world.

Financing of NSR

While financial structures of the New Silk Roads may seem furthest afield from NSR's People-to-People Connectivity; China's cultivation of new financial structures sees resonance in China's cultivation of newly organized People-to-People Connectivity. This can be explained most clearly by looking at the challenges China faces both in its Financial Integration with the world alongside the challenges China faces in the global cultural sphere. These challenges can be reduced to a single concept as discussed by Michel Foucault, Karl Marx, Antonio Gramsci, Louis Althusser, Jürgen Habermas, and Pierre Bourdieu. This concept is that of power and discourse. The relationship between power and discourse in the context of NSR financing can be most easily understood by recognizing that nations which exert the highest degree of control over geocultural discourse then hold the greatest amount of geopolitical and geoeconomic power. The inverse is also true, in that nations that hold the most geopolitical and geoeconomic power then find it easier to control geocultural discourse.

Up until the turn of the Twenty-first century, Western countries have contributed the most capital to global financial institutions and therefore have held the greatest voting power, more capable then of controlling decisions about where funds should be invested. This value cannot be decided upon as something that is equally valuable to all countries and regions of the world. An infrastructure project in one region will not yield the same amount of value for a distant region not included in supply chains created by or maintained by this infrastructure project. Therefore, value must be established, and is usually done so by controlling interests. To give a specific example, while the Karot hydropower project in Pakistan was an important project for the region, it benefits China with its controlling interest in the Gwadar Port in Pakistan, as well as the roadways and railways that China has also built along the China-Pakistan-Economic-Corridor. These benefits are greater for China than they are for the United States or Japan; who are both disengaged from the New Silk Road's most developed economic corridor to date. Therefore, the Asian Development Bank (ADB), with Japan and the US each with 15% controlling interest will not be willing to establish the value of the Karot hydropower project and will outvote China's 6% interest in the ADB by more than 500%. Therefore, China has had to provide new investment avenues for the New Silk Roads, so that it could have more 'say' in decision making within global financial institutions, granting more control to China over conversations about what is valuable and what is not.[24]

This is also the case with People-to-People Connectivity. People run on value. As people, we are always making judgements about what is valuable and what is not. Whether it's what we should eat in order to stay healthy, who we should associate with in order to obtain social capital, or what art we should look at or buy in order to keep our minds and spirits refreshed; we are always making judgements. This is obvious. What is not obvious, however; is how this value is established. Chances are, what we consider valuable is also considered valuable by others in our social milieu, that is, with other people who share our 'values.' These values are the project of our metaphysics, philosophical orientation, the novels and poems we've read, our education, as well as our political and economic institutions. Chinese culture has managed to modernize while retaining much of its original value system, which is perhaps why China's behavior in global markets baffles other actors whose values diverge with China's. We will discuss this more Chapter Three of this book, where we discuss political economy of culture.

Requiring yearly USD1.5 trillion (plus another USD 0.2 trillion tacked on for climate change mitigation) to complete these five pillars of projects; China needs money. The International Monetary Fund (IMF) and World Bank (WB), however, are dominated by the Global North, both in terms of leadership and voting power. So, in June of 2015, China instituted the Asian Infrastructure Investment Bank (AIIB), based in Beijing. Membership is open to the world, and funding goes exclusively to Asian infrastructure projects, in or out of BRI projects.[25] The Silk Road fund, then, was created to finance projects in countries along the Silk Road Economic Belt and the Twenty-first Century Maritime Silk Road. Most of the capital in this fund is Chinese capital; and its funding priorities consist in infrastructure, industrial cooperation, and resource development.[26]

Established in 1966, the Asia Development Bank has been committed to creating a stronger Asia Pacific region, specifically targeted at decreasing the income gap between the region's richest and poorest. The

[24] See: Hong Liu, Kong Yam Tan, and Guanie Lim, eds., *The Political Economy of Regionalism, Trade, and Infrastructure:Southeast Asia and the Belt and Road Initiative in a New Era* (World Scientific Publishing Company, 2021).

[25] Kashmeri, *China's Grand Strategy*, 17–18.

[26] Tom Miller, *China's Asian Dream: Empire Building along the New Silk Road* (London: Zed Books, 2017).

Silk Road Fund was set up by China as a state-owned investment fund in December 2014, when USD $40 billion was allocated for the fund. The fund's first investment went into the $1.65 billion Karot hydropower project in Pakistan, along with other hydropower projects in the region. In July 2015, the New Development Bank (NDB) was also created as a global development bank. It is funded and created through the five BRICS nations: Brazil, Russia, India, China, and South Africa. Its headquarters are in Shanghai, and along with its sister institution AIIB, it operates in spaces also occupied by the Asian Development Bank and the World Bank. Then there are several banks invested in New Silk Road infrastructure projects. The Bank of China allocated USD $100 billion between 2016–2018 towards NSR projects; while CITIC Bank allocated USD $130 billion, without specifying any time frame. The China Development Bank is also very involved, originally in infrastructure, but now also in funding resource acquisition by state-owned firms in Africa, Venezuela, Russia and Brazil.[27]

The World Bank, Asia Development Bank, and the International Monetary Fund are all configured around Western economies and markets. Thus they are made to integrate smoothly into Western value systems, and these value systems are propped up by sets of discourses which reflect Western economics and markets. These institutions neither value a Chinese development agenda, nor the discourses which develop into and out of this Chinese agenda. Thus, China has had to seek other methods of financing the New Silk Roads, because these new roads and belts will integrate regions according to a Chinese-driven agenda, meeting with fierce opposition from the United States and its allies, such as Japan and India.

Conclusion

The Silk Road is a compelling geocultural imaginary.[28] Recent discoveries at the Sanxingdui archaeological dig-site just outside of Chengdu,

[27] "Silk Road Fund's 1st Investment Makes China's Words into Practice—Business—Chinadaily.Com.Cn," accessed October 10, 2021, http://www.chinadaily.com.cn/business/2015-04/21/content_20497821.htm.

[28] Tim Winter, *Geocultural Power*. 'Geocultural power' is cultural power on a global scale. This emphasis upon cultural power displaces a hard/soft power axis.

capital of Sichuan province in Southwest China suggest that a tangential Chinese civilization not based in the Central Plateau region of the Han, but in the Southwest region of the Shu, had early traffic with West, Central, South and Southeast Asia.[29] Another layer of this imaginary derives in the Chinese Han dynasties (213 BCE-220 CE), when Buddhism travelled along the Silk Road from India to China; around the same time that Christianity climbed out of Northeast Africa and Western Asia into the Caucasus, Europe, and Central Asia. We mentioned earlier the travels of Buddhist monks and scholars from the second through the eleventh centuries, travelling long distances along the 'Silk Road,' and we also explained how there was always more than one 'road.' After the Buddhist Road, there was the Mongol Road with influence travelling what were really networks of roads and shipping lanes throughout the Islamic and Christian regions, with clergy, adherents, merchants, migrants, and soldiers conducting many real exchanges which by now we can only imagine.

The New Silk Roads being built by China today are not so imaginary. Indeed, they constitute a massive project building policy, facilities, trade, financial and People-to-People Connectivity throughout the globe.[30] Global North narratives of the New Silk Roads seem engineered to protect a geopolitical narrative which excludes China's Community of Common Destiny. Global North narratives ignore millennia of interconnectivity of policy, facilities, trade, finance and culture involving China and its neighbouring regions until the mid-1800's, that is up until the Great Divergence, when Western powers wrested the axis of power away from Eurasia towards Europe.[31] China's own narrative is Sino-centric and alarming to the Global North, which will be reluctant to lose control over material and cultural flows of power. Developed nations will continue to seek ways to prevent China and its allies from re-taking a place at the helm of global governance.[32]

29 "'Bizarre' Sanxingdui Ruins: A Tale of Cultural Integration," accessed October 10, 2021, https://www.prnewswire.com/news-releases/bizarre-sanxingdui-ruins-a-tale-of-cultural-integration-301260276.html.

30 See: Miller, *China's Asian Dream*.

31 See: Pomeranz, *The Great Divergence*.

32 See: Kashmeri, *China's Grand Strategy*.

CHAPTER 3

People-to-People Connectivity Along the New Silk Roads

In January of 2021, a White Paper was released, "China's International Development Cooperation in the New Era," which stated that human resources, aid, public goods, and agricultural development, as well as climate change mitigation, "outnumbered industry and economic infrastructure projects in the Belt and Road from 2013–2018."[1] Liaqat Ali Shah, the Head of the Policy Division for Trade and Industry Cooperation at the Centre of Excellence, China Pakistan Economic Corridor (CoE-CPEC) at Pakistan's Ministry of Planning, has stated that infrastructure and energy projects along CPEC are completed, underway, or progressed in their planning; and that funding and programming for CPEC socio-economic programs will increase in percentage.[2] If claims made in this White Paper are true for the period 2013–2018, that trend may be expected to remain at least stable, if not strengthen. Yet these programs and the umbrella they fall under, People-to-People Connectivity (P2P), are poorly understood outside of China. In the second part to his

[1] "Full Text: China's International Development Cooperation in the New Era," accessed October 11, 2021, http://english.www.gov.cn/archive/whitepaper/202101/10/content_WS5ffa6bbbc6d0f72576943922.html.

[2] "Lecture: Liaqat Ali Shah, Centre of Excellence, China-Pakistan Economic Corridor," Assessment of China's Belt and Road Initiative, accessed October 11, 2021, https://www.uvachinabriproject.com/event/2021/2/18/liaqat-ali-shah-centre-of-excellence-china-pakistan-economic-corridor-date-amp-time-tbd.

S. Kidd, *Culture Paves The New Silk Roads*,
Contemporary East Asian Visual Cultures, Societies and Politics,
https://doi.org/10.1007/978-981-16-8574-3_3

Image 3.1 2016 Chengdu Up-On International Performance Art Festival, an example of public–private People-to-People Connectivity in Chengdu's fine arts sector.

2005 book, *Reassembling the Social: An Introduction to Actor-Network Theory*, Bruno Latour discovers an equivocation:

> The adjective 'social' designates two entirely different phenomena: it's at once a substance, a kind of stuff, and also a movement between non-social elements. In both cases, the social vanishes. When it is taken as a solid, it loses its ability to associate; when it's taken as fluid, the social again disappears because it flashes only briefly, just at the fleeting moment when new associations are sticking the collective together.[3]

[3] Latour, Bruno, *Reassembling the Social: An Introduction to Actor-Network-Theory* (Oxford: Oxford University Press, 2005), 159, https://www.amazon.com/Reassembling-Social-Introduction-Actor-Network-Theory-Management/dp/0199256055.

Cultural considerations are as fluid as the social, and the moment we try and take stock of them by taking measurements, we lose sight of the gestalt and relational nature of culture; while often misreading the qualitative factors from the vantage point of specific discursive register. New or old Silk Road narratives are global, local, and mercurial; composed of local pockets of documentation threaded together into narratives that serve agenda or ideologies that vary considerable from region to region.[4] Belt and Road cultural flows are fluid and hard to grasp, adding to the opaque nature of the New Silk Roads fifth pillar, *Minxin xiangtong* 民心相通 (People-to-People Connectivity). The other four pillars of Policy Coordination, Facilities Connectivity, Unimpeded Trade and Financial Integration are much easier to measure and analyse. Quantitative analysis of these other four pillars provide analysis which is explicitly political and economic in nature, but must also be understood as implicitly cultural in aspect. This study reintegrates culture, politics and economics as part of a meta-discipline adjacent to the emerging field of cultural political economy, in order to analyse how People-to-People (P2P) connectivity works, what it means, and why it's essential for the other four pillars of NSR to function in the long term.[5]

Fifth Pillar in the Context of China's Theory of Fives

Thinking in Fives

Five is an important Chinese semiotic number. The New Silk Roads are made up out of five pillars, and one of the first formalised poetic genres was the five-syllable quatrain. The oldest system of fives, still very much in use today, especially in Chinese medicine, is Yin-yang Five Element Theory (*Yinyang wuxing xueshuo* 阴阳五行学说). Five Element Theory describes relationships and interactions between all systems of heaven, man, and earth. The theory includes two separate cycles of the same Five Elements, each constituting a map of relations that either revolve

[4] Phillipe Foret and Andreas Kaplony, "Conclusion," in *The Journey of Maps and Images on the Silk Road* (Leiden: Brill, 2008).

[5] Pan Yaling, "Promoting Bilateral People-to-People Exchange Amid Rising China-US Strategic Competition," *China Quarterly of International Strategic Studies*, 5, no. 2: 161–176, https://doi.org/10.1142/S2377740019500143.

in clockwise circular movement giving rise to one another (Creation Cycle); or move from one to the other element in the shape of a five-pointed star (Ko, or Destructive Cycle). In the Creation Cycle we see wood give birth to fire, fire to earth, earth to metal, metal to water, and water to wood, which begins the cycle anew. In the Ko Cycle, wood controls earth, earth controls water, water controls fire, fire controls metal, and metal controls wood. During the Western and Eastern Han dynasties, five-element theory provided guiding principles by which ministers advised the emperor, people lived their lives, and art was made. In modern times, the practical application of these Cycle theories dealing with the Five Elements is found in Chinese traditional healing techniques, from pharmaceuticals to acupuncture. These principles as developed and practiced today in Chinese philosophy, medicine, astro-cartography, and socio-economic theory have roots in Yinyang Five Element Theory within Daoist and Confucian contexts. Due to the conjoined nature of Confucian and Daoist discourses throughout China's history, we often see a hybrid of Confucian and Daoist Five Element Theory develop from its Pre-Qin origins, once again disseminated widely in the Song dynasty, with Zhu Xi's Neo-Confucian School of Principles (*Lixue* 理学).

In a Chinese Five Element version of political economies, culture (communications) can be likened to the *qi* 气 (air) of natural ecologies. *Qi* helps the limbs of the body to act in coordination with one another, as communication helps the individual to co-exist with others in communities. People-to-People Connectivity builds and sustains the four other pillars of NSR as a cultural force helping to coordinate various publics and their governments throughout NSR regions. Overemphasis on top-down Policy Coordination, industry-oriented Facilities Connectivity, commercial goals of Unimpeded Trade, and Financial Integration of flows of capital; without attention given to education, human resource development, and labor flows; creates an imbalance through the entirety of China's Belt and Road networks. This imbalance blocks healthy feedback loops and adjustment mechanisms. While education, human resource development, and labor migration are the alpha and omega of People-to-People (P2P) connections, cultural and creative industry flows are also very important. As well, post-COVID-19 P2P programming is largely dedicated to medical aid diplomacy, including China's P2P medical knowledge-transfer and training programs. As of early 2021, the lion's share of Chinese P2P focus is placed upon COVID-19 and other disaster relief efforts throughout Belt and Road regions, such as Southeast Asia

(Malaysia), Africa (Sierra Lione, Niger, and Zambia), as well as in Latin America (Cuba) and Oceania (Fiji).

People-to-People connects publics along the New Silk Roads, harvesting cultural, political, economic, and social capital from these exchanges, all of which cathect as what Tim Winter coins 'geocultural power.' In his book by that title, Winter posits the Silk Roads as a:

> geocultural imaginary and a form of geocultural power. It is argued that the Silk Roads provide China with a unique platform for exercising its geocultural advantage, and through history, culture, and heritage, we are seeing the forces of great-power diplomacy being exerted.[6]

Winter's research is mainly concerned with top-down People-to-People relations, that is, cultural policy which is top-down government conceived, directed and implemented. This book expands exploration to examine how top-down P2P programs mesh with grassroots 'bottom-up' cultural movements. We do also borrow from Winter's move away from considering China's cultural diplomacy purely as a mode of 'soft power,' shifting towards understanding these cultural efforts on the international stage rather as generative of 'geocultural power.' This is an effort to displace the discussion of Chinese culture from the soft/hard power axis, which is preferred for international affairs and cultural diplomacy discussions, but not as helpful for discussions which gravitate towards other disciplines, such as cultural geography and other sociological and cultural studies.

Translation Issues

Pillar/通	*Original Chinese term*	*Official English translation*
1	政策沟通	Policy Coordination
2	设施联通	Facilities Connectivity
3	贸易畅通	Unimpeded Trade
4	资金通融	Financial Integration
5	民心相通	People-to-People Connectivity

[6] Tim Winter, *Geocultural Power,* 35.

Now we will address a few translation issues in New Silk Roads studies. It's important to note what's being lost in translation between the Chinese term '*tong* 通' and its English translation 'pillar.' Here, a state of flux, an exchange of energy is fixed and objectified as pillar.' This mechanism of reducing relational structures into objects is at the heart of much misunderstanding between Chinese and Western cultures. While *tong* 通 is a component character in each of the five pillars: i.e., *gou* tong 沟通 [coordination], *lian* tong' 联通 [connectivity], *chang* tong 畅通 [flow], tong *rong* 通融 [integration], and *xiang* tong相通 [connectivity]; translation of NSR 'channels' into 'pillars' leads to a misunderstanding of the relational nature of each of NSR's five engagement areas. The mis-translation engenders perception of these engagement areas as mere instrumental props (pillars) to hold up an overarching structure or portico, such as economic, military, and/or cultural hegemony.

Fears exist that China's geocultural power will gain too strong a momentum of outward spread (*wai tui* 外推), as the country strengthens its 'soft power' throughout Central and Eastern Europe, the Caucasus, Middle East, Eastern and Western Africa, South Asia, Southeastern Asia, Latin and South America, as well as the Arctic sea lanes. Instrumental in pushing for cultural integration (*tuidong wenhua ronghe* 推动文化融合), the Chinese Digital Silk Roads go even further than physical roads and belts in connecting all of these regions. China's cyberspace strives to remain Sino-centric, blocking Chinese access to Western platforms of influence, such as Facebook and Instagram, in an effort to tighten surveillance of online users, as well as to control discourses proliferating along the Digital Silk Roads. If People-to-People Connectivity is going to succeed as a driving mechanism for the New Silk Roads, this problem along the Digital Silk Roads of separate cyber-spheres will have to be addressed. Either there will need to be more integration, with mobile and satellite networks working in concert, or with digital global governance rules breaking down segregation between the Global North, with its networks, discourses and norms controlled by first-world nations, and the Global South, with its networks, discourses, and norms being increasingly built by and guided by China.

In the White Paper mentioned above, we also observe a commitment to South-South Cooperation, with the 2016 establishment of the Institute of South-South Cooperation and Development (ISSAD) at Peking University. Also, by 2019, the South-South Cooperation Assistance Fund had already collaborated with over a dozen international organizations including the World Health Organization (WHO), United Nations Development Programme (UNDP), United Nations Children's Fund (UNICIF), and the International Committee of the Red Cross (ICRC) to deliver on 82 projects to address agricultural development and food security, poverty reduction, health care, public health emergencies, human resource education and training, as well as aid for trade, refugee protection, and post-disaster reconstruction. Commitment to South-South development is in line with China being weary of a neoliberal international atmosphere in which China's discourses fail to gain traction; working therefore to build and stabilize a South-South alignment in which Chinese values and cultural priorities are not precluded from prevailing discourses.

Chinese P2P discourse often meets with cognitive dissonance in joining international conversations on political economy and geocultural flow. Some of the language China uses, such as 'harmonious,' 'win–win,' and 'special characteristics,' tends to not be taken seriously by foreign policy experts in the West. In some cases, the P2P disconnect is a natural result of early NSR policy emphasis upon government-to-government and top-down approach to cultural and creative sectors, as well as of close coupling of state and market. However, understanding various models of P2P engagement, i.e. places where top-down or government-to-government engagement is supplemented or replaced by other P2P typologies, is important when attempting to understand the potential of this pillar in sustaining New Silk Roads futures. Once we open up new typologies of People-to-People Connectivity, we then turn to 'soft power,' 'cultural diplomacy,' and '*Minxin xiangtong*.'

P2P Typologies, Soft Power, Cultural Diplomacy and Minxin xiangtong

2020 saw mutual closures of embassies in Houston, Texas and Chengdu, Sichuan, and state actors soft-pedalling cultural and public diplomacy. It is possible that political and economic conditions may worsen in a vicious cycle escalating from trade war into military engagement. Fortunately, non-state actors continue to implement grassroots bottom-up People-to-People development in a dearth of top-down cultural diplomacy. In a political economy of authoritarian media policy, civic media engagement and activist media provide important channels for dialog and feedback. Top-down approaches seek to establish cultural security (*wenhua anquan*

文化安全), which tends to mean cultural uniformity; whereas complementary, supplementary, and antagonistic grassroots approaches advocate retaining a *renwen jingshen* 人文精神 (humanist spirit) in Chinese culture, with its emphasis upon individuality, cultivating traditional Chinese values while incubating innovation in goods, capital, people, technology, and data sectors.

Cultural diplomacy serves as an important methodology in cultivating the Belt and Road Initiative's fifth pillar. When China refers to People-to-People Connectivity, it is often referring to public diplomacy as a form of cultural diplomacy, with the additional development of human resources in the cultural, service, tech and agriculture sectors. As China develops discourses on cultural diplomacy and People-to-People Connectivity, there is a certain amount of slippage in meaning as these terms travel away from and back to Western generated discourses, constantly being recycled through what Paul Gladston discusses as translation-appropriations.[7] It is therefore helpful to set a typology of People-to-People Connectivity.

Established P2P Typologies

People-to-People did not begin with the Belt and Road Initiative, nor is it unique to China. People-to-People as a part of cultural and public policy are a part of many nations' foreign policy, playing various roles. While the Belt and Road was not officially announced until 2013, a 2012 press release from the European Commission details the launching of People-to-People dialogue with China as engaging a new level of connection focused on education, culture, youth, research and multilingualism.[8] At the time, People-to-People was considered a 'Third Pillar' in China-EU cooperation. The first two pillars, the High-Level Economic and Trade Dialogue and the High-Level Strategic Dialogue had now moved into their third phase or Pillar, bringing people together with people.

[7] Paul Gladston: Aesthetic Modernities.

[8] "Education and Culture: EU and China Launch People-to-People Dialogue," Text, European Commission—European Commission, accessed October 11, 2021, https://ec.europa.eu/commission/presscorner/detail/en/IP_12_381.

One typology of P2P distinguishes People-to-People Connectivity from government-to-government connections.[9] This typology is basic and fails to encompass China's mechanisms of state-mobilized People-to-People programs that have primarily cultural objectives. To complicate matters, the English term People-to-People varies etymologically from the Chinese term *Minxin xiangtong* 民心相通. "Minxin 民心" refers to thoughts, feelings, and aspirations of the people. "Xiangtong 相通" means to interlink spatially, as in the case of inter-joining rooms leading onto one another, or to communicate. Put together, *Minxin xiangtong* signifies in much the same way as does Joseph Nye's soft power, as a mechanism by which to win hearts and minds, bringing the aspirations, thoughts and feelings of foreign peoples into alignment with one another. Thus we see the humanities-based and cultural orientation of NSR's fifth pillar which seeks to increase Chinese cultural power abroad by winning the hearts and minds of foreign populations; aligning the thoughts, feelings and aspirations of the Chinese people with those of foreign populations along the New Silk Roads. Kadir Jun Ayhan speaks of People-to-People as a form of diplomacy which is:

> intentional, political, and transboundary communication-based interactions between groups of people for public, rather than private interests that have or aim to have foreign policy implications. This definition excludes P2P interactions which are non-diplomatic, e.g., pure international exchanges which do not have political objectives or relevance to foreign policies, or anti-diplomatic, e.g., warfare activities.[10]

Ayhan's P2P interactions exclude much of what China includes in the Fifth Pillar of Belt and Road Initiative, such as providing public goods, as well as all private sector or public–private-partnership (PPP) People-to-People development. Ayhan's analysis also seems to exclude international cultural programming which does not have primarily political, economic, or military objectives. Although Ayhan's analysis does not fit our own exactly, its typology is very useful. In Ayhan's analysis, P2P connections are classified into two categories; the first of which

[9] "A Typology of People-to-People Diplomacy|USC Center on Public Diplomacy," accessed April 12, 2020, https://www.uscpublicdiplomacy.org/blog/typology-people-people-diplomacy.

[10] "A Typology of People-to-People Diplomacy|USC Center on Public Diplomacy."

is directional, distinguishing top-down from bottom-up P2P programming. Top-down interactions are designed as political initiatives meant to influence foreign populations. Here we see how Ayhan's typology has already advanced beyond the government-to-government/People-to-People binary mentioned above, allowing state-mobilised People-to-People diplomacy to target not foreign governments, but the populations these governments rule.

Ayhan goes on to divide bottom-up P2P diplomacy into three further categories: complementary, supplementary or adversarial. These three categories are defined according to their alignment with or divergence from home government political ideology and foreign policy. An example of bottom-up complementary People-to-People Connectivity aligning with or being initiated by home governments, is the development of a Silk Road Community Building Initiative (SRCBI), launched in April of 2019 at the second Belt and Road Forum for International Cooperation by the China Non-Governmental Organization, Network for International Exchanges (CNIE). Priorities for this new initiative include People-to-People Connectivity, cultural diplomacy, and human resource development.[11] This is an example of Chinese non-government organizations operating in the international sphere in alignment with and complementary to home government objectives, and this example is also largely in line with Ayhan's typology of diplomatic P2P connections, with a strong link between the SRCBI initiative and China's 2019s Belt and Road Forum for International Cooperation.

The next category of Ayhan's sub-typology of bottom-up P2P diplomacy is that of bottom-up supplementary connections. These supplementary programs aim to fill a vacuum of formal public diplomatic programs. We see such a vacuum opening up, for example, between China and the United States. The closing down of the Chinese embassy in Houston, Texas in 2020 which then precipitated the tit-for-tat closure of the US embassy in Chengdu, Sichuan will have long-lasting implications. The US consulate in Chengdu offered, besides visa and immigration services which facilitated labor flow between countries; a monthly lecture series on China-US cultural relations, open to the Chengdu local and expatriate communities. In the absence of government People-to-People diplomatic programming, the need for bottom-up private sector or public–private

11 "New Move to Promote BRI Cooperation in Romania-Belt and Road Portal," accessed October 11, 2021, https://eng.yidaiyilu.gov.cn/qwyw/rdxw/104467.htm.

partnership will increase. Examples of this sort of supplementary programming are Chengdu's Luxehills Museum and A4 Museum international artist residency programs. Funded largely by real-estate and private investors, these museums provide cultural programming in exclusive residential areas, in a strange reversal of the Western trend of real-estate value tracing artistic geographies. Whereas the earlier creative Western cities saw money follow the art; in this case, Chinese developers have studied the creative city model well enough to understand that building a vibrant museum, cultivating its collection, and providing funding for rich domestic and international programming, as well as children's arts educational programs builds immediate value into a new residential district. Artists are often unable to afford living at these residential developments, where studio space rentals in the Luxehills Arts Village, for example, value as high as 300,000RMB (USD $46,354) per year.

Adversarial P2P grassroots groups interact with foreign populations and leadership in ways that contradict or malign their home government political ideology and foreign policy. Adversarial P2P grassroots programming is found throughout certain Chinese international Diaspora seeking objectives and values at odds with Chinese government objectives and values. An example of this would be the international Falungong movement, all but crushed by the Chinese government at the end of the twentieth century, now underground abroad. There are also Chinese Christian groups within and outside of China who seek to promote Chinese values which are religious in nature, at odds with Chinese Communist Party atheism. Adversarial P2P bonds are also cultivated in some Chinese contemporary avant-garde art and cultural activities, both domestic and in Diaspora communities. These disseminate cultural messaging at odds with the Chinese state, such as democracy, free speech, "art for art's sake," as well as anti-market ideologies at odds with neoliberal political economies of culture. The work of most blue chip contemporary Chinese art stars, like Ai Weiwei, Gu Wenda, and Xu Bing, all emigres from China's arts sector, successfully drive value for China's art market, as well as making money for arts institutions worldwide by making artworks which communicate cultural messaging that is adversarial to the Chinese Communist Party (CCP). This increases the cultural capital of Chinese artists, and paradoxically, the value of China's cultural export. Diaspora dissemination of Chinese culture often carries with it ideologies and historiographies arising out of China's political and economic past, at variance with contemporary China's political makeup.

As of yet, this value stands largely unaccounted for in China's analysis of its own cultural and public diplomacy.

New Silk Road P2P Typologies

Working off of Ayhan's original formulations, then, we define People-to-People Connectivity as cultural programming, including health and humanitarian assistance, as well as academic, cultural and professional exchange, both domestic and international. This cultural programming can be either top-down or bottom-up. The former is both conceived and implemented by government actors. The latter consists in grassroots-conceived cultural programming implemented through private-sector channels. Complementary bottom-up P2P, then, is private-sector cultural programming which works to implement top-down government cultural programming, aligned with their own private-sector cultural objectives. Funding is often provided through the public sector, whereas supplementary bottom-up P2P cultural programming often exists in cultural spaces where both cultural policy and infrastructure are absent. Note that complementary and supplementary are not in opposition to one another. Supplementary P2P is not defined in relationship with top-down cultural programming. Rather, supplementary P2P is an intersectional approach, a triangulation of different forces (public, private, public–private) and methods for integrating these forces. Supplementary P2P programming produces cultural messaging as relational, not necessarily oppositional, to top-down P2P cultural messaging.

New Silk Road P2P Typology Examples

Top-down People-to-People Connectivity

Examples of successful top-down People-to-People programs in Belt and Road countries can be found in China's domestic education sector, which brings in large and diverse flows of intellectual and creative capital from Belt and Road countries, as well as from non-Belt and Road countries such as Western Europe, UK, and the US. Demographics of foreign-exchange students have changed since the initiation of Xi Jinping's vision of the New silk Roads as part of a 'Community of Destiny' for humankind. At Sichuan University, percentages of students coming from non-Belt and Road regions have fallen, while students coming from

South, East, Southeast, and Central Asia, as well as Africa make up a larger percentage of the foreign student body. The 211 and 985 Projects began in 1995 and 1998, respectively, to elevate academic standards in Chinese universities, creating elite universities qualified to engage in international cooperation and exchange. Note that these two educational programs each hoped to attract foreign students, and began long before the Belt and Road Initiative. As we mentioned earlier in connection with Min Ye's book on State-Mobilized Globalization, programs pivoting towards international development really took root during the development and implementation of the Western Development Project (WDP) and China Goes Global (CGG) initiative. Then, as BRI was announced by Xi Jinping in 2013, the BRICS University League and Double First Class University program helped poise China for an optimised future in creative and tech sectors by 2050. Other projects more specifically targeted towards the Belt and Road include the University Consortium of the Maritime Silk Road launched in Xiamen in October of 2018. This is an international university consortium comprised of over 60 universities from 17 countries and regions along the 21st Century Maritime Silk Road. Members of this consortium include the University of Sheffield, Sorbonne University, the University of Melbourne, the Victoria University of Wellington, University of California: Irvine, and Nanyang Technological University.[12]

China's foreign-exchange education sector, however, has met with challenges. Hanban/Confucius Institute has recently rebranded as the Center for Language Education and Cooperation (CLEC, *Zhongwai yuyan jiaoliu hezuo zhongxin* 中外语言交流合作中心). As of March, 2021, there are still 51 Confucius Institutes in the US, with 4 more scheduled to close. 69 have closed down since 2014, most of these in the past two years. Many of these have closed due to conflict of interest, not being able to receive any federal dollars from the Department of Defence if there is a Confucius Institute on campus.[13] New People-to-People

[12] "University Consortium of Maritime Silk Road Launched in Xiamen-Belt and Road Portal," accessed October 12, 2021, https://eng.yidaiyilu.gov.cn/qwyw/rdxw/69333.htm.

[13] "How Many Confucius Institutes Are in the United States? By National Association of Scholars|NAS," accessed October 12, 2021, https://www.nas.org/blogs/article/how_many_confucius_institutes_are_in_the_united_states.

programs can be seen in CLEC programming, such as its "People-to-People Honorary" contest which rewards and celebrates peoples' stories of cultural connection between China and other countries.[14]

Bottom-Up Complementary People-to-People Connectivity

Bottom-up grassroots complementary P2P is organic cultural programming in synch with and aligned with top-down cultural programming, and is often funded by top-down agencies and actors. An example of complementary cultural P2P programming can be found in the EU-China Literary Festival, which is financed by the European Union and hosted by China. Peter Goff, scholar on China's publishing sector at Leeds University, conceived of the literary festival and presented his working model to Brussels. Events such as the Fifth EU-China Literary Festival at the end of 2020 in Beijing serve as an example of multi-lateral P2P which, while conceived in a top-down manner, engages grassroots regional networks. The 27th event of this iteration of the EU-China Litfest was a talk moderated by Chinese curator Zhang Weina, able to provide contextual insights for remarks made by Dutch writer Daan Heerma Van Voss and Chinese writer Liang Hong. In this example of P2P relations, many nuances of China's culture were discussed in a non-polarizing way. The talk, titled "Complex Relations: People and Peoples, Past and Present" provided a platform for the Chinese Renmin University professor and the Dutch novelist/historian to discuss freedom, imagination, subjectivity and the role of politics in art. Liang Hong talked about freedom and imagination in devotion to exploring subjectivity. Goff is also the founder and former-owner of the Beijing, Suzhou, and Chengdu Bookworm Cafes, which hosted multiple annual iterations of the Bookworm International Literary Festival from 2007 onwards, which we will discuss below as an example of supplementary grassroots P2P.[15]

Another example of complementary P2P Connectivity is curator and art historian, Lu Peng's latest project in Chengdu arts infrastructure creation. Lu Peng is serving as chief academic consultant for the 2021 Chengdu Biennale. Chief curator for the biennale is Fan Di'an, chairman

[14] Confucius Institute U.S. Center, *2020 CIUS Center Annual Report*, 2021, https://www.youtube.com/watch?v=9vVIwo4oJz4.

[15] "The Bookworm (Bookstore)," in *Wikipedia*, May 16, 2021, https://en.wikipedia.org/w/index.php?title=The_Bookworm_(bookstore)&oldid=1023424147.

of the Chinese Artists Association and president of the Central Academy of Fine Arts. Producers include Chengdu Culture, Radio, Television and Tourism Bureau of Sichuan Province, and other sponsors include the public sector Chengdu Academy of Painting (Chengdu Art Museum), and Chengdu Urban Construction Investment Management Group Co., Ltd. Thus we see that while public actors hold the greatest stake in this massive international exhibition of over 500 artworks by nearly 300 artists, these public institutions are working in concert with private sector actors whose objectives are aligned with top-down government cultural programmers.[16]

Bottom-Up Supplementary People-to-People Connectivity

The Bookworm International Literary Festival, also run by Peter Goff, would be an example of supplementary grassroots P2P Connectivity, but in this case it would be supplementary, rather than complementary. The primary difference is in the funding direction, as the Bookworm literary festivals never received any funding from top-down agencies or actors. There was sometimes funding given by government organizations, but they would be consulates representing countries besides China. Most of the funding was provided by local businesses, both Chinese and foreign-owned. The Bookworm literary festival, as conceived of by Peter Goff and curated by Catherine Platt, who now organizes the Hong Kong Literary Festival, hosted writers from all over the world, flying them in to Beijing, Suzhou, and Chengdu for workshops and book talks. The Chengdu leg of the festival provides an example of cultural programming that arose in a dearth of Southwest China arts and cultural infrastructure. Funded by various foreign embassies, international schools, and other domestic and international actors, the programming enjoyed unprecedented freedom. The degree of diversity of both Chinese and international writers and artists present at the festivals was highly inclusive.

Another excellent example of grassroots P2P is the Chengdu Up-On International Performance Art Festival, organised by performance artist Zhou Bin and other members of the 719 Artists Alliance and other avant-garde curatorial entities operating in Chengdu. This festival is conceived

[16] "'Super Fusion-2021 Chengdu Biennale' Will Be Unveiled Soon—INEWS," accessed October 12, 2021, https://inf.news/en/culture/b1e6153915eeb098fb710349d9c186de.html.

by local artists and curators, hosting artists from countries throughout the world in eight iterations since 2008. Performances are held at a combination of sites throughout Chengdu's fine arts sector, museums, and universities. Taking advantage of the palatial grounds of Chengdu's new secondary campuses recently built for various universities on the outskirts of the city, these live performances have enjoyed a high degree of freedom, barring nudity and violence. Up-On festivals receive their greatest support in the form of grants from the A4 Art Museum, which gives upwards of 70,000 RMB (USD $10,846) annually to defray travel and materials costs for festival participants and artworks. The A4 Museum, located at Luxelakes International Ecological City, receives its funding from real-estate developers who appreciate the value of cultural programming as a draw for creatives and wealth creators to Luxelakes. These developers appreciate the value of funding arts infrastructure, which brings in high value human capital to Chengdu, and builds wealth in the region. A4 Art Museum, as a private sector museum, supports diverse cultural messaging and is highly inclusive, as is seen in its 2019/2020 survey exhibition of Southwest China performance art, *From Streets to Languages: Performance Art in Southwest China Since 2008*, curated by well-known Chengdu curator Lan Qingwei.[17] Lan Qingwei is a former student of internationally known Chengdu curator and art historian, Lu Peng. Lu Peng is one of the forerunners of bottom-up grassroots supplementary art programming, helping contemporary Chinese art to enter onto the international art market in the early 1990's with the 1991 Guangzhou Biennale, a biennale operating on a new-to-China business model of private investment. Patrons of the Biennale would receive artworks in return for their patronage, artworks whose values would be discovered and built by the international biennale.

Cultural Diplomacy, Soft Power, & Geocultural Power

A 2014 China Daily article cites Martin Jacques of Cambridge University as proclaiming a new trend, where countries (foreign publics and their

[17] "A4 Art Museum—2019 年 11 月 23 日, 新展「从街头到语言: 2008 年以来的西南行为艺术」「From Streets to Languages: Performance Art in Southwest Area of China Since 2008」," accessed October 12, 2021, https://m.facebook.com/666948357073948/posts/772008049901311/#_=_.

policy makers) are "more influenced by outside factors, including the growing connectivity of people."[18] These statements were made at a time when numbers of Chinese international tourists and students enrolled abroad were at their peak; in sharp contrast to post-COVID numbers today. This may suggest that non-state People-to-People actors are now setback, and China must spend more money on fifth pillar top-down P2P. In the example of complementary grass-roots we discussed above, namely that of the 5th EU-China Litfest, we mentioned an event where a Chinese curator was able to engage in thoughtful dialogue with a Dutch writer. In this dialogue the writer, Daan Heerma van Voss expressed, "that neither 'progress' nor 'freedom' is the purpose and coordinate of fictional and non-fictional writing," adding that 'progress' and 'freedom' strip away a political economy of culture where art serves the 'people' (*yishu wei renmin fuwu* 艺术为人民服务), shifting towards personal cultivation and education, and even 'art for art's sake (*yishu wei yishu* 艺术为艺术).'[19] Here we see how intimately connected culture and cultural products such as books and artworks are with politics and economics. While an official representative of cultural or public diplomacy would not be able to so directly talk about China's political economy, writers and curators often address such issues. These events provide valuable platforms for cultural experts involved in designing and implementing BRI's fifth P2P pillar. This type of state-mobilised public diplomacy, or 'non-state actorness,' in public diplomacy is under-researched.[20]

Joseph Nye first popularised the term 'soft-power' in 1991 with his book *Bound to Lead: The Changing Nature of American Power*.[21] In this book, Nye's discussion of power pivots on metrics used to measure

[18] Jiang Xueqing, "Concept of Diplomacy Expands to People-to-People connectivity—Business—Chinadaily.Com.Cn," accessed October 13, 2021, https://www.chinadaily.com.cn/business/2014-04/12/content_17429278.htm.

[19] "Liang Hong x Daan Heerma van Voss: Complex Relations: People and Peoples, Past and Present—Literary Festival," accessed October 13, 2021, http://eu-china.literaryfestival.eu/liang-hong-x-daan-heerma-van-voss-complex-relations-people-and-peoples-past-and-present/.

[20] Hankuk University of Foreign Studies and Kadir Ayhan, "Branding Korea as My Friend s Country: The Case of VANK s Cyber Public Diplomats," *Korea Observer—Institute of Korean Studies* 49, no. 1 (January 19, 2018): 51–81, https://doi.org/10.29152/KOIKS.2018.49.1.51.

[21] Joseph Nye, Jr., *Bound to Lead the Changing Nature of American Power By* (New York: Basic Books, 1990).

and envision how power works in the world. He illustrates a progression of mistakes resulting in the shifting of world power from one order to the next, beginning with mercantilists who saw Spain's gold and silver as sufficient to anchor their power. It turned out that Holland's commercial networks introduced a new metric of power, and France once again with its strong population base and sound administrative systems. Later, with a shift from the strength in a rural population, Britain's political stability and industrial revolution toppled yet another model of hegemonic power. Nye evokes Daniel Bell's 1987 analysis to name manufacturing and services in the information industries as the next metric of power. Writing in 1990, Nye places China alongside Russia as not yet not equipped to develop this kind of power.

In 2006, Nye then wrote "Think Again: Soft Power," where he clarifies his usage of the term as such by saying that "Soft power is cultural power partly."[22] Nye points to three sources for soft power being culture, political values, and foreign policy. A nation's culture must be attractive, its political values authentic, and its foreign policies seen as legitimate, with moral authority. China's monolithic and non-transparent image on the world stage gives foreign publics an uneasy feeling, making China's cultural products less attractive, and discounting their value with what is known by scholars preoccupied with this issue as 'cultural discount' (*wenhua zhekou* 文化折扣). As well, the political values reflected in these cultural products, while appealing more easily to Asian publics, stand out as alien, non-authentic, and in many cases, illegitimate outside of Asia. These reactions decrease China's soft power, forcing China to rely more heavily on economic, political, and military forms of hard power to achieve their objectives. Here, soft power can be described as a cultural power, a power which balances political, infrastructural, trading, financial, and military power. In this discussion, 'geocultural power' is a relatively more sophisticated concept than is 'cultural power,' in that while cultural power exists, like soft power, as a counterpoint to hard power, i.e., political, economic, and military; geocultural power contains both hard and soft power within it, employing the cultural characteristics and effects of all types of power as they deploy on a global scale.

Cultural export can help to diversify categories of understanding, giving multiple channels of intellectual access to a nation's branded

[22] Joseph Nye, Jr., "Think Again: Power—Foreign Policy," accessed October 12, 2021, https://foreignpolicy.com/2009/11/03/think-again-power/.

message. In 2004, Nye cites successful cultural exports from China such as Gao Xiangjian's Nobel Prize for Literature in 2000; blockbuster film *Crouching Tiger, Hidden Dragon;* Chinese basketball superstar player, Yao Ming; and China's manned space flights.[23] It's important to note, however, that Gao Xingjian was a Chinese emigre, self-exiled to Paris; Ang Lee, the director of *Crouching Tiger, Hidden Dragon* is a Taiwanese director educated in Taiwan and the United States; and both Yao Ming's game and China's space flights took place largely outside of China's ideological and national spaces. This points to a Western culture-centric view of soft power. This is to say, at least in the examples that Nye uses, cultural attractiveness is that which speaks directly to the values and cultural priorities of Western nations. The Western-centric nature of the soft power discussion is another reason why we gravitate towards using the notion of geocultural power as a macro-trend of China's geopolitical development.

Let us look, however, at how Chinese scholars have nuanced the soft power discussion. In contrast to Nye's three components of soft power, namely culture, political values and foreign policy, Hongyi Lai frames soft power as consisting of, "official discourse, culture, and to a lesser extent, trade."[24] An analysis of how Chinese intellectuals use the term reveals not only that the term is being used with increasing frequency; it is also clear that China has in fact modelled its definition of soft power upon Nye's conceptualization of it, going then further to add its own special characteristics in expanding the scope of the term. Even before the commencement of the New Silk Roads in 2013, China had already begun in the early 1990's to study, analyze and enhance Nye's notion of soft power. Authorities had long decided amongst themselves that a corresponding strengthening of soft power had to occur in step with China's economic and political rise in the world. 1998 saw China join in the United Nations Education, Science and Cultural Organization (UNESCO) Intergovernmental Conference on Cultural Policies for Development. In 1998, China held the Paris China Culture Week, and in 2000 there was the US Tour of Chinese Culture, followed by the China Festival at the Asia–Pacific Week in 2001 in Berlin. There was a

[23] Joseph S. Nye, *Soft Power: The Means to Success in World Politics*, 1st ed (New York: Public Affairs, 2004).

[24] Hongyi Lai and Yiyi Lu, "Introduction: The Soft Power Concept and a Rising China," in *China's Soft Power and International Relations*, ed. Lai, Hongyi and Yiyi Lu (London: New York: Routledge, 2012).

Chinese year in France from Oct 2003 to Jul 2004, a Chinese cultural tour in Africa, as well as a 'year of' exchange of cultures between China and Russia in 2006/2007.[25] However, China's cultural power lags significantly behind its hard power in forms of economic, political and military strength. It is possible that metrics for cultural attractiveness may shift again in the future, as populations and governments build discursive value for non-Western fields of normative culture and political economies.

While Chinese scholars publish prolifically upon the value of Chinese cultural ideals and traditions in creating a new world order, there tends to be a disconnect as to how exactly a Chinese 'harmonious' worldview translates into foreign policy, or how it informs political economics. This, compounded with mixed messaging between Chinese and Diaspora regions, reveals differences in Chinese cultural ideation of normative values. Strong control of official ideology exerted over Chinese culture tends to discourage innovation, which often involves a 'transgression' of genre boundaries, or blurring of categories (*fenlei bu ming* 分类不明). While innovation does not have to serve as the panacea that it does in Western trends of individualism in breaking with past traditions; innovation is useful in learning to cope with newly arising social conditions.

At the time of writing, there is a good deal of skepticism as to whether China really means well by other NSR nations.[26] China's top-down approach to creating and implementing policy in many cases involves making deals with leaders of other authoritarian nations, and critics observe that these personal relationships boost and strengthen the durability of these regimes. Many fear that China's main goals are to excavate raw materials and import Chinese labor into regions where populations are already struggling to find employment in jobs which create value for themselves or for their regional economy.[27] These mounting concerns call for Chinese geocultural development throughout New Silk Road regions;

[25] Mingjiang Li, "Soft Power in Chinese Discourse: Popularity and Prospect," in *Soft Power: China's Emerging Strategy in International Politics*, ed. Li Mingjiang (Lanham: Lexington Books, 2009), 21–44.

[26] Yelena Sadovskaya and Leah Utyasheva, "'Human Silk Road': The People-to-People Aspect of the Belt and Road Initiative," in *China's Belt and Road Initiative and Its Impact in Central Asia*, ed. Marlène Laruelle (Washington, D.C.: The George Washington University, Central Asia Program, 2018), 109–25.

[27] Bhavna Dave, "Silk Road Economic Belt: Effects of China's Soft Power Diplomacy in Kazakhstan," in *China's Belt and Road Initiative and Its Impact in Central Asia*,

in order to help local populations to grow more familiar with China's cultural priorities, political policies, and public goods in the region. Policy on People-to-People Connectivity must also cultivate mechanisms which identify problems as they arise, creating channels for crisis resolution. Aziz Burkhanov has written up a media review on the impact of China's NSR on Central Asian national identity issues; explaining that the public is much more critical of and divided on the initiative than are leadership. Burkhanov attributes this to relatively recent Sino-Soviet border conflicts, imbalanced demographics and lack of academic discourse on contemporary China.[28] This, again, could be remedied with more resources allocated towards China's development of cultural power in the Central Asian region.

Cultural diplomacy can be understood as a government's attempt to influence foreign policy by influencing a foreign public population.[29] Advocacy, cultural diplomacy, exchange diplomacy, and international broadcasting are important venues for the "exchange of ideas, information, art, language and other aspects of culture among nations and their peoples in order to foster mutual understanding".[30] Types of cultural diplomacy include all forms of creative production, such as exhibitions, educational programs, exchanges, literature, broadcasting, and religious outreach programs.[31]Soft power increases with the degree of alignment of a state's cultural values to global cultural values and ideology.

ed. Marlène Laruelle (Washington, DC: Central Asia Program, The George Washington University, 2018), 97–108.

[28] Aziz Burkhanov, "The Impact of Chinese Silk Road Strategy on National Identity Issues in Central Asia: A Media Review," in *China's Belt and Road Initiative and Its Impact in Central Asia*, ed. Marlène Laruelle (Washington, DC: Central Asia Program, The George Washington University, 2018), 153–61.

[29] Hwajung Kim, "Bridging the Theoretical Gap between Public Diplomacy and Cultural Diplomacy," *The Korean Journal of International Studies* 15, no. 2 (August 31, 2017): 293–326, https://doi.org/10.14731/kjis.2017.08.15.2.293.

[30] Nicholas J. Cull, "Public Diplomacy: Taxonomies and Histories," *The ANNALS of the American Academy of Political and Social Science* 616 (2008): 31–54, https://journals.sagepub.com/doi/10.1177/0002716207311952.

[31] J. Michael Waller, *Strategic Influence: Public Diplomacy, Counterpropaganda, and Political Warfare*, Revised edition (Washington, DC: Institute of World Politics Press, 2009).

Minxin xiangtong

Chinese theories on New Silk Road's fifth pillar discuss *Minxin xiangtong* 民心相通 as spreading Chinese culture outwards (*wai tui* 外推). Earlier on, China's *Minxin xiangtong* focus was on Cross Strait relations and communist countries. This focus has expanded to other regions of the world since Reform and Opening-Up (*Gaige kaifang* 改革开放), and even more rapidly so throughout eight years of Belt and Road Initiative, with over 140 countries now entered into diplomatic relations with China in regards to this massive project.[32] At present, we see China engage in People-to-People diplomacy in a similar manner to the European Union's activities in Central Asia. The EU has seen a 30% increase over the past seven years in funding provided to the region on behalf of the Development Cooperation Instrument (DCI) and European Instrument for Democracy and Human Rights (EIDHR). This recent increase in funding may be linked to China's New Silk Roads, to counter China's power in the region. EU's bilateral assistance goes towards "education, regional security, sustainable management of natural resources, and socio-economic development."[33] China and the EU, then, have a Comprehensive Agreement on Investment which provides unprecedented access to China's markets with unique transparencies in key sectors, especially as regards subsidies given to state owned enterprises (SEO).[34]

This dissemination of Chinese culture along the New Silk Roads operates along various continua such as language, values, religion, material culture, knowledge and science. Language, both its acquisition and dissemination, is key to *Minxin xiangtong* in order to allow the reciprocity of People-to-People cultural exchanges. Language dissemination was developed first, with the establishment of Confucius Institute language curricula throughout the world, beginning with the Western Development Project model of Chinese development in the 1990's and

[32] Shichen Wang, "China's People-to-People Diplomacy and Its Importance to China-EU Relations: A Historical Institutionalism Perspective" 4, no. 1 (2016): 19.

[33] "Central Asia|Fact Sheets on the European Union|European Parliament," accessed October 13, 2021, https://www.europarl.europa.eu/factsheets/en/sheet/178/central-asia.

[34] "Fact Sheet of the EU-China Comprehensive Agreement on Investment," Text, EEAS—European External Action Service—European Commission, accessed October 13, 2021, https://eeas.europa.eu/delegations/china/91230/fact-sheet-eu-china-comprehensive-agreement-investment_en.

early 2000's. Recent Chinese-language literature, however, emphasizes the increasing importance for Chinese enterprises along the New Silk Roads to acquire foreign languages in order to expedite not only this fifth pillar, but to more effectively develop other coordination priorities. Xi Jinping is quoted as saying that the successful development of NSR is contingent on common values, mutual understanding and mutual respect; all of which have much to do with understanding one another's language.[35] Language as a 'key to other cultures,' not only brings cultures closer together, but also "satisfies the service-chain."[36] We see here not only a theoretical desire to unlock other cultures, but also a very practical need to open markets and connect supply-chains. Once there is less of a linguistic barrier between cultures, it will be easier for China to not only 'spread' Chinese values outwards, but also to discover and develop common values.

Conclusion

In this chapter, we have identified NSR's fifth pillar of People-to-People Connectivities as the single most powerful instrument of geocultural power generation available to Xi Jinping and China's ruling CCP party. After first contextualising NSR's five pillars within a much older Chinese system of thinking in fives, we then set upon our first real discussion of the problems of intercultural communication that arise from translations. The five pillars are, in Chinese, not structural pillars, but rather flowing channels of interconnections. What gets lost in this translation is the native correlative systems type of thinking that China brings to the table of global governance. Transitioning, then, into a discussion of soft power, cultural diplomacy, and *Minxin xiangtong* (People-to-People Connectivity (P2P); we set out first an established typology of P2P before describing a more specialised P2P typology adjusted for Chinese use along the New Silk Roads. This revised typology, then, focuses on the two trajectories (top-down and bottom-up) of the original typology; but sifts

35 "习近平: 掌握一种语言就掌握通往一国文化的钥匙-搜狐新闻," accessed October 13, 2021, http://news.sohu.com/20140330/n397433669.shtml.

36 车向前 Che Xiangqian and 郭继荣 Guo Jirong, "跨文化外推视阈下的_一带一路_民心相通提升路径_车向前 Multi-Cultural Extrapolation and the Path to Strengthening Minxin Xiangton in One Belt One Road," *Journal of Xi'an Jiaotong University (Social Sciences)* 37, no. 142 (Summer 2017): 45–53.

out a third subset of the latter trajectory, that of adversarial P2P, although it can be suggested that this type of P2P is what is at work in some of the alternative cultural messaging conveyed by some contemporary Chinese artists such as Ai Weiwei, who simultaneously bring audiences closer to an understanding of Chinese culture while at the same time distancing international audiences from official CCP cultural ideology. We will discuss these types of alternative cultural messaging more in chapters four and five.

What is essentially at work in the distinction between top-down and bottom-up P2P is a differentiation between public-sector and private-sector cultural programming. We conclude that the ideal P2P model, that is, one which most effectively brings publics along the New Silk Roads closer to understanding and practising acceptance and toleration of differences and the 'otherness' of Chinese culture, is that of public–private partnership P2P programs. These are ideal because they can draw upon the resources of both public and private sectors, which are considerably different. While the public sector has authority and large institutions at its disposal, the private sector has greater flexibility with an ability to adjust to conditions which change quickly through time and space. Public–private partnership People-to-People programs can most effectively provide feedback loops which have the ability to change and regroup according to both market demand and public opinion. For these reasons, they have the ability to generate the most geocultural power.

CHAPTER 4

Political Economy of New Silk Road Culture

This chapter on China's domestic and international political economy of culture of the New Silk Road (NSR) has two main tasks. The first is to reconnect politics with economics, and the second is to connect political economies with cultural development when it comes to how we think about the New Silk Roads. These are each done for the purpose of better understanding China's political, economic, and cultural deployment throughout NSR partner regions. While political economy can be used as an effective lens through which to see and understand developments in of NSR's four pillars of Policy Coordination, Facilities Connectivity, Unimpeded Trade, and Financial Integration; adding the cultural component back into political economy affords us a full set of tools by which to understand NSR's fifth pillar, that of People-to-People Connectivity. Indeed, we begin to see that these connections between people, populations, and publics point to cultural power as the medium in which the other four pillars can be sustainably engineered and firmly embedded. After exploring China's political economy of culture, we then develop the view of the New Silk Roads as a 'spatial fix,' drawing upon existing literature in the field looked at from a cultural perspective.

Here we harvest our discovery from Chapter 3, that bottom-up cultural programming and arts infrastructure can be more effective in implementing, responding to, and providing feedback for international

S. Kidd, *Culture Paves The New Silk Roads*, Contemporary East Asian Visual Cultures, Societies and Politics, https://doi.org/10.1007/978-981-16-8574-3_4

cultural policy than top-down state-controlled cultural programming. Later, in Chapter 5, we will explore 'cultural discount' as a phenomenon which plagues China's cultural power abroad, when the value of China's cultural product is depreciated upon exiting China's national borders and ideological space. This is often due to the top-heavy nature of China's cultural programming and arts infrastructure, tightly bound with the public sector, as state leaders seek ideal cultural and ideological outcomes for not only domestic but international audiences. Now, as China 'goes global,' 'goes West,' and develops both Overland Economic Silk Belt and the 21st Century Maritime Silk Road; we observe instances where cultural programming and arts infrastructure fail at critical moments to engage foreign publics. Particularly since COVID-19, anti-Chinese 'disease vector,' 'china-threat,' and 'yellow peril' racism has been on the rise in the US and UK. In some instances, foreign governments have taken recent steps to ban or obstruct Chinese state efforts to disseminate cultural messaging. One example of this was the recent decision by U.K. regulators to ban China's primary international news channel, CGTN, from the air.[1] This momentous decision to cut off almost half a million U.K. Chinese diaspora from a Chinese perspective on world news was quite likely made because of the top-down nature of this state-controlled media source.[2] Critics believe that China's cultural messaging lacks sufficient independence from authorities in Beijing. China's authoritarian lack of engagement with civic media and communication as well as activist media misses opportunities to self-correct and optimize cultural messaging targeted at foreign publics.

Politics being the study of governments and states; and economics the study of production, consumption and distribution of wealth, these disciplines have much to do with one another. Indeed, they were not originally isolated. Classical political economy incorporated cultural studies into its models. It was when economics specialized into a distinct discipline that it was severed from qualitative cultural models and "semiotic topics were

[1] "Chinese State TV Station Barred from U.K. Airwaves—WSJ," accessed October 16, 2021, https://www.wsj.com/articles/chinese-state-tv-station-barred-from-u-k-airwaves-11612459277.

[2] United Nations High Commissioner for Refugees, "Refworld | World Directory of Minorities and Indigenous Peoples—United Kingdom: Chinese," Refworld, accessed October 16, 2021, https://www.refworld.org/docid/49749c907.html.

marginalized or abandoned."[3] In the case of understanding China's rise in global governance, it is important to step outside of "predominant liberal varieties of capitalism," which have arisen in isolated theoretical fields of politics and economics, into other models wherein state and market are in much closer relationship.[4] Ziya Öniş and Mustafa Kutlay (2020) define the 'Beijing Consensus' as, "the projection of a Chinese model of authoritarian capitalism, also referred to as 'state capitalism.'" The authors describe this model of authoritarian capitalism as, "a distinct variety with its emphasis on state-permeated corporate relations, indicative industrial planning, strategic use of state fiscal resources and financial statecraft, and a highly personalized network of capital accumulation." Studies such as this of the politics and economics of China and its Belt and Road Initiative (BRI) are undoubtedly precise and authoritative in their respective fields. However, they tend to occlude the integrated nature of political economy in China; further obscuring the role of NSR's fifth pillar, People-to-People Connectivity, in a rapidly shifting field of what Tim Winter coins as 'geocultural power.'[5]

China's Cultural Political Economy

Outside of China there is a consensus that, as markets are supposedly separate from the state, so culture has little to do with politics or the market. Western fine art sector modernist and even post-modernist arguments for 'purity' in artistic practice suggest that each artist is an island; free from ideology and profit-drive. The Western position seems to suggest that the artist operates in an aesthetic bubble, independent from economic or political variables. China's political economy of culture takes a very different view. Indeed, there are and have always been individual Chinese artists and thinkers advocating a version of 'art for art's sake,' with disenfranchised literati expressing the desire for individual freedoms, or hermit monks and other ascetics who have divested from cultural, political, and economic institutions. For example, contemporary performance

[3] Ngai-Ling Sum and Bob Jessop, *Towards a Cultural Political Economy* (Edward Elgar Publishing, 2013), 72.

[4] Ziya Öniş and Mustafa Kutlay, "The New Age of Hybridity and Clash of Norms: China, BRICS, and Challenges of Global Governance in a Postliberal International Order," *Alternatives* 45, no. 3 (August 1, 2020): 123–42.

[5] Tim Winter, *Geocultural Power*.

artist Zhou Bin, residing and working in Chengdu, the capital of Sichuan Province in the Southwest of China, recently declared in an interview that nothing, no social issue or crisis facing human civilization, was more important than the mere existence of a single drop of water.[6] His position is quite different from the Chengdu Praxis artists who argue that the meaning of art is entirely socially constructed, and that art's value inheres in its ability to mitigate and otherwise bring attention to the difficulties faced by common people in their day to day lives.[7] Thus, the triangulation of politics, economics, and culture is not the same for Zhou Bin as it is for the Praxis artists. While both camps practice performance art, and both have been educated in Western as well as Chinese approaches to performance art; Zhou Bin has adopted the approach of 'art for art's sake,' which isolates culture from the political economy within which it has grown; and the Praxis artists constellate culture, politics, and economics as tightly orbiting one another.

In the mid-1980s, at the peak of the Chinese '85-New Wave movement, Western cultural, philosophical, and artistic influences appeared in China in a less digested form than what we find now. Over the past three and a half decades in contemporary Chinese art, there has been a backlash nativist movement demanding that Chinese artists take back their own cultural, philosophical, and artistic traditions. Thus, artists and critics have concentrated on ways to integrate the essence of Western traditions together with that of Chinese traditions; into a more 'organic' contemporary Chinese art. While 'art for art's sake' and 'art for the people' camps both partake in these trends and developments; it is the latter, less cosmopolitan school which finds its own thinking forming the sturdier bridge between China's long tradition and contemporary moment.

A good illustration of this tradition can be found in China's traditional historiography, consisting in its 24 official dynastic histories which cover Pre-Qin ancient history through seventeenth century Ming dynasty. These historical texts were created at the behest of and under the supervision of the Chinese ruling class, and they generally provided bibliographies of all known books (both extant and lost), biographies of

[6] Zhou Bin, Unpublished in-person interview with Zhou Bin, October, 8, 2019.

[7] Sophia Kidd, "Poetically Performance Art Dwells: Poetry and Praxis in Southwest China," *Yishu Journal of Contemporary Chinese Art* 12, no. 2 (April 2013): 130–37.

leading political figures, writers, and scholars, as well as economic geographies. This integrated hermeneutic of culture, politics and art arises within the Chinese Confucian historical and textual tradition as authoritative, comprising the very conditions of legitimacy. Chengdu's Praxis artists, while practicing a relatively experimental form of art, can place their own efforts to integrate culture and politics within a continuum of classical Chinese aesthetics, closely in constellation with China's traditional cultural political economy.

Rival aesthetic approaches such as that of artist Zhou Bin have classical precedent as well. Yang Zhu (440–360 BCE) of the Warring States (5th to third centuries BCE) is thought to have formed a school of 'ethical egoism' which advocated a philosophy of living by and for the self (*wei wo* 为我). While we have no knowledge of Yang Zhu's aesthetic theory, we do know that the ethical teleological end of his actions were anchored in the self, rather than in either the social body or the government that rules that body.[8] While Yang Zhu was one of the 'hundred' philosophers and philosophical systems (*zhuzi baijia* 诸子百家), Confucianism had some hundred years to go before its own thought was adopted and institutionalized in the Western Han dynasty. After the various philosophical schools were thinned out through war, persecution, and famine; as Confucianism became the official ideology, Buddhist and Daoist discourse arose in conversation with and often in reaction to Confucian politics, economics, and culture. This is not to say that Confucianism gave rise to these other two main systems of Chinese thought, but that these two sets of discourses were formalized in a milieu of Confucianism.

These three systems of thought have continued to develop in parallel manner, sometimes antagonistic and at other times harmonious. Today this triad of philosophical, religious, ethical, and aesthetic systems are known as the Three Teachings (*sanjiao* 三教, *or Ru Shi Dao* 儒释道). In the famous *Zhengshi* period (正始时期, 240–249 CE) just after the fall of the Eastern Han (25–220 CE), Confucian scholars of what came to be known as *Xuanxue* (玄学) [Abstruse School] produced annotative commentaries of two Daoist texts, the *Zhuangzi* (庄子), and the *Dao De Jing* (道德经), as well as of the *Book of Changes* (*Zhouyi* 周易) which doubles as a Confucian and Daoist text. These books comprise what is

[8] John Emerson, "Yang Chu's Discovery of the Body," *Philosophy East and West* 46, no. 4 (1996): 533–66.

known as the three *xuan* (*san xuan*三玄). Confucians producing important annotations like these on *xuan* texts produced a discourse made up of both Confucian and Daoist semiotic elements. Then, as Buddhism arrived from India, the first translations into Chinese used Confucian and Daoist language to translate Indian Sanskrit concepts. This resulted in the linguistic confluence of Confucian, Daoist, and Buddhist ideas. Later, throughout the Six Dynasties into the Tang, Daoist priests and Buddhist monks engaged in official court debates in a bid to gain patronage and support from the emperor. These debates revealed the tricky nature of these discourses with lexicons largely indebted to one another, with semiotic 'hairs' constantly being split. Losing these debates would result in destruction of Buddhist monasteries in some periods, or Daoist temples in other periods. When Daoists won, the conditions of their monasteries and publishing facilities at their disposal improved radically, while the Buddhist temples were demolished, and their monks dispersed. When Buddhists won the debates, the opposite would happen, as Buddhist texts would flourish and reach wide audiences while Daoist temples were razed. We can see this official 'state' support of certain ideologies as a political economy of culture.

In the political economy of China today, the Three Teachings of Confucianism, Daoism and Buddhism are promoted by the Chinese Communist Party as a continuation of its *guoxue* 国学 [national teaching] movement. It is important to note that of the Three Teachings, it is Confucianism which serves as the substrate in which Daoist and Buddhist thought systems are 'grown' in a controlled ideological and cultural experiment. This has historically been the case, and today even more so. Buddhism, Daoism, as well as Confucian thought are tightly controlled within a wholly other ideological substrate of Communism. Thus, Confucianism in China today is a chimerical and non-stable approximation of what it has historically been.

Historical Roots of Western and Chinese Political Economy

When political economy first emerged in the eighteenth-century as a field of study, it was rooted in moral philosophy. Western political economy thinkers were preoccupied with questions of right and wrong, the role that should be played by desire in wealth production, and questions of freedom and human rights. Each of these thinkers spent time thinking these questions through in the formulation of their ideas of how governments should interact with production, consumption, and transfer of wealth. In many of these thinkers, we detect the roots of their moral philosophy in the Western philosophical tradition, i.e., in the Greco-Roman tradition, especially in the writings of Aristotle (384–322 BCE). Below, we will touch upon a few key late Renaissance through Enlightenment political economists and their contemporaneous cultural economies, extending our discussion as well to Scottish Enlightenment figures David Hume and Adam Smith, before shifting into a parallel timeline of Chinese political economy, with roots founded in early Confucian thought.

Brief Survey of Western Political Economists from Fifteenth–Nineteenth Century

Niccolò Machiavelli (1469–1527) advocated for allowing individuals to work towards their own self-interest. He considered self-interest to be an economic driver; an argument used today for capitalism. Machiavelli's influences were diverse and included sources that were not confined to Plato and Aristotle. He in fact diverged a great deal from both. In his dedication to the Prince Lorenzo de'Medici (1492–1519), Machiavelli states his intention to provide rules and regulations for princely government, in the continuance of a traditional and especially Aristotelian political philosophical tradition.[9] Machiavelli was himself the author of fictional works as well as poetry, including patriotic poetry. He served Lorenzo de'Medici, statesman and ruler ofFlorence, a leader renowned for his patronage of arts and letters. We can deduce that Machiavelli's political economy of culture, although he never used the term, would be one where power and official ideology had great influence upon the value of cultural product.

Francis Bacon (1561–1626) wrote the *Novum Organum, or true directions concerning the interpretation of nature*. We can see by this very title the influence of Greek thinker, Aristotle, whose work, the *Organon*, was a treatise on logic. Although Bacon is inheriting an Aristotelian tradition, in his own work he is creating a new system of logic which he believed was an improvement on syllogistic logic. Using his new 'Baconian method' of logic, the author of the *Novum Organum* famously sets

[9] Leo Strauss, *Thoughts on Machiavelli* (Glencoe, Illinois: The Free Press, 1958), 23.

forth his structure of the 'four idols of the mind'; in which we see how moral philosophy and political economic theory are closely interrelated. These four idols are foibles that the scientific thinker must avoid: idols of the tribe, cave, marketplace, and theatre. The idols of the tribe are mainly the will to look for and believe in non-empirical reasons for unexplainable phenomena. Idols of the cave are environmental and include social influences upon one's own empirical findings. Idols of the marketplace refer to the ambiguous and manipulative nature of language and names. Idols of the theatre are ideologies, or distorting meta-narratives.[10] In Bacon's life, mercantilist political economic policies throughout Europe helped Spain and Portugal to establish empires. Shakespeare's plays, written at this time, were written in vernacular, trending towards popular, rather than high, culture. Thomas Hobbes (1588–1679) wrote the *Leviathan* in France, where he had fled in following the deposed King Charles. His mother allegedly went into early labor over the fright of the Spanish Armada threatening the British shores. His life was then subject to the turmoil of British civil war, and his intellectual efforts culminated in a view that only an absolute sovereignty could preside over the free will of individuals whose minds were waking up to the truths of natural philosophy and empiricism. A scientific revolution was well underway, and France and Holland were seeing the glory of their own empires unfold across the earth. John Locke (1632–1704) wrote not only on political economic philosophy, but also on the philosophy of mind and epistemology. His description and structuring of consciousness as a continuity of self-identity has contributed a great deal to the Western model of self, identity, individuality, and subjectivity. He, unlike Hobbes, was an opponent of absolute monarchy, and spent several years in the Netherlands, where he worked on *An Essay Concerning Human Understanding* and other writings. Throughout this period of the Enlightenment, in the move from superstition and religion towards reason and empirical observations, humanism arose alongside a growing middle class, which itself thrived on new mercantilist political economies. The arts flourished in a trend away from high culture towards popular patronage of the arts. The bourgeoise model of arts patronage consisted of not only the old way of supporting single artists, but also in the purchase of ticket prices to see

[10] Francis Bacon, *The New Organon (Cambridge Texts in the History of Philosophy)*, ed. Lisa Jardine and Michael Silverthorne (Cambridge: Cambridge University Press, 2000), 40–43.

concerts and plays. Technological innovations such as the printing press and popular literature also flourished; with less top-down control being exerted by religious and state institutions.

The Scottish Enlightenment period saw economic growth due to the penetration of Scottish markets into the United States. David Hume (1711–1776) set forth ideas on private property as unequal distribution of property guaranteeing against laziness in industry and labor. He believed that equality would result in poverty for all. While he was a great supporter of a private sector, his belief in heavy taxation as a motivator for industry and labor also provided for the public sector's health. Hume also wrote on aesthetics, and in doing so created space for non-idealic beauty and tragedy in the arts. He, however, advocated for authority in aesthetic ideals, in order to lead the tastes of the masses. Hume's was probably the most mature political economy of culture, in that he allocated space to discuss the connection between power and culture as one that can be utilized by leadership in controlling the public's tastes.

Adam Smith's economic theories were monumentally important to British political economic theory, and later US capitalism. While many are familiar with Smith's economic theories, especially that of the 'invisible hand,' laid out in the *Wealth of Nations*; few are aware of the moral philosophical notion of 'self-command' that Smith laid out in another book, *Theory of Moral Sentiments*.[11] Indeed, in this book, Smith articulated that the success of market-based institutions is based upon whether or not these institutions are structured in such a way as to protect people from the market by enabling virtue in the face of corruption. This ethical dimension in Adam Smith is often ignored in narratives of political economy, and especially in global political economy as developed since the 1970s. Without this ethical dimension, we can draw no connection between economics and culture. However, once we include this ethical dimension, the aesthetic dimension is drawn in once again, and the cultural moment can constellate within political economy. Our last point on Adam smith is his emphasis upon land, labor, and capital as the three main underpinnings of a nation's wealth, which led to the 'spatial fix,' as colonial and imperial political economies of Britain and the

[11] Matthew Watson, "The Historical Roots of Theoretical Traditions in Global Politial Economy," in *Global Political Economy*, ed. John Ravenhill (Oxford: Oxford University Press, 2017), 26–51.

U.S. established global prominence. After briefly discussing Chinese theories of political economy, attempting to draw culture into the discussion; we will return to the notion of the 'spatial fix,' positing it as a crucial component of China's New Silk Roads.

Chinese Ming Through Late-Qing Period Political Economists

Now we'll look at Chinese political economists active throughout the same periods as figures we've just discussed, from Machiavelli to Adam Smith; while trying to draw useful connections between thinkers' ideas and their political economic milieu of cultural production. It's important to note that China's economy was the largest in the world throughout these periods, grouped with the Tang (618–907 CE) and Song (950–1278 CE) dynasties as one of three most prosperous periods in China's history. Salt, iron, tea and salt production had been privatized and wage labor was introduced. While the Ming Hongwu emperor had established his reign restricting foreign trade and forbidding maritime trade but for the import of silver bullion, the third Yongle Ming Emperor Zhu Di built large fleets in pursuit of an international tributary system subservient to the Ming empire's national power. The subsequent development of industry, urban centers, and the prowess of its fleets helped China to set up an extensive trade network both overland and overseas, with Japan and Europe as its top trading partners. It is this network of trade-routes which serve as the historical predecessor to today's 21st Century Maritime Silk Road.

Qiu Jun (邱濬, 1420–1495) was an advocate of Neo-Confucian thinking in the Song dynasty manner known as School of Principles (*Lixue* 理学). We see his debt to Confucian thought from the title of Qiu's main text, *Supplements to the Commentary of The Great Learning* (*Daxue yanyi bu* 大學衍義補). *The Great Learning* (*Daxue* 大学) is a central Confucian text, one of the 'Four Books' along with *Doctrine of the Mean* (*Zhongyong* 中庸), Mencius (*Mengzi*孟子), and the *Analects* (*Lunyu* 论语). Qiu focused on land reform, proposing to limit the amount of land a person could own to only that land which they, themselves, could cultivate. He also proposed a new model of currency standard, with silver, copper, and paper arranged in a hierarchy of value from greatest to least. With industry and commerce throughout the urban centers of the Ming Empire, it was necessary to bring silver in to deal with ever-larger financial transactions; while at the same time, the empire was so expanded, and trade so extensive, that paper currency was needed to keep freight lighter and more practical. According to some accounts, the fall of the Ming in the mid-seventeenth century was precipitated by a dearth of silver needed for currency; and this resulted from resistance to the idea of using paper currency, which was easy to counterfeit.[12] Qiu Jun was an advocate of overseas trade, being one of the first Chinese thinkers to consider the import and export of not just refined objects and materials, but even the most common. Qiu Jun, having been raised on the island of Hainan, was very comfortable with sea voyage, and thus was one of the most effective advocates for using maritime routes for grain transport, which had heretofore been transported through rivers and canals; mainly due to the fear of Japanese piracy along China's eastern seaboard. The Ming Dynasty was known for its vernacular turn in arts and culture. This can be seen as a logical development of urban cosmopolitan centers and a thriving economy supported by a merchant class.

Wang Yangming (王阳明, 1472–1529), born Wang Shouren (王守仁), was fifty years younger than Qiu Jun, and yet he, too, used the Confucian *Daxue* as a foil for his own, more heterodox, ideas. His engagement with Confucian ideas made him the most well-known Neo-Confucianist since Zhu Xi (朱熹, 1130–1200) of the Song dynasty. Engaging with the Confucian disdain for commerce, industry, and the working class in general; he taught that ideas were available to all human beings. In an almost Platonic twist, he spoke of ideas as 'patterns' which exist in all minds, farmer and scholar alike. The folk tradition reached its peak during the Ming, with folk religions contextualized within the 'Three Teachings' (*Sanjiao* 三教) of Confucianism, Daoism, and Buddhism. While Wang was a statesman, he wasn't best known for his political or economic ideas. Rather, it was his student, Wang Gen (王艮, 1483–1540), and Wang Gen's student, He Xinyin (何心隱, 1517–1579); as well as Li Zhi (李贽, 1527–1602) who made contributions to the history of China's economic thought. Wang Gen, an iron mill worker, led the school of Taizhou, easily gaining the following of salt workers and other working-class people. His contribution to economic thought was based primarily upon the idea of equal distribution of land. He Xinyin and Li Zhi were much more radical, both dying in prison, as their own life works spilled over into the late Ming restoration of Confucian orthodoxy. He and Li radically advocated

[12] Hu Jichuang, *A Concise History of Chinese Economic Thought* (Beijing: Foreign Languages Press, 1988), 453–54.

ideas of equality for women, and for the satisfaction of common desires. The Confucian ideas of social hierarchy (which excluded women from the hierarchy) saw desire as evil, necessarily subject to moderation. He Xinyin even advocated public ownership of all property, as well as unconditional love and care for all, not just one's immediate family. These ideas of universal equality and unconditional love had been expressed much earlier in China's intellectual history by the school of Mozi (470–c. 391 BCE) during the Spring and Autumn period. There were distinct regional cultural forces throughout the vast Ming empire, as there were during Mozi's time.

About fifty years later, in the late Ming/early Qing period, agricultural reformer Xu Guangqi (徐光启, 1562–1633) challenged the doctrine that certain plants could only grow in certain areas. This had heretofore created a lot of difficulty over especially grain transport; the political and cultural center of China generally being in the north while most of the food was produced in the fertile southeast region. He was one of the group of scholars who had studied in Macau with Italian Jesuit priest Matteo Ricci (1552–1633), learning thereby a great deal from knowledge streams arising outside of China. Xu's notion of agriculture, however, was not limited to rice paddies and other modes of horticulture. While placing horticulture at the core of agriculture, he also included sericulture, animal husbandry, and domestic industry. Later, and also straddling Ming and Qing dynasties; Wang Fuzhi (王夫之, 1619–1692), Huang Zongxi (黃宗羲, 1610–1695), and Gu Yanwu (顧炎武, 1613–1682) all emphasized the notion of 'thought of self,' an ethical notion somewhat akin to Adam Smith's 'self-command.' Wang, Huang, and Gu believed that industry and commerce were of tantamount importance, and supported the growth of the middle classes. They believed that the ancient ways of the Five Emperors and Three Kings were inferior to the ways of the present day; and that what Heaven had bestowed upon man had to be optimized, as the resources on earth had also to be optimized through industry and commerce. They were also quite nationalist, speaking of the difference between the Chinese and 'barbarians,' which probably had a lot to do with their loyalty to the fallen Ming, and rejection of the new Manchu Qing government.

In painting during this period, there were two streams. One was orthodox Confucian, and the other individualist and non-orthodox. With a non-Han Manchu ethnicity taking the Chinese throne during the Qing, much emphasis was paid to legitimacy. As is usually the case during these ideologically unstable periods of China's history, Confucian values took hold of the cultural and political sphere. However, with many Ming loyalists withdrawn and self-exiled from their official capacities, there was an interesting mix of the vernacular, Buddhist, and popular aesthetics permeating much cultural production at the time, with wealthy middle classes and systems of patronage providing alternative political economies of culture which the Qing was unable to entirely suppress.

Yan Yuan (颜元, 1635–1704) and Li Gong (1659–1733) between them formed an economic school of thought with their attack on wealthy classes and empty orthodoxy. They fully supported industry and commerce but had differing ideas on the hierarchy within which these classes fit. Yan Yuan's follower, Wang Yuan, put forth the idea that, outside of urban centers, only tillers should own land, pushing for doing away with rent-seeking behavior amongst the landed feudal gentry. Lan Dingyuan (1680–1733) also believed that industry was important for the strength of China's political economy. He was also strongly in favor of open shipping routes and international trade, although at that time there was great weariness amongst the Chinese about dealing with Westerners; and the Ming loss of Macau to the Portuguese was still a stinging point for those defending against protectionist political economists. Hong Liangji (洪亮吉, 1746–1809) spent much energy treating the problem of population, facing centuries of an instilled belief that a large population was always best. Hong, however, was one of the first to measure growth rates, which were bourgeoning due in part to new agricultural methods and raised the problem of inflation and decreasing wages for the people if population were to increase.

Wei Yuan (魏源, 1794–1857) was the "last thinker of the typical Chinese pattern of economic thought," although he advocated learning much about Western culture and political economic institutions. He focused on grain transport and the salt monopoly in the years leading to the first Opium War (1840–1842). After the war, he focused on promoting the development of industry and commerce so that production techniques could support the construction of ships and guns large and strong enough to beat the Western 'barbarians' at their own game. His love of democracy in the West, as well as the arts of prosperity drove him to admire the wealthy classes as makers of their own destiny. His devotion to growing the merchant classes was not for personal gain or affirmation; rather he advocated this economic growth and class disparity as crucial for the national economy. Wei's book, *The Geography of the Maritime*

Countries was the first scientific treatment about international trade. He has been called the "last of China's classic economic thinkers and the first Chinese pilgrim to the "holy land" of modern bourgeois economics."[13] By this time, Western economic theory with its roots in the Greco-Roman tradition had begun to integrate with Chinese economic theory with its own roots in the Confucian tradition.

New Silk Roads: A 'Spatial Fix'

Major domestic challenges faced by China include industrial structure imbalance, environmental problems, inequality among regions, income inequality, low domestic consumption rates, lack of jobs for white collar workers, and unsustainable economic development.[14] These problems have developed as side effects of China's hypergrowth over the past forty years, and now add to other challenges being faced regarding sustained future growth. While much literature on the New Silk Roads concentrates upon China's role in global governance as it reconstitutes the geopolitical imaginary, China's emphasis is upon its own internal problems and challenges. Thus, it is in this light that many insights into the New Silk Roads can be gained by viewing it as a 'spatial fix.'

One of the first to discuss a 'spatial fix' was Johann Heinrich von Thünen (1783–1850), nineteenth century German economist. Contemporary economic geographer David Harvey (1935–) devotes a chapter to the spatial fix in his *Spaces of Capital: Towards a Critical Geography*.[15] In this chapter he discusses thought on this subject in von Thünen as well as Karl Marx (1818–1883) vis a vis Hegel's (1770–1831) *Philosophy of Right*. Hegel, in the tradition of Western moral philosophy, uses a broad brush of speculative philosophy to describe a political-economic structure which places the family as microcosm at the center of society, by which is meant all societies across all regions of the earth. Hegel posits that the family is the unit run altruistically; while civil society was a free-for-all where individuals used other individuals to provide for their family.

13 Hu Jichuang, 526.

14 Cem Nalbantoglu, "One Belt One Road Initiative: New Route on China's Change of Course to Growth," *Open Journal of Social Sciences* 5, no. 1 (January 6, 2017): 87–99.

15 David Harvey, *Spaces of Capital: Towards a Critical Geography* (New York: Routledge, 2001), 284–311.

Hegel believed that market forces are ultimately destructive to social harmony. Profit is generated by harnessing other peoples' labor, and markets expand by the 'perpetual transformation of social needs' which create ever more needs and desires in other people. Hegel believed that the state must intervene to mitigate the tendencies of these destructive and expansive forces. The subjugation of the working classes to the systems and institutions built to maximize profit along these lines then deprives these lower classes of the benefits of an increasingly wealthy and sophisticated civil society. The inner tension of a society will then be alleviated by expanding markets in lands further away. Von Thünen, too, felt that the development of frontier territories would serve as a spatial fix, allowing otherwise impoverished families to gain land for themselves, and for markets to unload goods in markets which would otherwise be deprived of the benefits of these products. Industry could also find room for expansion in these frontier or foreign territories, allowing for further specialization of labor in civil society and the development of jobs for more sophisticated or managerial types of labor.

China's plan for the New Silk Roads provides solutions for domestic issues of industrial structure imbalance, environmental problems, inequality among regions, income inequality, low domestic consumption rates, lack of jobs for white collar workers, and unsustainable economic development. However, fixing these problems for China by spatially expanding the economic geography as a system will quite possibly lead to the superimposition of these tensions between private and civil life across a much larger playing board. That is to say, the nature of the system may not change, but the impoverished classes will now be located outside of China's borders, and the profit-seeking and rent-seeking behaviors created by the natural market forces in state-mobilized capitalism may merely find new, non-Chinese, victims. These constitute the fears of people and their leaders in states and regions along the New Silk Roads. Policy Coordination, Facilities Connectivity, Unimpeded Trade, and Financial Integration may lead down dark roads, unless leaders take precautions that the New Silk Roads are inclusive, ensuring a'win–win' for the publics concerned. 'Win–win' is the 'transcendence of a duality between public and private life,' as David Harvey points out:

> The evident tension between the family and civil society—between the private and public spheres of social life—can be resolved, in Hegel's view, only through the acquisition of a universalistic consciousness through the

> institutions of the modern state. The rational state, Hegel claims, can transcend the dualities of private and public life and so restore the broken unity of human existence through synthesis of the role of 'homme' and 'citoyen' which Rousseau had envisaged as ineluctably split asunder within the complex weave of bourgeois society.[16]

The 'Community of Common Destiny (*Gongtong mingyunti* 共同命运体)' of mankind spoken of by Chinese president Xi Jinping resonates with what Hegel called a 'universalistic consciousness' which transcends the dualities of the zero-sum game usually played in geopolitical development and colonial statesmanship. This book proposes that it is the fifth pillar of New Silk Road development, People-to-People Connectivity, which provides a heuristic for the NSR in which we can resolve tensions created by capitalisms rubbing up against each other. The key for Xi's 'Common Destiny' is cultural, public and People-to-People diplomacy, both top-down and grassroots. Spread of Confucius institutes, university and research centers, exhibitions, and cultural heritage tourism indeed pave the way for NSR's other four pillars. Appropriate policies focus on access to foreign markets; while fostering industrial zones and improving higher education as well as supply chains will help China to move up the global value chain.

Conclusion—New Silk Roads Political Economy of Culture

In his article "Value and Affect," Antonio Negri discusses the schism between politics and economics insofar as this split obscures reasonable analysis of the relationship between value and labor.[17] Negri points out that the economic relationship is a social one. Placing a spotlight on this social relationship proves economic theory to be ontological. In the following passage, political economy is framed by Negri as 'top down.'

> What has irreversibly changed, however, from the times of the predominance of the classical theory of value, involves the possibility of developing the theory of value in terms of economic order, or rather, the possibility

[16] David Harvey, 285.

[17] Antonio Negri and Michael Hardt, "Value and Affect," *Boundary 2* 26, no. 2 (1999): 77–88.

> of considering value as a measure of concrete labor, either individually or collectively. The economic consequences of this difficulty are certainly important, but equally important are its anthropological and social presuppositions. These latter elements are what I will focus on here—on this novelty that transforms the theory of value "from below," from the base of life.[18]

In Chinese higher education, humanities are interpreted and taught from an economic point of view. This is true from the study of classical and modern literature to the fields of sociology, politics and philosophy. Thus, Negri's thought of value, not just as an economic principle, but as a primary social principle, would not be seen as progressive or interdisciplinary, but as a basic principle upon which all others are built. Negri's theory of value, however, was taken from the 'base of life' earlier on in the formation of Marxist-Leninist political economics, and placed at the highest 'topos' of life, within the ideological sphere in control, as implemented to this day by the Chinese government. We want to examine what this top-down implementation of a proletariat-based value system looks like in the deployment of the People-to-People pillar of the New Silk Roads.

We have found that such top-heavy cultural policy is, in some instances, unable to maintain contact with the will of the peoples in its jurisdiction, especially when the channels for feedback in print and in social media are censored or shaped to optimize cultural messaging. In our last chapter on People-to-People Connectivity, we emphasized the importance of grassroots, or bottom-up, creative agents in the cultural sector. These work best as a supplement to government designed P2P programs. These private enterprises or public–private partnerships (PPP) localize centralized cultural policy to optimize policy interpretation according to region of implementation. Central government policies are sometimes intentionally vague, and thus adaptable, in terms of implementation, to regions and peoples of other regions within China and cultures outside of China. As

[18] Negri and Hardt, 77–78.

Michael Keane argues in his "Creative Industries in China: four perspectives on social transformation," creative economies divert economic attention from "the material to 'the people.'"[19] Here we see a similar tension developing within creative sectors of the economy, also known as 'creative economies,' one which equates the top-down/grassroots dichotomy with similar dichotomies in policy making as well as economic planning.

The New Silk Roads are often interpreted by Western pundits as seen through the lens of Western political economic narratives. As we have mentioned before, these narratives tend to keep politics separate from economics, further obscuring projects across all five pillars of the New Silk. Data gets presented through mathematical methodology which assume that economic actors act rationally and always to maximise personal benefit, a type of thinking which is very recent in human history, reaching full fruition in twentieth century capitalist economies. While this assumption appears to be objective, or value-free; it holds the presuppositional value that economic and political policies that maximise personal benefit are socially optimal.

The political economy of New Silk Roads oversees the social, economic, political, and aesthetic nature of its policies in general. Where Chinese systems administer along the New Silk Roads, cultural policy interpretation and implementation will vary from region to region. As cultural distance between China and each of these other nations and cultures is detrimental to the value of cultural exports, China must overcome this distance by building multi-purpose industrial zones, improving vocational and higher education, and nurturing networks between local creative brands and foreign marketing and distribution, channels.[20]

[19] Michael Keane, "Creative Industries in China: Four Perspectives on Social Transformation," *International Journal of Cultural Policy* 15, no. 4 (November 1, 2009): 431–43.

[20] Chung Van Dong and Hoan Quang Truong, "The Determinants of Creative Goods Exports: Evidence from Vietnam," *Journal of Cultural Economics* 44, no. 2 (June 2020): 281–308.

CHAPTER 5

Cultural Discount and Chinese Cultural Exports

China's creative industries and cultural production are charged with the task of strengthening the progress of China's cultural power worldwide. This is something other developed nations, for example the United States, have identified in their own practice as soft power development. American blue jeans, Coca-Cola, Hollywood films, and major network television series like *Law and Order* have changed the way publics throughout the world dress, drink, spend their leisure time, and think of justice. Through these cultural products, US culture has been able to transmit its own values and tastes, winning the hearts and minds of people through cultural power as a supplement to or replacement for political, economic, and military force. China seeks to do the same with their own culture, and it's proving difficult. The 'othering' of Chinese culture slows this process down, resulting in a trend that often sees devaluation of China's cultural export upon exiting China's borders. This is known as cultural discount (*wenhua zhekou* 文化折扣) and is a topic of much discussion amongst Chinese experts on creative and cultural industries.

S. Kidd, *Culture Paves The New Silk Roads*,
Contemporary East Asian Visual Cultures, Societies and Politics,
https://doi.org/10.1007/978-981-16-8574-3_5

Zhou Enlai (1898–1976) viewed culture as "an instrument of political and economic cooperation between China and the outside world."[1] While economic reforms beginning in 1978 that came with Deng Xiaoping's (1904–1997) Reforms and Opening-Up (*Gaige kaifang* 改革开放) have had over four decades to gain momentum and take shape; reforms in cultural management are still fairly new and have yet to take consistent shape at home and along the New Silk Roads. This chapter discusses to a basic extent some of the trade barriers, government policies, human resources, and marketing strategies that hold Chinese cultural export at a seemingly perpetual disadvantage. As mentioned in Chapter 3, China's People-to-People Connectivity must not be too top-down or authoritarian if it is going to appeal to publics in regions outside of Asia. Somehow, China must find ways in which to increase the value of its cultural export, and must do so by mitigating the problem of cultural discount (*wenhua zhekou* 文化折扣). These cultural discounts are less severe in the Global South, and this has to do with these cultures being more likely to share certain traditionalist cultural ideals with China, such as family values, patriarchal values, and aesthetic values. Publics living in the Global North, on the other hand, have in many cases transitioned away from these traditional values, and are less likely to consume Chinese cultural products which convey these values. When 'othering' is extreme, as is the case with China, this extends beyond culture, into political and economic 'othering.' For example, recent Central and Eastern European (CEE) pushback against Huawei 5G networks significantly hampers New Silk Roads development, especially in the initiative's second pillar of Facilities Connectivity (*Sheshi liantong* 设施联通). Without Huawei's networks working in tandem with China's financial technology (Wechat and Alibaba) and satellite systems (Beidou), China lacks the digital networks needed to administrate smart cities and other logistical infrastructure (wet and dry ports, rail, and roads). This pushback strengthens as the US-Biden administration renews strategic partnerships with other nations in the Global North seeking to counter China's global influence via political and economic means. As these partnerships gather momentum, the battle then loops back onto the cultural playing field, and China's cultural trade deficit is exacerbated with an increased devaluation of its cultural export. An international atmosphere of 'china threat,'

[1] M.S. Olimat, *China and Central Asia in the Post-Soviet Era: A Bilateral Approach* (Lanham: Lexington Books, 2015), 47–54.

'yellow peril,' and 'an increasingly aggressive Beijing,' must be met with greater efforts on China's behalf to strengthen The New Silk Road's fifth pillar of People-to-People Connectivity. These efforts include redoubling public diplomacy (especially cultural and medical diplomacy), as well as strengthening and internationalising creative sector developments both at home and in regions along the New Silk Roads.

Creative Industries: A Question of Control

Xi Jinping stated in his 2014 speech at the Forum on Arts and Literature that art should be of 'high quality' while at the same time functioning as propaganda. The appearance of the word 'propaganda' is uncomfortable to Westerners, with its connotations of manipulation, lack of criticality, and top-down heavy-handedness. In its its extreme form, propaganda stands to be labelled as 'brain washing.' In China, however, 'propaganda (*xuanchuan* 宣传)' is not a dirty word, meaning something akin to the Western use of the terms 'marketing' or 'dissemination.' Semantics aside, Xi clearly intends in his speech for art to serve the people by conveying cultural messaging that lines up with Chinese Communist Party values. This measure of 'quality' diverges vastly from aesthetic ideals and cultural values held by publics and governments of the Global North, the publics of which tend to view art as independent from both the market and the state.

Although Theodor W. Adorno (1903–1969), Max Horkheimer (1895–1973), and other social and critical theorists of the Frankfurt School exposed the ideological power of mass culture; many cultural critics and social scientists today are still disengaged with the term 'cultural economy.' The idea that art and culture operate in tandem with economic, political, and military power is still foreign to most outside of certain niches of academia. 'Cultural economy' appears to make artists feel uncomfortable, as if 'culture' were some refuge from daily commerce, and as if daily commerce had not already penetrated into every crevice of our cultural activities. Teaching a few years back in Germany to students of international affairs and political science, the expression 'cultural economy' raised eyebrows and hands, and extra time was spent laying the foundations of this conversation in hopes of a more integrated approach to understanding China's own use of culture as a political tool.[2]

In his discussion of cultural industries, David Hesmondhalgh defines these industries as anything that capitalizes on ideas or cultural and creative resources as 'creative capital,' focusing on core creative industries of media, ads, publishing, and computer tech.[3] For him, creative industries were characteristically posed with the following four problems: risky business; creativity versus commerce; high production/low reproduction costs; and semi-public goods. Resolutions to these problems include the following five: misses are offset against hits by building a repertoire; concentration, integration and co-opting publicity; artificial scarcity; and loose control of symbol creators, but tight control of distribution and marketing.[4] Others, such as John Howkins have a looser definition of 'creative economy' as including all financial transactions in creative products, defining then these 'creative products' as a "good or service that results from creativity and has economic value."[5] The United Nations Conference on Trade and Development (UNCTAD) definition of creative economic activity is "any economic activity producing symbolic products with a heavy reliance on intellectual property and for as wide a market as possible." These include "upstream activities" (traditional) and "downstream activities" (market-oriented advertising, publishing, etc.)[6] The UNCTAD "Classification of Creative Industries" lays out the following types of Creative Industry in four categories.

Category	*Types of creative industry*
Heritage	Traditional cultural expressions (arts, crafts, festivals, and celebrations)
	Cultural sites (archaeological sites, museums, libraries, exhibitions, etc.)
Arts	Visual arts (paintings, sculptures, photography, and antiques)

(continued)

[2] John Howkins, *The Creative Economy: How People Make Money from Ideas* (London: Penguin Books, 2001), 348, H.

[3] See David Hesmondhalgh, *The Cultural Industries*, Second Edition (Los Angeles: SAGE, 2007).

[4] David Hesmondhalgh, 17–24.

[5] John Howkins, *The Creative Economy: How People Make Money from Ideas*, 447.

[6] "Creative Economy Report 2010," 2010, 422.

(continued)

Category	*Types of creative industry*
	Performing arts (live music, theatre, dance, opera, circus, puppetry, etc.)
Media	Audio-visuals (film, television, radio, other broadcasting)
	Publishing and printed media (Books, press, and other publications)
Functional creations	New Media (software, video games, digitized creative content)
	Design (interior, graphic, fashion, jewellery and toys)
	Creative services (architectural, advertising, creative R & D, cultural and recreational)

Cultural and Creative Industries Along the New Silk Roads

China's development of creative industries and organs of cultural production along the New Silk Roads optimizes the likelihood that foreign peoples along the New Silk Roads will gain an understanding of Chinese culture. Best case scenarios see these publics internalize Chinese culture, which reduces the tendency to 'other' the new cultural influence. Conversely, in gaining a greater understanding and grasp of the markets through which it disseminates cultural products; China seeks to optimize its cultural messaging to further engage foreign publics. As this book argues, it is the fifth pillar of the New Silk Roads, that of People-to-People Connectivity (*Minxin xiangtong* 民心相通) that develops this cultural power. It does this in ways that includes the spread of Confucius Institutes, university and research centers, student exchange programs, cultural weeks and cultural days, exhibitions, music concerts, poetry readings, tourism, film, television, publishing, gaming software, and social media. The building of value into Chinese cultural exports changes the perceptions of cultural consumers along the New Silk Roads. As China experiences the severity of cultural trade deficits, and its efforts at "going out" *zou chu qu* 走出去 promote multi-level and expansive communication with other nations; People-to-People Connectivity cultivates geocultural power which then facilitates the other four 'harder' pillars of BRI: Policy Coordination (*Zhengce goutong* 政策沟通), Facilities Connectivity (*Sheshi liantong*), Unimpeded Trade (*Maoyi changtong* 贸易畅通), and Financial Integration (*Zijin tongrong* 资金通融).

In his report at the Thirteenth National Congress of the Communist Party of China (CPC) (October 1987), Deng Xiaoping made a series of tweaks to the notion of 'socialism with Chinese characteristics.' It was at this time that Deng was able to purge nearly a hundred older generational party members who were resistant to market reforms set in motion by Reforms and Opening-Up which had commenced nine years earlier at the Third Plenum of the Eleventh Central Committee of the CPC in 1978. Officials who resisted market-oriented reforms and bourgeois liberalism were discharged in favor of a younger more liberal-minded generation of reformists. Reports given at the Thirteenth National Congress saw the following semantic changes, each of which may refer to nuanced policy change meant to affect the trajectories of political, economic and cultural arenas.[7] Placing 'socialism with Chinese characteristics' as the pedestal upon which to exhibit new conceptual works of political economic expression; a series of derivatives appeared as the: 'road of," "theory of," "praxis of," "basic route of," "fundamental politics of," "democratic governance of," "macroscopic business of," and "great banner of" socialism with Chinese characteristics. Each of these nuanced trajectories served as possibilities for new conversations about China's political economy as represented by the CCP. This newly evolved political economy saw the "fundamental principles of Marxism in tandem with China's modernization." It was "rooted in China's contemporary scientific socialism," and more importantly for our discussion of China's political economy of culture; it was a "unified understanding" held not only by "all party members," "but also every Chinese person"; a fundamental strengthening of the coming together of *all thought*. Deng Xiaoping's reshaping of the original vision of socialism with Chinese characteristics was meant to be a re-evaluation and "re-understanding" of a newly forming political economy, scientific-socialism, and philosophy. Indeed, this political economy was meant to manage not only markets and politics; but also *sixiang wenhua* 思想文化 (literally 'thought culture'). While Western market-theory was being incorporated into this new socialism; its key

7 "中国特色社会主义: 概念演变与内涵升华–理论–人民网," accessed October 18, 2021, http://theory.people.com.cn/n/2013/0116/c49157-20216946.html.

characteristic was and still is this official thought guidance provided by the CCP.[8]

Min Ye, in an excellent treatment of the Belt and Road Initiative as an evolution of China's earlier Western Development Program (WDP) and China Goes Global (CGG) initiatives; analyses China's political economy from 1998–2018. She speaks of the New Silk Roads as spearheading what she calls 'state-mobilized globalization.'

> The system consists of different authority structures and power centers – political leadership, central agencies, state capital, and local governments. There is considerable fragmentation and negotiation between the leadership and the agencies, between the state and state capital, and between the center and local governments. There are also complicated interest groups and functional separations inside the political authority, across different state agencies, across SOEs [State Owned Enterprises], and across local governments. In short, in contrast to the image of a coercive and effective authoritarian system, the Chinese state system is structurally fragmented.[9]

This analysis of the fragmented and complicated nature of China's political and economic structures is especially helpful in understanding how to look at and talk about Belt and Road policy, implementation, pushback, and subsequent revisions as comprising an integral feedback loop. This feedback loop between centralised planning and localised implementation benefits from varying degrees of policy clarity. This 'fuzzy' policy allows for creative implementations in the process of State Mobilized Globalization (SMG). Let's keep this in mind as we now look at the relationship between culture and China's political economy over the past 70 years. We will briefly examine the varying degrees of control exercised over the cultural sector during this time, arriving at how the political economy of culture along China's New Silk Roads expresses and reinforces China's cultural ideals, and how these ideals may in fact worsen the 'othering' of Chinese culture, and increase 'cultural discount' as well as China's cultural deficit.

[8] "中国共产党领导是中国特色社会主义最本质的特征-新华网," accessed October 18, 2021, http://www.xinhuanet.com/2020-07/15/c_1126241149.htm.

[9] Min Ye, "The Belt Road and Beyond State-Mobilized Globalization in China 1998–2018," 7.

'Art in Service of the People' or 'Art For Art's Sake'?

When the communists came into power in 1949, Chinese artists were seen as a force of cultural production. Throughout the 1950s this meant that artists were supposed to take back the force of visual representation from bourgeoise abstraction and other Western 'spiritually polluted' (*jingshen wuran* 精神污染) modes of depicting the world; and follow the Soviet-style of 'social realism.' Representations in print or on canvas were made to mimic reality as it was collectively and socially perceived as accepted 'reality.' This 'realism' promoted communist cultural ideals of a collective and shared reality which saw things 'as they were,' with no hidden class warfare embedded in the visual or written text. During the 1960s, throughout the Cultural Revolution, 'revolutionary romanticism,' which characterises propaganda posters of the period, adopted social realism in ways which depicted and encouraged the revolutionary fervour of the Chinese proletariat classes. Mao and his 'Gang of Four' wanted people to dig even deeper into their commitment to Communist ideals; and to find the resolve to again purge Chinese society of anything Western or bourgeois, anything intellectual or 'highbrow,' anything abstract, or anything otherwise signaling cultural ideals at variance with the cultural ideals of the Chinese Communist Party. Artists were given employment within the party, and in the biographies and catalogues of older contemporary Chinese artists today who began their career in that period; one sometimes sees that they got their start working in the propaganda departments painting large posters for neighbourhood councils.

With Deng Xiaoping's Reform and Opening-Up, as international markets opened up trade routes for foreign electronics and cars; cultural commodities arrived, and with them the philosophical concepts shaping the cultural ideals that informed those cultural commodities. 'Samizdat' versions of works by Western philosophers such as Friedrich Nietzsche and Jean-Paul Sartre, as well as catalogues and books of Anglo-American and European art flooded underground cultural networks. The first batch of Chinese art students, classes of 1978 and '79, initiated conversations still developing in China's critical discourse today. At the time, artists often engaged with theoretical systems such as existentialism and structuralism, and developed their own nascent bodies of artwork informed by pop art and other Western schools of art. Many of these same graduates had been sent down to the countryside during the Cultural Revolution; or had grown up with their parents who had been sent down to rural areas. Many of these artists had grown up working in factories, rather than going to grade school; and then returned to the cities to study in newly opened universities then flush with the circulation of entirely foreign philosophical ideas, aesthetic modalities, and cultural ideals. This unique set of socio-historical conditions predisposed a generation of Chinese contemporary artists to adopt and adapt foreign ethics and aesthetics in unique ways. Chinese intellectual and aesthetic translation-appropriations of Western schools of thought and art created considerable space for changing these modes of thought and artistic creation. Thus, Chinese existentialism and pop-art cannot be explained as a carbon copy of German existentialism or New York pop art. Variants of these ideas and modes of artistic creation have informed a unique body of contemporary Chinese art, one which commands high prices on the international art market today. It was in the mid-1980's that numbers of Chinese artists turned away from 'art for the sake of the people' towards 'art for art's sake.'

'85 New Wave

The explosion of new art forms in China during the mid-1980s was not only due to Chinese artists' exposure to Western ideas; but equally if not more importantly to these artists' ability to revisit their own traditional culture without punitive repercussions. Not only were Western philosophical, cultural and aesthetic ideals seen as bourgeoise spiritual pollution; but China's own classical philosophical, cultural and aesthetic ideals were also seen as corrupting an otherwise simple and utilitarian consciousness. This had been brewing since the turn of the twentieth century in China, when various Chinese intellectuals returned from study abroad and began to advocate throwing out the Chinese system of written characters in favor of a Romanized alphabet. These intellectuals also advocated tossing out Chinese classical styles of ink-wash painting (*shuimo hua* 水墨画) in favor of Western oil painting, argued that ink-wash painting no longer represented Chinese reality. These claims about reality are seen as crucial in making meaningful social, cultural, economic or political change.[10]

[10] Sophia Kidd, "Realism in China's Contemporary Moment: Chen Anjian's Transport Teahouse Oil Painting Series," *Yishu Journal of Contemporary Chinese Art* 17, no. 6 (2018): 52–67.

The '85 New Wave artistic movement saw multiple lines of aesthetic enquiry reach full flower in an amazingly short period of time. Some of these lines of inquiry include: 'art for art's sake,' 'art that serves the people,' 'art as exploration of existence,' and 'art as resistance.' As mentioned above, 'art for art's sake' makes claims most diametrically opposed to 'art for the sake of the people,' and thus is most radical in China. Consider how this contrasts with Western art, wherein 'art of resistance' would often be considered the most radical type of artistic practise. Even in today's contemporary Chinese art world, 'art for art's sake' is seldom understood or given any meaningful critical treatment by either domestic or international arts writers. 'Art as exploration of existence,' whether from a down-to-earth perspective or from a metaphysical one, also gets glossed over or misread by many Chinese critics, and often by international writers as well. This could be due to the tendency (both domestically and internationally) to over-value Chinese art's ability to either bolster (domestically) or subvert (internationally) the Chinese government. 'Art that serves the people' is sometimes also 'art as resistance,' but not always, as the former can serve social functions which align with Party cultural ideals; and the latter can serve social functions by advocating for ideals at variance with Party cultural ideals.

From Mao to Xi: Two Landmark Speeches 1942 and 2014, Setting Aesthetic Policy Milestones

Two landmark speeches in modern and contemporary China dealing with the political economy of culture are those given by Mao Zedong at Yan'an in 1942, and Xi Jinping at the Beijing Forum on Literature and Art 72 years later, in 2014. Xi Jinping's speech during the Beijing Forum refers to the past in order to stress the element of continuity in legitimacy for the CCP's rule and relevance.[11] In this speech, Xi developed an integral art theory presenting guidelines for artists to follow. In 1942, Mao had stated that, "There is in fact no such thing as art for art's sake, art that stands above classes or art that is detached from or independent of

11 "A Year After Xi's Landmark Speech on the Arts, Some Things Get Left Out—WSJ," accessed October 18, 2021, https://www.wsj.com/articles/BL-CJB-27898.

politics."[12] He was addressing the notion of 'art for art's sake,' draining it of any value for the CCP's political economy of culture. Xi, however, in 2014, does not address this notion of aestheticism head on, but rather says that, "Literature and art are the bugle call for the advance of the times, are most able to represent the spirit of an era, and are most able to guide the mood of an era."[13] Federica Mirra summarizes Xi's theory of art, which was only released to the general public one year later, into five main points. First, art is needed to realize the Chinese Dream (*Zhongguo meng* 中国梦). Second, it must be full of praise for Chinese culture, as well as for its people. Third, art should not be made by an artist for elite purposes, but rather for the people. Art must be produced within a hermeneutic creative process that informs the artwork by learning from the people. Fourth, whereas from Mao critiqued China's 'four olds' of old ideas (*jiu sixiang* 旧思想), old culture (*jiu wenhua* 旧文化), old habits (*jiu fengsu* 旧风俗), and old customs (*jiu xiguan* 旧习惯) as evils of an obsolete past; Xi believed that artists should praise China's past by making works that integrate old with the new. Lastly, Xi believes that the Party is the 'guarantor' for art and literature, meaning that the Party will be accountable for art produced during its watch, and thus maintains the right to control its production. We see in Xi's aesthetic theory that art is instrumental to politics, and China's economy is controlled by and tied up with its politics. Thus, contemporary Chinese art, literature and culture are inextricably tied up in China's political economy.

Alignment of China's Cultural Ideals with the CCP

Xi's art theory as stated in 2014, one year after the announcement of both Belt and Road in Kazakhstan and Indonesia, respectively; places culture as an integral part of the instrumental use of ideology in building an internationally active socialist state. Present at his speech were: China Writer's Association Chairwoman Tie Ning, China Peking Opera Association Chairman and Shanghai Peking Opera Theatre and Art Director

[12] "Talks at the Yenan Forum on Literature and Art," accessed October 18, 2021, https://www.marxists.org/reference/archive/mao/selected-works/volume-3/mswv3_08.htm.

[13] Federica Mirra, *Art Theory in Xi Jinping's Policy: M.A. Thesis* (Leiden University, 2016).

Shang Changrong, Kongzheng Song and Dance Ensemble First-Level Playwright Yan Su, China Association of Fine Arts Vice-Chairman and China Academy of Fine Arts Director Chang Xuhong, China Association of Dance Chairwoman and National Theatre Dance Art Chief Inspector Zhao Rusu, China Writer's Association Vice Chairman and Shanghai Municipal Writer's Association Vice Chairman Ye Xin, and China Film Association Chairman and China Drama Academy First-Level Performer Li Xuejian; all of whom gave addresses.[14] Thus we see that writing, performing arts (theatre, opera, and dance), fine arts, and film are crucial underpinnings in the cultural fabric of China, or in the very least in the cultural fabric of cultural production, as ebbs and flows of a cultural narrative shaped by CCP ideology.

What are China's cultural ideals? This is the topic of hundreds of volumes on the subject produced both inside and outside of China, by Chinese writers, Chinese diaspora, and writers who have no ethnic connection to or lived experience in China. The answer is different from volume to volume, and more so as the perspective shifts from period to period, and vantage point to vantage point. For our own purposes, we need to understand which Chinese cultural ideals have and will continue to come to bear upon peoples in nations along the New Silk Roads, both overland and maritime, both virtual and physical, and within our international cultural imaginary of the ancient as well as New Silk Roads. We also need to select those cultural ideals which translate poorly into other languages, cultures, and especially non-Asian cultures.

Zhang Lihua of the Carnegie-Tsinghua Center for Global Policy prioritizes harmony, benevolence, righteousness, courtesy, wisdom, honesty, loyalty and filial piety as those principles which drive China's foreign diplomacy.[15] These would then be cultural ideals as exported from the cultural core of Chinese society. Other core concepts not mentioned in this list would be social capital (*guanxi* 关系), interdependence, unity, and 'face.' Harmony [*hexie* 和谐] is an important concept, and it

[14] "Xi Jinping's Talks at the Beijing Forum on Literature and Art," *China Copyright and Media* (blog), October 16, 2014, https://chinacopyrightandmedia.wordpress.com/2014/10/16/xi-jinpings-talks-at-the-beijing-forum-on-literature-and-art/.

[15] "China's Traditional Cultural Values and National Identity—Carnegie-Tsinghua Center—Carnegie Endowment for International Peace," accessed October 18, 2021, https://carnegietsinghua.org/2013/11/21/china-s-traditional-cultural-values-and-national-identity-pub-53613.

could be epitomized in the expression *he er bu tong* 和而不同, which we introduced earlier. It stresses unity composed of many differences. According to the Chinese notion of *he er bu tong*, a cultural universal is made up of diverse peoples who maintain cultural particulars. How the Chinese ideal of *he er bu tong* plays out, for example along the New Silk Roads, varies from region to region. In China, where NSR originates at Xi'an and along the South Eastern Seaboard in cities such as Quanzhou, the mandate of mandarin as the 'common language' (*putonghua* 普通话) throughout China has been seen as problematic. As ethnic minority languages in China have begun to disappear, policy changes have seen increased emphasis upon the study of ethnic minorities and their languages. However, an understanding of a dead or dying language is not the same as keeping that language alive in minority populations. Outside of China, in New Silk Roads policy, Xi emphasises the need for enterprises engaging in international affairs, whether political, economic, or cultural; to learn foreign languages in order to facilitate People-to-People Connectivity (*Minxin xiangtong* 民心相通). This issue, as well as the issues of translations and language service are seen as key issues in fifth pillar development.

Each of the cultural ideals listed by Zhang are also those of the Chinese Communist Party; and of them; benevolence, righteousness, courtesy, wisdom, honesty, and loyalty are also seen as virtues in not only other Asian cultures, but also non-Asian cultures. They are integral to implementing both the golden rule, 'do unto others that which you would have done unto yourself,' as well as its Confucian variant, 'do not do unto others that which you would not have done unto yourself.' Filial piety, however, and the Confucian theory of five cardinal relationships (*wulun* 五伦) which institutes social hierarchies of ruler—minister, father—son, older brother—younger brother, husband—wife, and mutual trust in friendship; is being purged from the list of cultural ideals in Western neoliberal societies. It is still however, a cultural ideal in Asia, including East Asia, Southeast Asia, and Central Asia, as well as in African and South American societies, among others. For this reason, Chinese cultural ideals translate more easily across Chinese borders whilst travelling into these regions. When the ideals of filial piety or hierarchical relationships hit Western shores, however, the value of cultural imports into which these ideals are embedded tends to deteriorate.

Before we move on to discussing how the political economy of culture is employed in signifying these cultural ideals, I will also touch upon the

Chinese cultural ideals of social capital (*guanxi*), lian 脸/mianzi 面子 (face) and '*subtlety* (hanxu 含蓄).' A grasp of this last term is essential to understanding the art of subtlety in Chinese communication styles. The word *hanxu* can be used as a verb or an adjective, and can be defined as 'to contain' or 'to embody,' referring to an implicit and indirect mode of communicating. What is left unspoken contains the kernel of the meaning. It is this tendency of Chinese communication style which makes it a 'high-context' way of expressing meaning. According to Fang and Faure, Chinese cannot really be understood outside of its full cultural context. This is linked with the discussion of Chinese culture as a collectivist culture.[16] Just as the identities of individuals in Chinese society are largely socially determined by other individuals in their various communities; in a similar way, we find the meaning of single words or memes largely determined by the contexts in which they are spoken. On a deeper and more complete level, the analogy extends to ancestor worship and the belief that one's identity is not only determined by other living individuals in our communities; but also, by the dead who have come before us. Likewise, in Chinese communication, the meaning of a word or a meme is determined not only by other expressed meanings; but also, largely by meanings that have not been overtly expressed, or have been expressed by that word in other older contexts, i.e. that which is left unspoken is essentially in many cases the true gist of what has been spoken. Literally, *hanxu* is made up of two characters; *han* 含 and *xu* 蓄, the first term means to contain; and the other, *xu*, has a larger range of meaning which includes not only the sense of having a store of something, but having cultivated that something with an energy or posture of mental and spiritual reserve. This term appears in some of China's oldest texts, such as the Book of Documents (*Shangshu* 尚书) and the *Book of Odes* (*Shijing* 诗经), both key texts in the Confucian classical canon. Much later in the Qing and early Republican periods, the word came to refer to hair, and the growth of hair; expressing the link in Chinese culture between hair and ancestors, where cutting one's hair was akin to cutting off a finger; both cardinal sins against one's parents, who gave us this body, the flesh and hair of which belongs as much to our ancestors as to ourselves.

[16] Tony Fang and Guy Olivier Faure, "Chinese Communication Characteristics: A Yin Yang Perspective," *International Journal of Intercultural Relations* 35, no. 3 (May 2011): 320–33.

The Chinese cultural ideals of interdependence and unity, then; can be traced back to this need to contextualize not only one's subjective existence, but also one's linguistic expression, within a greater whole; otherwise the meaning of the word or message is incomplete and distorted. *Guanxi*, then, is an approach to human interaction based upon Chinese communication models. *Guanxi* systems of interconnection and mutual indebtedness are created and maintained in order to get things done in a system where institutional rigidity and inscrutable hierarchies create the need for back-channels, workarounds, and hacks in order to get things done or obtain the results one needs to obtain. While the collective nature of Chinese social order seems to be what is most associated with *guanxi*, or social capital, it is important to note that *guanxi* operates at individual as well as social and organisational levels. In the West, 'networking' operates in a similar manner as does the notion of social capital, an asset which an individual brings with him or herself upon entering the professional realm. The *guanxi* an individual wields builds the value of that individual for an organisation, because this value will be absorbed by the organisation as part of its operational power, i.e. the ability to get things done despite red tape, institutional rigidity, and hierarchical inscrutability.[17]

While *guanxi* and *hanxu* are complicated notions to grasp, the Chinese cultural notion of 'face' is even harder to maneuver. Face has two elements, '*lian*' and '*mianzi*.' The latter can be obtained through individual effort and achievement, the former is entirely contingent upon not only how others perceive one's reputation (*mianzi*), but also how one perceives and feels about how others perceive you. For the Chinese, both *mianzi* and *lian* are constantly formed and performed in a social context. *Mianzi* is achieved more purely through one's actions in relationship to one's profession and social position; but *lian* must be worked at constantly, with the popular term these days in China, '*shua lian* 刷脸' meaning to 'wipe face' like a credit card through the social machine all day and night on social networking apps and out in social scenes. While in the West we also suffer from FOMO (fear of missing out), for largely social reasons, needing to 'be there' and 'in the know' in order to achieve the goals we want to achieve in social and organisational contexts; the

[17] Yi Zhang and Zigang Zhang, "Guanxi and Organizational Dynamics in China: A Link Between Individual and Organizational Levels," *Journal of Business Ethics* 67, no. 4 (October 5, 2006): 375–92.

major difference between these Chinese and Western notions is the way in which value is accrued. This goes back to *hanxu*, in valuing reservation, indirectness, and even the unspoken. This subtlety operates not only in the accruing of value, but also in the accrual of meaning, as in narrative style. Cultural products consist in not just manufactured goods, but also meaning and value. With Chinese cultural products expressing meaning and producing value in ways so different from Western cultural products; it grows apparent how Chinese cultural products get discounted as they cross Chinese borders, conveying cultural values that translate poorly outside of Chinese and other Asian contexts. This disparity in the value of cultural products vastly increases cultural discount of China's cultural exports, such as film, TV, publishing, or other forms of popular culture.

While Xi Jinping's China is finally seeing the bans on forms of religion in China lift, as film, television and publishing organs produce cultural programming including Buddhism and Daoism as valid aspects of what it means to be Chinese; people in China are still very cautious about when and to whom they express their belief systems. A recent experience translating for an organization wanting to publish a journal on Three Teachings scholarship saw the journal's application for publication refused. The Three Teachings in contemporary Chinese thought are those of Confucianism, Buddhism, and Daoism, and this journal was to focus upon all three. Although there was no reason given, it may have been because of journal's potential to deviate from the Party's atheist orientation. Thus, the Party's weariness of endorsing Buddhist and Daoist ideals of withdrawal from official service or questioning of materialism keeps a reign on cultural messaging that strays from authoritarian scientific-materialism and atheist ideology. While other Asian societies can accept Confucian cultural ideals, they would also be looking for more traditional (less Communist) religious ideals in their cultural products, be these ideals integrating Buddhist, Daoist, Muslim, or other systems of non-atheist belief. Non-Asian societies are sometimes stuck in a nostalgia for an older China, one from before the Opium Wars, when the emperor kept scores of concubines as Buddhist and Daoist monks roamed courts and hermits hid in the hills. The more China's Communist Party restrains the cultural narrative away from this nostalgia, the more value its cultural exports will continue to lose.

Contemporary Chinese Art as Exceptional Domestic and International Cultural Product

International Branding

Later, we will discuss regional difference in contemporary Chinese art, bringing our focus by the next chapter to Southwest China's contemporary arts production in the light of New Silk Roads development. For now, let us dwell briefly on the international branding of contemporary Chinese art. This branding has developed, in some senses, as a political weapon used by Western arts institutions and the neo-liberal ideology these institutions serve. Vilification of the Chinese government and the mythology of the Chinese artist as rebel-hero adds value to Chinese contemporary art for collectors in the West and within China. This vilification then also serves to decrease the cultural power of China's cultural and creative industries abroad; thereby advancing the reach and geocultural power of Western global governance. It can be argued that any exposure is good exposure, however, and ultimately China has benefitted by having this (albeit negatively) branded channel for its cultural export of contemporary Chinese art.

Let's look at a brief sketch of exhibition history in the US of main contemporary Chinese artists. Two epicenters for these exhibitions are in the San Francisco Bay area and in New York, notably at the Guggenheim Museum. Beginning in the late 1960s, Zhang Daqian had his first exhibition at the Stanford Museum, and then another half a decade later at the Asia Art Museum of San Francisco. Other main exhibitions include the *1998: A Century of Crisis: Modernity and Tradition in the Art of the Twentieth Century China*; curated by Julia Andrews and Kuiyi Shen, held in conjunction with *China 5000 Years: Innovation and Transformation in the Arts*. Both exhibitions were held at sites associated with the Guggenheim.[18] In that same year, with more visibility than Shen and Andrews' exhibition, was Gao Minglu's *Inside Out: New Chinese Art*, organized by the Asia Society New York, covering contemporary Chinese art development from 1989–1998. This featured at the Guggenheim, travelling then to the SFMOMA and the Asian Art Museum. After this, the next

[18] Jay Xu, "Presentation of Chinese Contemporary Art in the United States" (Unpublished "Aliens" exhibition panel discussion, Stanford University, November 22, 2019).

major blips in the US narrative of Contemporary Chinese art occur in 2013 with Maxwel Hearn's curatorial effort *Ink Art: Past as Present in Contemporary China*, at New York's Metropolitan Museum of Art. Then, in 2017, Alexandra Munroe curated *Art and China after 1989: Theater of the World*.

While Xu Bing and Cai Guoqiang are two of the very few Chinese artists given a solo exhibition at major US venues, note that both of these artists have spent a large part of their lives outside of China, namely in New York. Xu Bing's *Word Play: Contemporary Art* was held in 2001 at the Freer-Sackler Galleries in Washington, DC. *Cai Guoqiang: I Want to Believe*, at the Guggenheim, was eight years later, in 2009. There are networks throughout the world, each with their own Chinese contemporary art historiographies. These accounts of history often feature lesser-known but equally important exhibitions. *Avant-garde Chinese Art* was held in Beijing in 1989 as well as at the City Gallery in New York, going then to Vassar College Art Gallery in Poughkeepsie, NY. The touring exhibition familiarized audiences with Chinese Ai Weiwei and other members of the Stars art group. In 1989 *The Stars: Ten Years*, a third Stars exhibition at Hanart TZ Gallery in Hong Kong, refamiliarized us with the same artistic milieu. Also in 1989, Huang Yongping, Gu Dexin, and Yang Jiechang traveled from China to Paris for the exhibition *Magiciens de la terre* at the Centre Georges Pompidou, curated by Jean-Hubert Martin. In 1991, *I Don't Want to Play Cards with Cezanne* and *Other Works: Selections from the Chinese "New Wave" and "Avant-Garde" Art of the Eighties* at the Pacific Asia Museum in Pasadena, CA was curated by Richard E. Strassberg. These are the main exhibitions responsible for creating the contemporary Chinese art narrative known to scholars in the West.

The domestic attention to and the international demand for contemporary Chinese art escalated after the event at Tiananmen in 1989. Southwest Chinese curator and art historian Lu Peng curated the Guangzhou Biennale in 1991, showing a diverse geography of China's experimental art alongside blue-chip Chinese contemporary artists. Successful exhibitions in that same year, such as *Exceptional Passage* (Fukuoka, Japan); and auctions (Christie's, Hong Kong) attest to the popularity of contemporary Chinese artists' original take on both traditional Chinese and Western styles of all periods. The 1993 45th Venice Biennale codified the Chinese roster of 13 blue-chip contemporary artists: Zhang Peili, Yu Youhan, Yu Hong, Xu Bing, Wang Ziwei, Wang Guangyi, Sun Liang, Song Haidong,

Liu Wei, Li Shan, Geng Jianyi, Feng Mengbo, and Fang Lijun; consulted by Chinese art critic, Li Xianting. *Mao Goes Pop* (Sydney, 1993), and *Fragmented Memory: The Chinese Avant-Garde in Exile* (1993, Wexner Center for the Arts, The Ohio State University, Columbus, curated by Julia F. Andrews and Gao Minglu) gave audiences a chance to understand Chinese cultural political economy through the lens of social, political, and aesthetic dissidents of the Chinese state. In 1993, an Andrew Solomon article "Their Irony, Humor (and Art) Can Save China" was the cover story of New York Time Magazine. In this article, Solomon traces China's avant-garde back to Chinese art critic Li Xianting, quoting "Old Li":

> "Idealism?" Lao Li said at one point. "I hope that a new art can appear in China and that I can help it. Pre-'89, we thought that with this new art we could change the society and make it free. Now, I think only that it can make the artists free. But for anyone to be free is no small matter."[19]

This cover article by Andrew Solomon constituted a huge success for Chinese cultural export, conveying in a world-class news format two things. One, that Chinese civilization was capable of producing global meaning and values; and two, that these values are structured by meaning which engages positively with neoliberal Western cultural political economics. Thus, the success of the contemporary Chinese fine art sector both contributed to and caused cognitive dissonance within China's global political and geocultural power. While Western art critics and reporters spoke of Chinese appropriation of Western art forms and visual languages, what these writers often missed was an analysis of traditional Chinese aesthetic theory, as well as the regional nature of these aesthetic theories in China over the past millennia. For the next nearly three decades, these artists coming up from the Stars artist lineage then took over the contemporary Chinese art narrative, appearing again and again throughout the world: Cai Guoqiang: *Flying Dragon in the Heavens* (1997, Denmark), *Red and Grey—Eight Avant-Garde Chinese Artists (1997, Singapore), 47th Venice Biennale, Harald Szeeman's Fourth Biennale d'Art Contemporain de Lyon (1997, Lyons),* and

[19] "Their Irony, Humor (and Art) Can Save China—The New York Times," accessed October 18, 2021, https://www.nytimes.com/1993/12/19/magazine/their-irony-humor-and-art-can-save-china.html.

Documenta X (1997, Kassel) are only a few examples. Also notable at the turn of the Twentieth century are greater efforts to research and promote contemporary Chinese art. In 1997 we see The Annie Wong Art Foundation founded in Vancouver, BC, dedicated to "promoting and expanding international recognition and understanding of contemporary Chinese art."[20] Around that time a website titled *Stir-Fry: A Video Curator's Dispatches from China*, chronicled Barbara London of the MoMA New York in her travels and encounters with media art and artists in Beijing, Shanghai, Hangzhou. The writing of these chronicles is shrewdly balanced, every positive description of the details of Chinese peoples' lives seemed contrived to balance depressing socio-historic forces.

Over two decades later, the map provided by London of a previously smooth art territory has now grown increasingly striated. Today international art branding focuses less on first-tier cities such as Beijing and Shanghai, now following the new flow of arts infrastructure and funding into frontier regions such as Southwest China, with centers in Chengdu (capital of Sichuan), and Chongqing (one of four federal municipalities in China, alongside Beijing, Shanghai, and Tianjin). We will focus on art museums in Chengdu and Chongqing cities in Chapter 6, as we discuss the influences of New Silk Roads cultural policy on frontier.

Domestic Branding

We'll start this section with Reform and Opening-up, or rather in the year preceding it. In 1977 there was an exhibition known as the *National Art Exhibition to Enthusiastically Celebrate the Inauguration of Comrade Hua Guofeng as the Chairman of the CCP and the Chairman of the Central Military Commission and to Enthusiastically Celebrate the Great Triumph of Smashing the Gang of Four's Scheme to Usurp the Party's Power*. We see by the title of this exhibition the use to which contemporary art is being put in that year, and the ideas it is meant to disseminate. With the Cultural Revolution finally over, the National College Entrance Exam had been reinstated. The Central Academy of Fine Arts, Central Academy of Arts and Crafts, and the Beijing Film Academy were all reopened in that same year. Then in 1978, the China Federation of Literary and Art

[20] Asia Art Archive, "Introduction of the Annie Wong Art Foundation," accessed October 18, 2021, https://aaa.org.hk/en/collections/search/archive/zheng-shengtian-archive-reports-admin-documents/object/introduction-of-the-annie-wong-art-foundation.

Circles resumed. Late that year the United States and China issued a Joint Communique on the Establishment of Diplomatic Relations Between the People's Republic of China and the United States of America. 1979 saw the resumption of the Central Academy of Fine Arts journal, *Fine Arts Research*. *World Art* kicked off its publication with an article by Shao Dazhen. "A Brief Introduction to Modern Art Schools in the West" went a long way towards a renewed narrative of Western modernist art. Another new journal started up in that year, *Chinese Art*, including painter Wu Guanzhong's article, "Formalist Aesthetics in Painting," reinvesting Chinese discourse in the socially constructed elements of art with its apposite consideration of subjectivity in relationship with 'non-ideological' 'art for art's sake' aesthetic elements. According to University of Chicago arts professor Wu Hung, this article kicked up significant debate at the time.[21] The 1979 first *Stars Art Exhibition* is infamous for having been shut down at its original location, then moved to Huafeng Studio in Beihai Park under the protection of Jiang Feng, chairman of the Chinese Artists' Association as well as Liu Xun, leader of the Beijing Artists' Association. We see immediately after Deng Xiaoping's sweeping liberalization of markets, an impulse to match this tempo in economics with an equally rapid liberalization of ideology in the arts. At the National Art Gallery, the *Fifth National Fine Arts Exhibition* held the first major art exhibition since the Cultural Revolution. It should be noticed that paintings honored with awards were oil paintings done in the social realist style; namely Cheng Conglin's *Snow on X Day X Month* and Gao Xiaohua's *Why*. However, while this genre was identified with leftist political economies of culture; the content of these paintings expressed more existential ennui, signaling a new subjectivity on the arise amongst artists pursuing questions not directly connecting with national ideologies.[22] While critical aesthetic debate continued concerning the purpose of art as well as the relationship between content and form; domestic historical narratives of contemporary Chinese art were being challenged and reworked. One of the strategies taken by Chinese arts institutions at that time was to translate-appropriate Western narratives. An example of this can be seen in the 1982 National Art Gallery exhibition of *The Hammer*

[21] Wu Hung and Peggy Wang, eds., *Contemporary Chinese Art: Primary Documents (MoMA Primary Documents)* (New York: The Museum of Modern Art, 2010), 409.

[22] Lu Peng, *The Story of Art in China: From Late Qing through Today 美术的故事: 从晚晴到今天* (Guangxi: Guangxi Teachers Normal University Press, 215AD), 315–53.

Collection from the U.S.: 500 Years of Important works. The National Cultural Palace in Beijing's *Expressionist Paintings from Germany* was also held in that year.

As the eighties progressed, the will for artistic experiment gained critical mass. In 1983, exhibitions in Xiamen, Fujian (*Five Artists Exhibition*), and at Fudan University (*Experimental Painting Exhibition: The Stage 1983*, and later known as the *Ten Artists Exhibition*) were both shut down within days of opening. We see later that year, at the Second Plenary Session of the 12th Central Committee of the CCP, that a campaign is initiated to 'Cleanse Spiritual Pollution,' meaning that authorities believed that individual artists and intellectuals had mistaken economic liberalizations for an indication that complementary ideological reforms were underway. By 1984, Deng Xiaoping was inspecting the Special Economic Zones of Zhenzhen and Zhuhai, as China's planned economic expansion developed through liberalization of markets. These liberalizations also saw the coastal cities of Beihai, Dalian, Fuzhou, Guangzhou, Lianyungang, Nantong, Ningbo, Qingdao, Qinhuangdao, Shanghai, Tianjin, Wenzhou, Yantai, and Zhanjiang open to foreign investment. Notice that none of these cites, be them special economic development zones or merely opened to foreign investment; are in the Southwestern region of China, our focus in Chapter 6. Note, however, that without infrastructure, the Southwestern cities of Chengdu in Sichuan and Kunming in Yunnan did manage to host a 1983 exhibition of Paintings by Edvard Munch which had first opened at the National Art Gallery. This speaks to the strong cultural and artistic development in the region which has historically insisted upon its place on the creative and intellectual map of China. Also, in 1983 the Sichuan People's Publishing House commenced the publication of *Marching Toward the Future*, publishing original and translated writings as well as artworks.

By 1985, critical discourse was strengthened by the journal *The Trend of Art Thought* out of Wuhan in Hubei province. Li Xianting, still very active today in critical discourse on art and thought in China, was on the editorial board through its dissolution two years later. Gao Minglu took up a position on the editorial staff of the journal *Art*; and the journal *Jiangsu Pictorial* picked up its pace to publish monthly articles on almost exclusively Chinese contemporary art. In 1985, what has come to be known as the '85 New Wave' kicked off the explosion of experimental art happening in China at that time, which includes the famous Huangshan "Symposium on Oil Painting" in Jingxian, Anhui. The symposium was organized by the Research Institute of Fine Arts at the Chinese National Academy of Arts, the Anhui branch of the Chinese Artists Association, the Central Academy of Fine Arts, the Beijing Fine Art Academy, and *Art History and Theory*; inviting predominantly young oil painters and theorists to discuss critical aesthetics.[23] This is also the year in which more experimental avant-garde art forms begin to take (albeit side) stage. The Rauschenberg Overseas Culture Exchange exhibition at the National Art Gallery in that year saw the US artist invited to give lectures on his experimental artistic practice. The experimental group Zero out of Hunan held a group exhibition at the Fuxiangyiyuan in Changsha, commencing a performance artwork consisting in a march to Lhasa. In April of 1986, at the "National Symposium on Oil Painting", Gao Minglu added great weight to the moniker '85 New Wave with his talk "'85 Art Movement," going a long way to codifying the work of young artists groups arising at this time. Also in this year, and important for constructing a narrative of Southwest China's contemporary Chinese art; was the *Red, Yellow, and Blue: Modern Paintings by Young Sichuan Artists* exhibition held in Chengdu. As well, the Southwest Research Group was founded in Kunming, including such artists as Zhang Xiaogang and Ye Yongqing. The *Xiamen Dada—Exhibition of Modern Art* was held at the Xiamen Art Museum, an exhibition which is not as famous as the event held later in the same year of 1986, in which artists involved in the exhibition set their artworks on fire in the square. An important exhibition held that year at the National Art Gallery, the *Group Exhibition of Young Hunan Artists* (sponsored by *Fine Arts in China*), pulled together the disparate activities of the youth collectives active at that time; namely the Leishi Painting Society, Painter Group, Zero Art Group, Wild Grass Painting Society, Overpass Painting Society, and the Huaihua Group. Lasty, in this epic year of 1986, an event dedicated exclusively to performance art was held at Peking University, *Concept 21, Performance Display*, celebrating an art form which is to this day held in circumspect by art institutions and professionals in China.

In 1987, we see a culminating crisis. The Central Committee of the CCP issues a *Notice Regarding Issues of the Current Opposition to Bourgeois Liberalism*. The Ministry of Propaganda issued an order prohibiting national academic events, cancelling what was being planned as the first

[23] Wu Hung and Peggy Wang, *Contemporary Chinese Art: Primary Documents (MoMA Primary Documents)*, 412.

nationwide modern art exhibition. The Chinese United Overseas Artists Association, made up out of expatriate Chinese artists throughout the US and America was then founded in New York. Ai Weiwei is one of the original members. It was also at this time that Chinese and international narratives of contemporary Chinese art were somewhat in sync; as for example in 1987, when Xu Bing was celebrated with a solo exhibition at the National Art Gallery where he showed, for the first time his *Book from the Sky* (shown at that time as *A Mirror to Analyze the World*). In February of 1989, the landmark exhibition with 186 artists showing 193 artworks titled *China/Avant-Garde* opened at the National Art Gallery. What's notable is that the exhibition was curated by critics, bringing together arts and intellectual infrastructure in a way that may have overwhelmed the political economy of culture in China at that time. A 'gunshot incident' reminiscent of Chris Burden's own 'gunshot incident' precipitated the exhibition being closed for the first time on its opening day. With martial law declared and the scene dispersed at Tiananmen by mid-June of 1989, the journal *Art's* editorial board was restructured, and *Fine Arts in China* ceased publication.

In the Southwest of China, centering in Chengdu throughout the 1990s, the activity of the 719 Artists Alliance went largely under the radar, except for its work in its manifestation as Keepers of the Water, organized by American water activist and performance artist Betsy Damon. The Keepers of the Water performances actually received a warm welcome by officials, media and the populace, who generally appreciated the socially active and constructive message of the performance events. Key artists in these Southwest China groups include Dai Guangyu, Zhu Gang, Liu Chengying, and Zhou Bin, the latter of which had started out his career as an oil painter at Yuanmingyuan art village in Beijing before moving to Chengdu.

Heading into the mid-nineties, we continue to see a lot of cultural exchange between China and other countries. Journals were still rolling on, *Fine Arts Literature*, compiled by Peng De, was published by Hubei Fine Arts Publishing House. *Avant-Garde Today* 今日先鋒 began publication by SDX Joint Publishing. The *Third Modern Chinese Art Research Documents Exhibition* 中国当代艺术研究文献资料第三回展 was held at East China Normal University, focusing on experimental forms such as installation, environment, and performance. Also in that year, avant-garde *Black Cover Book* 黑皮书 was privately published and circulated underground, edited by Zeng Xiaojun, Ai Weiwei, and Xu Bing, with Feng

Boyi as text editor. Zeng Xiaojun and Ai Weiwei subsequently edited and privately published the *White Cover Book* and *Gray Cover Book* in 1995 and 1997, respectively.

By 1995, see a confluence of Western and Chinese ideologies, styles and moneys come together in Chinese creative production. However, in that same year, we see some kickback forming a foundational swell, with the founding of The Spiritual Civilization Steering Committee in Beijing. When the word spiritual (*jingshen* 精神) is used in official Chinese discourse, this is usually a red-flag indicating on the ideological level. Keeping in mind that the official religion of the CCP is atheism, the closest thing there is to spiritual beliefs is ideology, and the CCP's ideology is dialectical Marxism/scientific materialism. Thus, any ideology which establishes value on levels of subjective agency or other metaphysical orientations are cast into the box of 'spiritual pollution.' Meanwhile, the official approch of embracing market strategy was to consolidate market forces by supporting the publishing industries in helping to determine an official discourse on art that was influential enough to determine market value and control ideology. In 1998, Xinhua Bookstore teamed up with thirteen art publishing firms to publish a 48-volume *Collected Works of Chinese Modern Art*. This was part of a larger project going by the title *Classification of Chinese Fine Arts*. Meanwhile, experimental practices both in terms of artistic production and curatorial events were taking place more commonly in basements and other off-site locations, and despite the low-key under the radar approach, were still being cancelled. For example, Xu Ruotao and Xu Yihui curated *Persistent Deviation/Corruptionist* in a building basement way out on the outskirts of the Third Ring Road in Beijing. It was closed on day two of its run. At this time, Ai Weiwei and collaborators were involved in building such spaces as the China Art Archives & Warehouse on the outskirts of Beijing; and curating such events as the *Fuck Off/Buhezuo fangshi*, which Ai Weiwei curated with Feng Boyi as an effort to defy the Shanghai Biennale, then in its third and commercially successful iteration of 1999. The performative nature of this *Fuck Off* event kicked off what was to become a vast shade cast over the body of performance art, which over the next two decades was forced to change its moniker from *xingwei* 行为 art (literally 'behaviour art') to *xingdong* 行动 or *xianchang* 现场 (action art and live art, respectively), in order not to have its events, promotional materials and associated ephemera flagged as politically 'sensitive' (*mingan* 敏

感). Thus, as we see a swelling of tides meeting up on the Chinese mainland, Chinese diaspora and other international actors were making efforts to develop a narrative which would preserve values in alternative cultural messaging.

2001 was a big year, in which China won its bid for the 2008 Summer Olympic Games. Shanghai hosted the Ninth Asia–Pacific Economic Cooperation (APEC) Economic Leaders Meeting, and China became part of the World Trade Organization (WTO). It was also in this year that contemporary art in Southwest China reached the critical mass necessary and sufficient enough to host a biennale; as Liu Xiaochun, Gu Zhenqing, Huang Xiaorong and Feng Bin organized the First Chengdu Biennale. It was funded in part by the Jiazhou California Industrial, Ltd., reflecting how art institutions at the scale of the biennale reflect other market and investment models outside of the arts, even depending upon them for survival. Also in this year, the Chengdu Academy of Painting held the symposium, *Academic Exchange Exhibition of Contemporary Prints.* While we do see arts infrastructure finally receiving enough funding to scaffold events into existence; in the Southwest there was, as there still is today, over twenty years later; an unwillingness on behalf of either private or public investors in arts infrastructure to experiment with non-traditional art forms, i.e., anything but painting. True, by the time the Chengdu Biennale arrived at its fifth iteration in 2011curated by Lu Peng; there was a good deal of installation and video on the floor of its expansive and multi-location halls. There was even a performance artwork by Chengdu North Village artist Wei Yan to celebrate opening day ceremonies. However, this was perhaps the single event of its magnitude in two decades to include such a fringe art medium as performance art to be witnessed by audiences of an officially sanctioned and well-funded arts exhibition. This is especially the case in the years following the 2004 Edict Forbidding Performance Art issued in Chengdu after an artwork involving nudity, @42, by He Liping, went viral, causing government backlash and censure.[24]

24 Sophia Kidd, "Conceptual Archaeology: Performance Art in Southwest China," *Yishu Journal of Contemporary Chinese Art* 10, no. 3 (June 2011).

Conclusion

Thus far we have developed an understanding of how Chinese cultural ideals have been crafted into a narrative which suits the Chinese Communist Party. This model of shaping a cultural narrative is the anticipated and even natural result of a political economy of culture which sees culture as an instrument of ideology, a vessel into which cultural messages are poured and then served domestically and internationally. We have also discussed how publics, especially in the Global North, hold that vessel to their lips and dislike the taste in their mouth. It is possible that as the Chinese state raises the attractiveness of its profile internationally in regions along the New Silk Roads by coming to the economic aid of these people; this elixir will taste better, especially in those regions of the Global South. However, this kind of economic 'hard power' is expensive and will not take root without a complementary cultural 'soft power.' By engaging in multi-lateral cultural exchanges, China would be able to raise the value of its cultural exports while advancing their economic and political agenda abroad. Not only would those dreaming the 'Chinese dream' be able to see the quality of their lives increase, but the building of the New Silk Roads would be able to obtain a new level of sustainability and cooperation with foreign peoples in the fulfilment of what Chinese President Xi Jinping hails as a 'Common Destiny' for all humankind.

Contemporary Chinese artists have pushed the margins of what is true, good, and beautiful in China's cultural narrative. By cultivating this diversity in China's cultural narrative, these artists have created a financially and culturally successful niche for China's cultural export. Much of this artwork has been created and marketed outside of China, by political dissidents and other Chinese diaspora; but this is changing. In our next chapter, we will dive deep into the fine art museum sector in Southwest China to explore how artists and arts administrators within China's national borders have spent the past few decades cultivating these diverse cultural narratives in a dearth of arts infrastructure funding. More importantly, we will discuss how these artists and arts administrators are dealing with the new influx of New Silk Road funding into China's Southwest creative economy.

CHAPTER 6

Contemporary Art in China's Southwest Frontier New Silk Road Region

In 2000, when an international delegation of curators toured for 15 days throughout Hangzhou, Shanghai, Beijing, Guangzhou, Taipei, and Hong Kong, dialoging with artists, critics and curators in each of these urban centers; nobody went to the Southwest of China. There was simply not enough money in arts infrastructure in Southwest China to make it stand out. That is, until most recently, with the implementation of New Silk Roads cultural policy. Today, Sichuan, Yunnan, and Guangxi Provinces are targeted for cultural funding, as the Southwest is recognized as a political, economic and cultural hub in the pivot into Central, South and Southeast Asia's New Silk Road regions.

This chapter continues the conversation begun in Chapter 5 about Chinese fine art as an exception to China's problems of cultural discount. The devaluation of Chinese cultural product as it crosses national borders results in a cultural trade deficit (*wenhua maoyi chizi* 文化贸易赤字), especially with Western nations. Chinese populations consume more foreign cultural product (film, television, publishing, etc.) than foreign populations consume Chinese ones. As China's southwest region serves as a pivot in the movement Westward (true West, through Central Asia), we focus on this region as we seek to create a domestic sample of how China's political economy of culture influences both artists and art markets in micro-regions of China. After briefly contextualizing the fine art sector as

S. Kidd, *Culture Paves The New Silk Roads*,
Contemporary East Asian Visual Cultures, Societies and Politics,
https://doi.org/10.1007/978-981-16-8574-3_6

one among many other cultural and creative industry segments in the region, we then limit our discussion geographically even more so, by selecting Chengdu and Chongqing as our cities of interest. We inflect the discussion of the fine art sector towards its margins as we focus on avant-garde creative production. This is productive for two reasons. Firstly, it shows us how top-down cultural forces in China's political economy operate upon creative production by either incorporating or excluding experimental and anti-establishment forms of art. Secondly, as we find that the mechanisms of control generally succeed in depriving Chinese avant-garde artists of access to already scarce arts infrastructure, we look at the recourse avant-garde artists have available to them in order to sustain their creative practice.

In April of 2018, I conducted field research on Southwest art museums, hoping to discover whether or how private sector investment and New Silk Roads funding bodies influence museum administrative practices and curatorial choices. This field research was conducted during a research residency at Luxehills Museum in Chengdu, Sichuan. I specifically chose this museum for its practice of focusing on work produced by avant-garde artists living and practicing in Southwest China today. We will discuss how my initial research question regarding avant-garde artistic and exhibition practices was deflected in order to avoid political and aesthetic sensitivities. We will also discuss answers given to a survey amongst Chengdu and Chongqing museum directors as well as other arts professional in the region. Additionally, we'll look at transcripts of the symposium which concluded my two week residency, to which these directors were invited to meet and discuss how New Silk Road policy influences their choices for exhibition rotations, public education, and collections.

Cultural Discount and Deficit

While the poetics of the Silk Road are dreamy and exotic, the politics of the New Silk Roads are not. At the time of writing, China's international image across the Global North is tanking as the US and its allies in the Indo-Pacific region create a consensus which accuses China of overstepping its territorial rights, being guilty of genocide and coercion in border territories, and being unqualified as agents of global governance. Discussions of China's diverse culture and history are dismissed in favor of simplified narratives, postures and headlines which solely address top-down geopolitical issues. The complexity of the political situation, obscured by media spin on all sides, takes up most of the available bandwidth non-China experts have in thinking about China. Which means that few non-China experts are actually thinking about the day-to-day lives of Chinese people at all, but are rather cogitating spectacular images and representations of world powers, of governments jostling over policy, infrastructure, trade, and financial technologies. Again, as we have pointed out in previous chapters, fifth pillar thinking, or thinking about People-to-People Connectivity along the New Silk Roads, is lacking. Without these conversations opened up, the cultural power China seeks to cultivate through successful People-to-People Connectivities is diminished.

Here we detect a psychological and aesthetic gulf between a poetic dream of the Silk Road and the political reality of China's New Silk Roads.[1] The disparity or distance between the China of Buddhism, tea and pandas, and the 'real' one we read about in the Western media, causes psychological and cognitive dissonance. Many who would otherwise be interested in learning about such an old and interesting culture prefer to ignore Chinese people and their culture, allowing the political and economic aspects of China's international presence to dominate the narrative. This exacerbates the 'cultural discount' we discussed in our last chapter, resulting ultimately in a greater 'cultural deficit' between China and countries with publics who are influenced by Western media models, models that attempt to erode the significane of China's culture. This cultural suppression erodes China's international cultural confidence.

This mechanism of center-periphery cultural suppression that exists when looking at China in the world, is internally mirrored within China in regards to frontier regions. Frontier regions of China, such as China's Southwest, face suppression of their cultural ecologies not only abroad, but also within greater China. In the Southwest of China, an area which has long played second fiddle in China's domestic cultural policy development; foreign actors are arriving with the new funding, culture-surfing into the region and reaping the benefits of arts and culture infrastructure funding present for the first time in China's history of thousands of years. These foreign actors, as we'll explain below, act in concert with top-down

[1] Harm Langenkamp, "Contested Imaginaries of Collective Harmony: The Poetics and Politics of 'Silk Road' Nostalgia in China and the West," in *China and the West: Music, Representation, and Reception*, ed. Yang Hon-Lun and Michael Saffle (University of Michigan Press, 2017), https://doi.org/10.2307/j.ctt1qv5n9n.

People-to-People Connectivity programs to bring artistic, cultural, and ideological implants into the Southwest region. These implants, partly because they do not arise organically with the local arts and culture ecology, wither not long after the foreign actors have collected their money and kudos and returned home. Local artists, especially avant-garde and otherwise marginalised artists, continue on as before, albeit somewhat enriched, without arts and culture infrastructure.

Chengdu's Fine Art Sector as One Area of Cultural Policy Funding

We focus upon China's Southwest region in order to demonstrate a working model of cultural production (*wenchuang* 文创) as an integral part of the earlier Western Development Program (WDP, *Xibu da kaifa* 开发). This model has simultaneously been a part of the China Goes Global (CGG, *Zou chu qu* 走出去) policy, and can be seen in similar international efforts and other economic structures in NSR regions outside of China. According to Michael Keene, expert on China's creative industries, the term 'cultural industries' was first used formally in China in 2001 in language used to reform China's cultural system. Just two years later this reform became a national strategic goal, and the term 'creative industries' was first used formally in Shanghai. In 2007, Chinese President Hu Jintao declared that:

> A basic system of public cultural services will cover the whole society, the cultural industry will account for much more of the national economy and become more competitive internationally, and a more abundant supply of cultural products will be available to meet the people's needs.[2]

It wasn't until 2009, however, that these industries became a focus point of a set of key economic strategies.[3] This was the result of much debate and discussion amongst academics and cultural policy makers on the nature of China's cultural trade deficit, a debate which operated in tandem with similar internal Chinese Communist Party debates about

[2] "Hu Jintao's Report at 17th Party Congress," accessed October 18, 2021, http://www.china.org.cn/english/congress/229611.htm.

[3] Michael Keane, *Creative Industries in China: Art, Design, and Media* (Cambridge: Polity Press, 2013).

China's soft power which both fuelled and were prompted by Chinese President Hu Jintao's use of the term. In these earlier discussions of soft power, usage was contextualised as a defensive move, a levy constructed against the stripping away of China's cultural rights. As Michael Keane phrases it in his discussion of Hu Jintao's use of the term, this soft power was an important part of China Goes Global, while "cultural security symbolized strengthening the fortress."[4] This national cultural security (*guojia wenhua anquan* 国家文化安全) required that China's cultural trade deficit be addressed. This is still underway, with even more focus as China develops its cultural presence through People-to-People Connectivity in New Silk Road regions.

The Sichuan Cultural Industry Development Report (2019) describes six levels in its approach to developing culture along the region's frontier as well as throughout global cultural markets. The first strengthens the overall brand of Sichuan's cultural heritage, especially its ancient roots in Shu and Ba civilization, two civilisational 'cores' which are seen in recent media surrounding new discoveries at Sanxingdui as contemporary rivals of Han Chinese civilization. The second develops rural areas, film and television, as well as ecological and health practises. A third focuses on developing Sichuan's revolutionary culture; that is, the history of the People's Liberation Army, or Red Army, in Sichuan. A fourth strengthens local folk festivals and performance, cultural heritage sites, and the collation and preservation of classical texts. The fifth area of focus includes developing national and international brands for local cultural products such as bamboo, cuisine, Sichuan theatre, as well as Ba and Shu folk culture products. The last area of cultural production pushes out into further peripheries, looking specifically at Chengdu and Guang'an, as well as Sichuan's autonomous Tibetan region in the West of the province[5] (Table 6.1).

2017 was the first year in which Sichuan figured as a national 'center' for cultural production. In this year, eight key earners in Sichuan's cultural industries included: media/film/television, innovation/design, contemporary fashion, music/art, textual/travel, information services, expo/exhibition/advertising, and education/consulting. Notable, in the

[4] Ibid., 31.

[5] Xiang Baoyun 向宝运, ed., *Annual Report on Cultural Development of Sichuan* 四川文化产业发展报告 (Beijing: Social Sciences Academic Press, 2019).

Table 6.1 2017 Cultural industries production, added values, and increase in percentage of production [6]

8 Key Areas	*Value added (100,000,000 RMB)*	*Percentage*	*Increase (% since 2016)*
Totals	687.97	100	28.91
Media/film/television	80.51	11.70	2.03
Innovation/design	160.10	23.27	22.59
Fashion	55.13	8.01	79.49
Music/art	27.54	4.00	27.47
Texts/travel	41.00	5.96	36.38
Information services	271.99	39.54	28.71
Expos/exhibitions/advertising	23.99	3.49	70.75
Education/consulting	27.71	4.03	68.56

2019 Annual Report of Cultural Development of Sichuan, there isn't much mention of contemporary Chinese art. After going carefully through the report, one sees that most mention of art had to do with internationalising local folk brands and culture, which is indeed important for the regional cultural aspects of Sichuan to contribute to China's overall cultural narrative. The only mention of fine arts, however, was in the report's Appendix, section six of the document. This mentioned that on November 2nd, 2019 the Pompidou Center and Mao Jihong Foundation collaborated with the Chengdu Chinese Culture Dissemination Group and the Chengdu Chinese Culture Exhibition Dissemination and Cultural Development, L.L.C.

We will be discussing this particular exhibition at length below, identifying such 'cultural implants' as this one to be crucial in global flows of capital and value which suppress local arts ecologies. The collaborative and funding bodies listed in this report do vary from the information provided in the Cosmopolis 1.5 exhibition catalogue. This could be due to organisational changes within the public and private sector groups (Chengdu

[6] Zheng Zhengzhen, "Regional Reports," in *Annual Report on Cultural Development of Sichuan* 四川文化产业发展报告, ed. Xiang Baoyun 向宝运 (Beijing: Social Sciences Academic Press, 2019). An additional note to this table is provided: "Figures provided for texts/travel category only include texts/travel activity in relationship to tourism industry creative industries. Similar figures related to categories of tourism industries in connection with sports do not coincide with figures provided here".

Media Group, Chengdu Chinese Culture Dissemination Group, and the Chengdu Chinese Culture Exhibition Dissemination and Cultural Development, L.L.C.) after the printing of Centre Pompidou's exhibition catalogue.[7]

Cultural Implant: Pompidou's Cosmopolis Chengdu Biennale

The Southwest of China has always been a border territory. The Han, one of this nation's fifty-six ethnic groups, accounting for 92% of the population, has cultivated a cultural, economic, and political narrative for millennia centering around the nation's capital. Before the Yuan dynasty Mongols conquered the Han in the thirteenth century and moved China's political centre to present-day Beijing, China's capital was regularly located just south of the Yellow River in the Central Plains. Alternatively, when northern Xianbei and Xiongnu tribes moved down into these plains, the Han pushed south of the Yangzi River, establishing their capital in Jiankang (modern day Nanjing), or in Hangzhou and Kaifeng, as during the Song dynasty. In all cases, however, Southwest China has been a hinterland, a place to flee to during war or exile, and at best a place of commerce in exotic goods such as tea, horses, and brocade silk. As such, China's Southwest has tended to be culturally marginalized, and its people considered so uneducated and uncouth that their own intellectual, spiritual, and artistic heritage has generally been occluded from the China's cultural narrative. This holds true as well for contemporary Chinese art.[8]

[7] Yan Xianlei, "Appendix: Chronology of Main Sichuan Cultural Production Events," in *Annual Report on Cultural Development of Sichuan* 四川文化产业发展报告, ed. Xiang Baoyun 向宝运 (Beijing: Social Sciences Academic Press, 2019).

[8] China has not always been a united empire. The period after the fall of the Eastern Han in the second century CE until China's reunification by the Sui dynasty in the sixth century CE constituted a period of great disunity that began with the Three Kingdoms period (one of the Kingdoms being the Shu, located in Southwest China today) and fragmented further through the Six Dynasties period, with six successive dynasties locating their capital at modern-day Nanjing, in the South. This period is also known as the Southern and Northern Dynasties period, with the six Southern dynasties south of the Yangzi River and sixteen successive and contemporary kingdoms located north of the Yangzi River.

What brings the recent wave of arts representatives and creative actors to Chengdu, then, is not necessarily the art, or even the artists, nor the curators and critics, much less the ethos or art ecology of the region, but the unprecedented amounts of money pouring into Chengdu, as one of the two largest urban centres in Southwest China (the other being Chongqing, just two hours east by speed rail). Meanwhile, the entire creative infrastructure of Chengdu's fine art sector, which has been active and thriving, if not somewhat self-contained since before China's' 85 New Wave Movement in the mid-1980s, enjoys the unique humiliation of foreign actors coming in to build the region's new arts infrastructure.

One example of this occurred at the end of 2019, in the large-scale Chengdu *Cosmopolis #1.5*. This huge affair which commenced with the Chengdu mayor being flown to Paris for conferences with the Centre Pompidou, resulted in a public-private partnership venture with the Guangdong-based Chinese Mao Jihong Arts Foundation (owners of the Fang Suo Commune bookstores). The Mao Jihong Foundation was one of three principal collaborators in the Biennale (the third being the state-owned Chengdu Media Group). The organizers spent, in total, the better part of a year in Chengdu, laying the groundwork for planning, installing, and documenting the Biennale. A mix of French and Chinese organizers/curators spent this time in Chengdu to assiduously follow the trail of information about contemporary art in Southwest China that has made its way out of the region via national and international media. Following this breadcrumb trail, the Cosmopolis team met with principal Chengdu curators such as Lu Peng and Lan Qingwei, among others. Lu Peng is well known regionally, nationally, and internationally for his role as a curator of contemporary Chinese art who focuses primarily on Beijing and Shanghai-based blue chip Chinese artists. Lu has also championed Sichuan schools of art, such as the Scar Art and Native Soil movements, including such blue chip artists as He Duoling and Zhou Chunya. Lan Qingwei, a student of Lu Peng's, although largely accomplished in Chengdu, has begun to extend his influence outside of this context into the greater sphere of China's contemporary art scene. Lan Qingwei's focus is more experimental than Lu Peng's, having featured performance art and new media artists in his exhibitions along with relatively established forms such as painting and sculpture. After meeting with *Cosmopolis #1.5* organizers, it didn't take long for Lu Peng and Lan Qingwei to figure out that what the Pompidou and Mao Jihong wanted, however, was not their well-honed expertise on the Southwest art scene, but, rather, their connections and interns. Meetings did not continue, and this may be where the initial disconnect that evolved between *Cosmopolis #1.5* and the Chengdu art scene originated.

Neither Lu Peng nor Lan Qingwei nor any of the Southwest curators, museum directors, or critics I spoke with in connection with *Cosmopolis #1.5* held positive views on the Biennale, although my own interviews and contacts are not by any means comprehensive as regards Chengdu's diverse art ecology. In fact, many Chengdu arts professionals were unaware of the Biennale until well into its run; that is, well after the Biennale's artistic director and chief curator had flown back to Paris, following some opening talks at the Fangsuo Commune Bookstore. The curator was unavailable for interviews, not to be found at most of the ensuing dozens of talks, lectures, workshops, artist residencies, concerts, and other events organised for what was an amazing extravaganza of international contemporary art.

However, while the Chengdu creative community was alienated by this particular Biennale, the public was not. Paying 98 yuan per ticket (approximately $14 USD), a steady flow of mostly young urban professionals and creatives poured through the main exhibition hall of *Cosmopolis #1.5*. The Biennale did succeed at exposing thousands of viewers to global art discourses—among them, sustainable urban development, class warfare, gender, ecological crises, and technological power disparities. With its research-based curatorial approach, *Cosmopolis #1.5* was unprecedented in Chengdu, evoking a great deal of discussion among academics and creative professionals about how to secure sustainable development in Southwest China. *Cosmopolis #1.5* accomplished the tackling of major social, economic, and political issues throughout its four component parts—its main exhibition; the architectural pavilion Water and Future Life; Urban and Rural, consisting of offsite village projects by two collectives—Colombia's Arquitectura Expandida and Indonesia's Gudskul; and the X Music Festival.[9]

While the artworks and programming of this Biennale were intelligent, informative, and even influential, *Cosmopolis #1.5* may have been more appropriate in a first-tier Chinese city, such as Shanghai, where the local and the global have already become homogenised. Resources spent by the

[9] Sophia Kidd, "To Be or Not to Be a Biennale: On Art Ecologies, a Review of Centre Pompidou's Chengdu Cosmopolis #1.5: Enlarged Intelligence," *Yishu Journal of Contemporary Chinese Art* 18, no. 4 (2019): 45–56.

local government on this Biennale may have been better spent on local arts infrastructure, as well as upon vocational training to enable local arts professionals to grow along with the city. This would help raise the value of Southwest contemporary art on its own terms, as a thriving community able to add diversity to the international arts ecology as China pivots toward the Middle East, Europe, and Africa in that multi-billion *yuan* project known today as the Belt and Road Initiative, or as we most often refer to it here, the New Silk Roads. Although the Southwest has always been a border territory, it no longer need be marginalized.

Native Southwest China Art Ecology

In order to discuss Southwest China's art ecology, I focus here on findings from a research residency conducted from April 1–17th, 2018 on museums in Chengdu and Chongqing, China. This was arranged through a privately funded research residency at the Luxehills Museum and Art Village. There, I worked with the Museum Director and two museum staff. These three served as researchers, consultants and translators. The first job we undertook was the translation into Chinese and consequent re-wording of my original research aims and proposal. In the first part of this section, I will present observations and analysis of the rewording and omission of original content from the abstract to this paper as I worked with Chinese museum staff. Second I will talk about the survey developed with museum staff and distributed to Chongqing and Chengdu museums and art museums. Third, I will discuss the symposium held at the end of my residency attended by museum representatives, artists, critics as well as other local creative professionals. In doing so, I will make some observations and give brief analysis of speeches given and discussions held at this symposium.

Preliminary Findings & What Got Lost in Translation

The first job we undertook was the translation and consequent re-wording of my original research aims and proposal, in order to prepare materials and invitations for a symposium which would conclude my residency. For cost and time efficiency, we felt it would be easier to convoke an assembly of museum representatives than it would be for me to visit each museum one by one. Our second objective was to distribute a survey with 10 questions that could be given to museum representatives in addition to, or in lieu of, attendance at our symposium.

The transformation in the text of my research aims and objectives, after multiple consultations with museum staff, will give some indication of the difficulties of conducting field research in China, where self-censorship is part of an effort to adhere to a strict set of unspoken rules to avoid offending anyone in order to gain as wide a research base as possible. Our aim, for example, was to make the survey useful to all kinds of museums, and to all art museums which did and didn't exhibit avant-garde artwork. Thus, while I had originally wanted to research Lu Peng and Lan Qingwei's experimental curation, it was decided to take out references to specific museum directors or to avant-garde art. While I started out asking questions specifically about marginalized artistic and exhibition practices, what we ended up going for in the end, was an understanding of funding sources of various museums and the roles these museums recognised for themselves in society. Language used to express government 'notice' rather than 'surveillance' was meant to open the survey and symposium to museums which would not be willing to take part in a conversation which spoke directly of, or commented on, government ideological intervention at Chinese museums. If we focused on avant-garde art in our research proposals, not only would non-art museums refrain from coming, but many publicly funded art museums would also fail to respond. It was made clear to me that this was an uncomfortable topic, albeit an important one.

Also, mention of culture as an instrument of social, economic and political change was removed. Specific labelling of museums as 'role-takers' in representing NSR was also removed. Ascribing too much agency to museums in China also appeared problematic. While European Marxist and ideological critique would naturally grant or recognise power in institutions of representation, such as museums; Chinese Marxist theory (at least in official rhetoric) steers away from 'causal' relationships, preferring 'correlation' or 'inter-connectedness'. Although we see intentionality in China; i.e. using culture as an instrument and museums as organs of cultural representations; these observations are meant to remain implicit and not explicitly pronounced.

Chengdu and Chongqing Museum Sectors

In frontier regions of China that have lacked arts and culture infrastructure, it is often the case that private real-estate developers take on the responsibility of building arts infrastructure. This is also the case in Chengdu, and the Luxehills and, later, Luxelakes housing developments at the Southern fringe of this city of 14 million have each built and operated contemporary art museums that have operated longest and most consistently in this city. Creativity and luxury brand the residential tracks, with organic food available at the village center and children's art education programs available at the museum. In the case of these two Chengdu museums, developers invest year-by-year, funding extensive programming and exhibitions (Tables 6.2 and 6.3).

In the space of a few days, a list of participating art museums was composed of those who responded in a timely manner to our symposium invitation. Of the Chengdu art museums listed above, the following accepted our invitation: Chengdu Blue Roof Art Museum (New Hall), Guanghui Art Museum, Chengdu Modern Art Museum, Luxehills Art Museum, Sichuan University Art Museum, Chengdu Ni Bang Museum of Ceramic Art, and Winshare Art Museum. Chengdu Modern Art Museum, represented by Huang Xiaorong at the symposium, no longer has a brick and mortar location. I have included it in our study for the role it has played in Chengdu contemporary art development, being responsible for the first Chengdu Biennale in 2001, co-curated by Huang Xiaorong. Since the closing of the physical exhibition space, Huang Xiaorong operates in Chengdu's cultural and creative sectors as a consultant, independent curator, and art critic. To emphasize the institutional genealogy of Chengdu's museum sector and local biennale tradition, I have listed Huang Xiaorong in context with this seminal Chengdu arts institution in addition to his role in the Chengdu arts community as art critic and consultant on matters being discussed that afternoon. All Chengdu and Chongqing museums to participate in our symposium were those already within our personally affiliated institutional networks.

Discussion of Surveys Answered by Symposium Participants

Surveys were distributed one week prior to the symposium, and most of them were collected in person, on the day of the symposium. The survey asked for the name of the participant, and eleven names were given,

Table 6.2 Proposed sample of Chongqing and Chengdu museums

Chongqing Museums (13)	*Chengdu Museums (12)*
重庆中国三峡博物馆 Three Gorges Museum	金沙遗址博物馆 Jinsha Site Museum
重庆红岩革命历史博物馆 Chongqing Hongyan Revolutionary Museum	三星堆博物馆 Sanxingdui Museum
重庆自然博物馆 Chongqing Museum of Natural History	四川博物馆 Sichuan Museum
重庆大韩民国临时政府旧址陈列馆 Provisional Government of the Republic of Korea Site Exhibition Hall	成都武侯祠博物馆 Chengdu Wu Hou Shrine
重庆三峡移民纪念馆 Chongqing Three Gorges Immigration Memorial	四川丝绸博物馆 Sichuan Silk Museum
北碚区博物馆 Beibei District Museums	成都永陵博物馆 Chengdu Yongling Museum
卢作孚纪念馆 Lu Zufu Memorial Hall	
四世同堂纪念馆 Four Generations Memorial Hall	
梁实秋纪念馆 Liang Shiqiu Memorial Hall	
晏阳初纪念馆 Yan Yangchu Memorial Hall	
抗战时期荣誉军人自治试验区陈列馆 War of Resistance Against Aggression Period Honored Soldiers Autonomous Experimental District Exhibition Hall	
国立复旦大学重庆旧址 Former Wartime Period Fudan University Site)	
重庆巴渝民俗博物馆 Chongqing Bayu Folk Custom Museum	成都博物馆 Chengdu Museum

(continued)

Table 6.2 (continued)

Chongqing Museums (13)	*Chengdu Museums (12)*
聂荣臻元帅陈列馆	成都杜甫草堂博物馆
Marshal Nie Rongzhen Exhibition Hall	Du Fu Thatched Cottage Museum
钓鱼城历史文物陈列馆	鹿野苑石刻艺术博物馆
Exhibition Hall of Historical Relics of Diaoyucheng	Mrigadava Museum of Stone Sculpture
铜梁区博物馆	朱成博物馆
Tongliang District Museum	Zhu Cheng Ancient Sculpture Museum
刘伯承同志纪念馆	成都永陵博物馆
Comrade Liu Bocheng Memorial Hall	The Royal Tomb of Wang Jian
奉节县白帝博物馆	成都泥邦陶瓷艺术博物馆
Fengjie County Baidi Museum	Chengdu Ni Bang Museum of Ceramic Art
重庆抗战遗址博物馆	
Chongqing War of Resistance Against Japanese Aggression Site	

Table 6.3 Proposed sample of Chongqing and Chengdu art Museums

Chongqing Art Museums (15)	*Chengdu Art Museums (15)*
Changjiang Museum of Contemporary Art	成都当代美术馆
重庆长江当代美术馆	Chengdu Museum of Contemporary Art
重庆缙云书画院	麓湖·A4美术馆
Chongqing Puyun Museum of Painting and Calligraphy	Luhu Art Museum
龙美术馆 (重庆馆)	四川大学美术馆
Long Art Museum (Chongqing Location)	Sichuan University Art Museum
GCA 星汇当代美术馆	成都花园 (成都市美术馆)
GCA Xinghui Contemporary Art Museum	Chengdu Art Academy Art Gallery
罗中立美术馆 (四川美术学院美术馆)	何多苓美术馆
Luo Zhongli Art Museum (Sichuan Fine Arts Institute Art Museum)	He Duoling Art Museum
CAEA美术馆	福宝美术馆
CAEA Art Museum	Fubao Art Museum
重庆美术馆	妙音阁·云艺术美术馆
Chongqing Art Museum	Miaoyin Pavillion: Yun Art Museum
	(Yan Cheng)
坦克库·当代艺术中心	四川中国书画美术馆
Tank Loft Chongqing Contemporary Art Center	Sichuan China Paintings and Calligraphy Art Gallery
原·美术馆	红美术馆: 成都国际文化艺术中心
Essence Contemporary Art Museum	Red Art Museum: Chengdu Int'l Cultural Ctr
王琦美术博物馆	文轩美术馆
Wang Qi Art Museum	Winshare Art Museum
华人当代美术馆	高小华美术馆西南民族大学艺术学院美术馆
Chinese Contemporary Art Gallery	Gao Xiaohua Art Museum: Southwest Minzu University
黄桷坪当代美术馆	麓山美术馆
Huangjueping Contemporary Art Museum	Luxehills (Lushan) Museum

(continued)

Table 6.3 (continued)

Chongqing Art Museums (15)	*Chengdu Art Museums (15)*
重庆市群众艺术馆	成都蓝顶美术馆 (新馆)
Chongqing People's Museum	Chengdu Blue Roof Art Museum (New Hall)
重庆文联美术馆	花样年·知美术馆
Chongqing Literary Federation Art Museum	Huayang Zhi Museum
重庆大学艺术学院	四川美术馆
Chongqing University Art Museum	Sichuan Art Gallery
星汇当代美术馆	宽云美术馆
GCA Galaxy Contemporary Art Museum	Kuanyum Art Museum
	诗婢家美术馆
	Shibijia Art Museum
	许燎源现代设计艺术博物馆
	XLY MoMA

while two answerers chose to submit the survey anonymously. We also asked for the name of the museum institution represented, the questionee's position at that institution, as well as the length of time he or she had served in that capacity within the institution. Of the eleven answers given concerning years served within a certain position at an institution, nearly half had worked there less than five years, nearly a quarter had served for between five and ten years, while fifteen percent had worked ten or more years within that capacity. All but one of thirteen institutions represented were non-profit institutions, with one creative cluster being a for-profit organisation. With thirteen surveys collected, all but one represented unique institutions, with two Sichuan University Art Museum representatives each filling out one survey (Table 6.4).

When asked whether the answerer was aware of any specific museum exhibitions dealing with the subject of the New Silk Roads, eight out of thirteen either answered in the negative or left the answer blank. The representative of the Sichuan Institute of Fine Art gave the most detailed answer, giving three examples: the New York Metropolitan Museum of Art *Chinese Art of the Qin and Han Dynasties, 221 BCE–220 CE*, held from April 13–July 16, 2017, the National Museum of China *Qin and Han Civilizations*; and the Sichuan Institute of Fine Arts *Long Silk Road: Feasting with All Nations*. The representatives of the Nibang Ceramic Art Museum and the Luxelakes A4 Art Museum cited the Chengdu City Museum's *Dunhuang Art*, *Land of Tianfu* and *Silk Road Culture Special Exhibitions*. The representative of the Sichuan University Art Museum mentioned that the township of Mianzhu had held an exhibition centered around the folk art of *Nianhua* painting, to disseminate traditional art

Table 6.4 List of museums and organizations answering surveys

Sichuan Arts Museums	*Chongqing Arts Museums*	*Other (Sichuan)*
Sichuan University Museum of Art	Chongqing Bayu Folk Museum	Mintown Creative Community
Chengdu Modern Art Museum	Sichuan Institute of Fine Art Museum of Art	
Nibang Ceramic Art Museum	Chongqing Galaxy Contemporary Art Museum	
Chengdu Blue Roof Art Museum	Yangtze Art Museum	
Luhu A4 Art Museum		

forms. One of the two answerers who submitted anonymously listed a Sichuan Provincial Museum exhibition of Indian and Chinese sculpture.

When asked to describe what they perceived the New Silk Roads as being, nine out of thirteen answers were provided. All eight of these answers indicated that the New Silk Roads were a top-down government directive. One answerer indicated that this top-down directive was totally unrelated to art; three addressed solely its cultural and social aspects; while five answers discussed the interaction between the political, economic, and cultural aspects of the New Silk Roads. I give the answers below, as they are nuanced and interesting enough to display in full.

Unrelated to art & culture	*Solely cultural and social*	*Political, economic, and cultural*
"Totally unrelated to art"	"A concept which refers to Chinese culture being exported on the government level"	"It's political, economic, and cultural."
	"Promote communicability between society and culture"	"Fundamentally economic and political; secondarily cultural with domestic and international policy; built on national conditions."
	"This is a government directive. The government will use NSR for purposes of advocacy. They culturally disseminate, using NSR to pass through all cultural aspects"	"First of all it is an extension of Chinese political and economic expansion. It is an effort to integrate economically with Europe and Asia, in order to obtain greater economic advantages and resist American economic hegemony. Secondly, this is a large measure to export Chinese culture.

(continued)

(continued)

Unrelated to art & culture	*Solely cultural and social*	*Political, economic, and cultural*
		"NSR is of extreme importance right now as a direction and way of thinking in China, greatly influencing our lives. NSR uses the symbols of the ancient Silk Road to initiate external (foreign) collaborations, and to adjust our (domestic) development and economy. This is the larger picture. When it comes to my own work, I find myself as a local experiencing this as well. Right now we must all focus on how to develop our Southwest region's art ecology research, to figure out how to better integrate our museums into society; helping our city's optimal development" NSR is a concentrated expression of the will of a country's power and institutions."

At the onset of this symposium, held on April 13, 2018 at 3:00 pm, I gave a presentation which stated my research aims and objectives (the edited and translated version). I have described above that my original research aims and objectives had been 'translated' both 'linguistically' and 'culturally' in order to appeal to a greater number of potential attendees to our symposium. In this process, I discovered that I was not going to be able to go forward with my original aim of using primary source materials including interviews and new data to focus on avant-garde activities and actors associated with museums in the Southwest China. My original research aims and objectives had been displaced.

Summary and Analysis of Short Speeches Given by Symposium Attendees

At the symposium, we had one artist, four critics, three researchers (including myself), twelve museum representatives and one creative cluster founder/CEO.

Position, Institutions, Public/Private Status of Attendees at the Symposium

Position	*Institution*	*Public/ Private*
Artist	Highlands Art Village	Private
Critic	Independent, Chengdu based	Private
Critic	Independent, Chengdu-based	Private
Critic	Independent, Chengdu-based	Private
Critic, Curator, former Museum Director	Chengdu Modern Art Museum	Private
Associate Professor, PhD in Economics	Chengdu University	Public
Senior Researcher in the a position funded by the Swiss National Science Foundation	Laboratoire d'Anthropologie Culturelle et Sociale (LACS) at the University of Lausanne	Public
Curator	Chengdu Blue Roof Art Museum	Private
Manager of Operations	Guanghui Art Museum	Private
Museum Director	GCA Galaxy Contemporary Art Museum	Private
Acting Museum Manager	CAEA Art Museum	Public
Deputy Museum Director	Sichuan Institute of Fine Art Art Museum	Public
Museum Director	Lu Shan Art Museum	Private
Museum Director	Sichuan University Art Museum	Public
CEO	Mintown	Private
Museum Director	Chengdu Nibang Ceramic Art Museum	Private
Front Museum Hall Director	Winshare Art Museum	Public/Private
Operations Manager	Long Art Museum (Chongqing branch)	Private
Representing Lan Qingwei, Museum Director	Guanghui Art Museum	Private

An Artist's Perspective

There being only one artist present, it is fair to suggest that any findings from this one attendant would not be able to represent how Southwest China artists think or feel about the New Silk Roads in their region. However, having spent over a decade in the region working with, interviewing, researching, and writing about artists in this region; I can say that the artist's response, while more extreme than most; is representative to some extent. It is important to note that the artist is an anti-establishment avant-garde artist, and thus does not represent those artists who are happy with China's political economy of culture, especially that reflected in New Silk Road cultural policy. While the artist is not an establishment artist, he is very successful with rich patrons in the real-estate sector, and he exhibits widely in both private and public museums throughout China, despite being asked to sometimes pull artworks from exhibitions. His artworks are accepted into exhibitions about as often as they are rejected for their sensitive political and social content.

The artist's input at the symposium bordered on the irate. He objected to my subject matter, and to my suggestion that top-down government cultural policy had any relationship to 'real art.' He stated that if he didn't know me personally, he would suspect that I was holding this symposium on behalf of the Chinese government, as a propagandistic effort to promote New Silk Road cultural policy. He was equally pessimistic about Chinese museums' ability to maintain academic standards with their research, or objectivity within their collections. He doubted that the truth could ever be arrived at, even at a symposium such as we were attending that day. While he refused to admit any substantive connection between NSR cultural policy and 'real culture,' he stated that without culture, the New Silk Roads could never bring about a 'win-win' within or outside of China.

Critics' Perspectives

All four of the critics present at the symposium have been working within the region for the past two decades. As the Southwest region has been a culturally and artistically marginalized region up until the recent influx of NSR funding, most artistic discourse has been avant-garde in nature. Thus, these four critics have focused upon avant-garde art production, and their experience with the creative and fine arts sector is with a largely privately funded and operated sector. As we shall see, this predisposes each critic to approach the topic of NSR cultural and artistic influence from a largely pessimistic point of view.

Each of these critics decried the lack of funding in the arts throughout the past two decades of the region's economic and cultural development. They identified museums as either ideological tools for government actors, or subject to personal tastes and whims of private collectors. They lamented the lack of objectivity as well as academic standards for research. Critic 1, having been part of the curatorial team responsible for Chengdu's first two Bienalles in the early aughts, was most articulate about how public and private sectors interfaced, and observed that as funding did trickle into the region for public arts and cultural infrastructure, there was a class system being exacerbated by the New Silk Roads, which was demarcated by ideological boundaries. For each of these speakers, NSR was seen as an authoritarian force which isolated sensitive subject matter, depriving it of a platform for discussion; and forced the closure of open experimentation in nascent artist clusters and villages. They were equally pessimistic about the role that private sector investment played in the arts, with Critics 2 and 3 becoming visibly emotional and their voices pitching as they yelled in complaint about how museums served the needs and objectives of real-estate developers. Their use of the word 'spiritual' in describing the corruption and lack of objectivity in the region's cultural sector reflected Southwest China's less commercial approach to art as I have experienced it. Where there has always been very little money, the region still a rich and vibrant cultural and artistic milieu; materialism does not gain purchase as easily. Thus, when it arrives, this materialism will be seen as antagonistic to more substantive or 'spiritual' aesthetic values.

Museum and Other Institutional Representatives' Perspectives

Representatives of public and private museums as well as the city's most successful creative cluster were less emotional than artists and critics present at the symposium. Their statements were more balanced and objective, in line with their professional status within arts and culture management. For example, the representative of the public/private Winshare Art Museum admitted that there was a lack of objectivity when it came to exhibition rotation and exhibitions. He attributed this, however, to the short history of Chinese art museums; suggesting that a period of development is natural for a museum sector within only a few decades of history, in the best of cases. The representative of the GCA Galaxy Contemporary Art Museum agreed with this assessment, adding that Southwest China museums had an even shorter history than museums in first tier cities such as Beijing and Shanghai. Huang felt that NSR funding would bring critical mass to the Southwest museum sector, and with it more experience and professionalism.

A representative of the Sichuan Institute of Fine Art Museum pointed out that the museum he represented had over 3,500 artworks in its collection, a relatively high number for the region. Collections had been established to the point to where, in his opinion, more attention should be paid to creating the right conditions for preserving the collection. This advanced level of consideration for the works of art in the collection indicates the level of professionalism being reached at that institution. He also mentioned that the government was urging the Institute to collaborate more widely with international institutions outside of China, citing Turkey and Italy as countries with whom collaborations had already been undertaken. The representative of the Chengdu-based Sichuan University Museum of art (not to be confused with the Chongqing-based Sichuan Institute of Fine Art), followed up with a point about the importance of preservation. He suggested that the lack of attention given to preservation of works of art has to do with the nascent level of awareness of art's value outside of immediate market conditions. That is to say that contemporary art in China, with only three to four decades of development, does not exist within a stable continuum of value. Collectors, arts institutions, and arts professionals are all experiencing art markets as rapidly shifting, and thus feel unable to track market indicators in a systematic way. This representative pointed to Western arts institutions as already investing much more in preservation efforts. This had to do, he added, with more stable value systems within which contemporary art is contextualised. He spoke to exhibitions which were created under the rubric of and with funding from New Silk Road cultural policy, pointing out that cultural and fine art objects which are exhibited in New Silk Roads exhibitions are supported by plenty of funding, but have value within an isolated system which is not integrated, or otherwise organically contextualised, within contemporary art markets.

The representative of the Blue Roof Museum, one of Chengdu's oldest and most successful contemporary art institutions, spoke at the greatest length about various case studies having to do with New Silk Road funding and the Southwest region's collaboration with international arts institutions abroad. Although the museum is privately funded, the representative had a good deal of knowledge about the Cultural Bureau's interaction with academic arts institutions; listing a number of exhibitions including ones in Australia and Egypt. He spoke of a binary condition, which saw NSR funding expanding the Southwest region's domestic and international influence while at the same time narrowing the scope of contemporary art away from experimental modes of artistic production and exhibition. Furthermore, NSR funding often narrowed the scope of exhibitions to exclude contemporary art altogether, preferring to exhibit and educate publics about cultural heritage as contextualised in New Silk Road cultural narratives.

Another representative of the Sichuan Institute of Fine Art Museum of Art discussed the institution's focus on research into Chinese contemporary art since the 1980's. He was no stranger to the navigation efforts necessary for integrating top-down cultural narratives into the curriculum, while at the same time cultivating cultural energies as they arose both within the student body and in the region. He spoke of exhibitions inspired and funded by NSR cultural policy that he had been a part of in Europe, including one in Sweden and in Frankfurt. He had spent the better part of a month in Frankfurt as part of this cultural exchange and felt that it had been very fruitful. One observation he made was that people outside of China had very little understanding of Chinese contemporary art within China, especially of contemporary art in the Southwest China region. He hoped that greater efforts would be made to investigate various modes of expression in Chinese contemporary art, and was optimistic that more international cooperation would facilitate these investigations.

The representatives of the Guanghui Art Museum and the Long Art Museum Chongqing branch each spoke from the vantage point of having ample private funding. In both cases, emphasis was first upon collections, and only second upon exhibitions and public education. The Guanghui Art Museum had not yet opened, and was in the second year of a preliminary phase for collecting. The Long Art Museum already had a successful base in Shanghai and, with its experience in that first tier city, was already established as a taste-maker within international art markets. The latter discussed how NSR and other top-down cultural policy had the effect of weakening momentum, and of getting in the way more than helping. This reflects the attitudes of arts institutions in regions where private arts and cultural institutions are plentiful enough to do without public art infrastructure. Guanghui's representative spoke of museums as sites of intellectual and cultural production, places where the spirit of the people is cultivated. For this reason, she argued, diversity is of the utmost importance.

The last symposium speakers I will discuss here include two scholars. One taught cultural production at Chengdu University, and the other was a Canadian researcher on earthquake reconstruction and allocation of public goods in Sichuan province. I will also discuss comments contributed by the founder and CEO of a successful creative cluster in Chengdu. The Chengdu University professor spoke to a couple of points made by other speakers. In response to the artist's indignation at New Silk Road cultural policy interfering in the lives of artists by dictating tastes or ideological orientations; she suggested that the New Silk Roads constituted a 'blind spot' for the art world, or at least for artists who insisted upon seeing a separation between culture and political economics. She also affirmed another point made earlier, about the West's thinking both about Chinese contemporary art and Chinese political economy. The Canadian researcher spoke of the influence that New Silk Road cultural policy would inevitably have upon the region, both from in the public sector of arts and cultural infrastructure, but also on property values and the cost of housing. The creative cluster representative spoke from the sole perspective of one who invests personal capital into a successful creative cluster, seeking to minimise not only importance of public and private funding upon the arts, but also the importance of the museum sector altogether. His point of view was that arts and culture should be concerned entirely with the communities it served, as a proletariat good which was generated by and served everyday communities, rather than contained within the 'white cube' of an arts institution.

Conclusion

This chapter on contemporary art and the museum sector in Southwest China is the heart of this book. Here we have continued the conversation developed in Chapter 5 about China's problem of 'cultural discount,' and 'cultural trade deficit.' We have also looked within China's borders at one of its frontier New Silk Road regions to see how top-down government cultural policy in regards to NSR has influenced artists and arts professionals, particularly as regards the museum sector, in the Southwest of China. We have also seen ways in which the public arts sector interacts with the private in the curation, exhibition, promotion, and preservation of contemporary art. In order to contextualise this discussion of Southwest China's arts ecology, we also discussed how cultural implants, such as the *Cosmopolis 1.5* exhibition put on by the Centre Pompidou in collaboration with extra-regional as well as local government actors, fail to serve local arts ecologies in the long term. The export of arts funding to foreign and extra-regional actors fails to build sustainable arts and culture infrastructure within the Southwest regions. On the other hand, the notoriety of artists exhibited is promoted and organizational networks that develop around such a large-scale exhibition do build value for Southwest China art markets. Thus, local artists and arts professionals do benefit, albeit in an indirect manner. It remains to be seen how much or to what extent local actors benefit from this added value. Perhaps a hint lies within the vocational training that interns working for Cosmopolis organizers received whilst working with foreign actors in the experience of facilitating the large-scale exhibition. Perhaps some of these interns will go on to develop professionally whist working in the fine arts sector of Chengdu. It is important to add that just before this book is going to print, Chengdu is preparing to hold a large-scale biennale in 2021 without the aid of any foreign actor. It will be curated by a well-known Chinese curator, Fan Di'an, and Lu Peng is serving as one of the principal co-ordinators of the event, which is publicly funded. Exhibition works by artists all over the world, a total of over 300 works will be exhibited by over 200 artists. I anticipate that this will be more effective than was Cosmopolis #1.5 in cultivating China's Southwest's art ecology and building lasting arts infrastructure in the region.

In examining three main areas of data derived from my 2018 research residency at Luxehills Museum (working with museum staff on translating research aims and objectives, the survey, and a symposium), we see that the answers concerning NSR influence upon the Southwest China museum and fine art sector are not cut and dry. Experiences of NSR cultural policy vary according to the role various actors play, i.e. artists, critics, museum professionals. At the moment, NSR cultural funding in the Southwest resembles pouring water onto scorched desert sand. There has been such a dearth of arts and culture infrastructure for so long, and the museum and fine art sector is still in its nascency. Thus, it will take some time to determine the real results of this funding. One thing that we can observe, however, is that some funding is better than no funding. As it is, the avant-garde have always been under the radar, and will remain there for some time to come. I conclude that this will be much the same in regions outside of China, as NSR cultural policy creates more extensive inroads into international regions along the road and belt. Local arts ecologies will be mostly left alone, unsupported as they have been, while actors who are able to benefit from top-down government People-to-People cultural programming, be they local or not, will do so because of their language ability, international networks, and ambition along these lines. There is a danger in these areas, as there is in Chengdu and Chongqing, that history will exclude the local heroes, so to speak, as narratives of contemporary art as well as cultural heritage evolve under the umbrage of the New Silk Roads. However, recent developments, such as the 2021 Super-Fusion Chengdu Biennale are promising, and could signal real transformations in the way the fine art sector is being handled in New Silk Road frontier regions.

CHAPTER 7

New Silk Roads People-to-People Connectivity in Cultural Centers Along the Old and New Silk Roads

In our last chapter, we went deep into one of China's frontier regions, focusing on the museum and fine art sector of the Southwest cities of Chengdu and Chongqing. We did this as a case study, examining the effects of the center upon the margins in China of New Silk Road cultural policy. While we cannot say with any certainty that these trends will reproduce as Chinese cultural policy extends to New Silk Roads regions outside of China, we do suggest that this will be the case. As we hope that future studies will be conducted, here we map some of the urban cultural centers of the New Silk Roads, suggesting the most optimal sites for such future study.

This chapter presents research on material and intangible cultural exchanges between China and its top trading partners along the old Silk Roads and New Silk Roads. We revisit the geography laid out in Chapter 2 of this book, where we gave an introduction of New Silk Roads geography. This time we focus on cultural centers of both the overland Silk Road Economic Belt and the seagoing 21st Century Maritime Silk Road. We explore cultural relations between China and certain of these cultural centers to demonstrate how geocultural power, cultural heritage, and cultural diplomacy are being utilized in a bid to facilitate China's development of the New Silk Roads. Keeping in line with our objective, we begin here to illustrate how the People-to-People component of the

S. Kidd, *Culture Paves The New Silk Roads*,
Contemporary East Asian Visual Cultures, Societies and Politics,
https://doi.org/10.1007/978-981-16-8574-3_7

Belt and Road Initiative plays out in some of the key urban centers of these New Silk Roads.

Just as the ancient Silk Roads were not a cut-and-dried pathway through the desert and mountains from China to Europe; the New Silk Roads constitute a complex network of overland and maritime trade routes. The old Silk Roads arose organically over centuries, even millennia; brought into being through the political economies and cultural trajectories of multiple governments and peoples. They were much simpler than their modern counterpart, involving mainly overland routes from China through Central Asia and overseas via Chinese ports to Southeast Asia and as far as Africa. The New Silk Roads are a gigantic and complex project brought into being over a period of not yet a decade in its present form, and no longer than two or three decades, if one counts the China Goes Global and Going West initiatives as earlier iterations of the same trajectory. These New Silk Roads are elaborate, and if one keeps in mind how integral these supply chains are and will be to the global economy; then there isn't an urban center in the world that goes unaffected by them.

Thus for the purposes of this chapter, to give a sense of how culture is paving the New Silk Roads, we sketch out selected urban centers, focusing on what China is contributing to their vibrancy today in connection with cultural heritage, as well as other creative and cultural industries. In order to create some symmetry to this discussion, we focus on urban centers that roughly approximate the route of the old Silk Road with its urban centers at Xi'an, Dunhuang, Samarkand, Merv, Balkh, Constantinople, Ctesiphon, Taxila, Damascus, and Rey. Thus we will look at New Silk Road urban centers at Beijing, Riyadh, Delhi, Islamabad, Kabul, Ankara, Istanbul, Damascus, Jerusalem, and Astana. In order to somewhat update the discussion, however, to remain relevant to the actual geography of important New Silk Road urban centers, I also touch upon Moscow, Bishkek, Kuala Lumpur, Djibouti, and Duisburg.

Beijing, China

In April of 2019, the mayor of Beijing, Chen Jining, declared Beijing's intentions to deepen international cooperation along the New Silk Roads, opening to simultaneous sister-city relationships with twenty-one nation capital cities. These efforts are financed by the Asian Investment Bank and New Silk Road Fund. This is part of a greater effort to bring major

Silk Road cities together throughout China, the Middle East and Europe. Adding substance to the One Belt One Road fifth pillar of People-to-People Connectivity; these efforts include investment in cultural and creative businesses in sister Silk Road cities. Incubation centers and high-tech zones, the likes of which have been built all over China in the past couple of decades, are being developed in these sister cities. Incubation centers and hi-tech zones, unlike their analogues in other pillars of OBOR, seek to meet global challenges using cultural and creative resources. In higher education, thirty-two Beijing academic research institutions have been designated as training centers for One Belt One Road academic exchange students, bringing students for scientific vocational training into China with One Belt One Road scholarships.

China's cultural and creative industries are most advanced in its nation's capital, with film and television production in this city staffed with young creatives educated at the best universities worldwide. CCTV-4 broadcasts a daily column throughout Asia, Europe and the United States by the name of *Homeland Dreamland*, targeted at Chinese diaspora as well as foreign nationals.[1] Programming includes travel reporting and discovery. An imprint column of *Homeland Dreamland* is *One Belt One Road*, a daily programmed module initiated in August of 2016 employing dozens of production staff, interviewing subjects around the world in New Silk Roads regions.[2] Programming thus far has focused on people and regions in China, Sri Lanka, Laos, Iran, United Arab Emirates, Kenya, Myanmar, Tanzania, Ethiopia, Cote d'Ivoire, Nepal, Philippines, Belarus, Germany, Netherlands, Poland, Serbia, Bulgaria, Romania, Belgium, Tajikistan, China-Kazakhstan border, Kazakhstan, Austria, Hungary, Czech Republic, Russia, Greece, Italy, South Africa, Ukraine, Switzerland, Azerbaijan, France, Chile, Ecuador, Peru, Turkey, Uzbekistan, Georgia, Zambia, Algeria, Morocco, Nigeria, Spain, Mauritius, Zimbabwe, Senegal, and Namibia. This list of countries featured in CCTV-4 One Belt One Road programming is listed in its order of initial broadcast date, beginning in 2016 and listed up through January of 2020. This programming focused on domestic development in China, through

[1] "远方的家 （中央电视台中文国际频道大型日播旅游栏目） _百度百科," accessed October 18, 2021, https://baike.baidu.com/item/%E8%BF%9C%E6%96%B9%E7%9A%84%E5%AE%B6/10434512.

[2] "一带一路（大型系列旅游节目）_百度百科," accessed October 18, 2021, https://baike.baidu.com/item/%E4%B8%80%E5%B8%A6%E4%B8%80%E8%B7%AF/19926646.

the South China Sea, to Africa, throughout the Middle East and Europe, to countries as far flung as Chile and Peru.

Meanwhile, in Beijing, there are festivals conducted to bring awareness of the One Belt One Road to the general population; such as *Beijing's One Belt One Road Intangible Culture Style* with interactive maker-space projects by which the general population can take a hands-on approach to understanding the value of cultural heritage along the New Silk Roads.[3] *One Belt One Road Loves Beijing* (May 18–Sep 4, 2018) was a large scale event coordinated by the Beijing Municipal News Offices and China International Broadcasting and Television Online Broadcasting, to bring local and foreign populations together for discussion on the New Silk Roads.[4] In 2018, Beijing University also established the One Belt One Road Institute.[5]

COVID relief includes PPE supply as well as education about the virus, such as training in prevention measures. Vaccine donations have comprised what is possibly China's most successful measure of diplomacy thus far. However, prior to COVID, Beijing had already vamped up the Health Silk Road as way of promoting Chinese culture in the form of Traditional Chinese Medicine (TCM) abroad, establishing bases along the New Silk Roads for this large scale cultural and medical dissemination. Roots for this network are established at the China TCM Institute Guan'anmen Hospital and the United States National Health Institute Oncology Institute in collaboration with the International TCM Oncology Alliance, Gansu Health Plan Committee TCM Center in Kyrgyzstan, Guangzhou TCM University, TCM Center established in Malawi, Africa, Jiangsu Provincial TCM Institute, TCM Center in Paris, France, Heilongjiang TCM University Middle East and European TCM Center in Hungary, Beijing TCM University, TCM Center in St. Petersburg, Russia, Hunan TCM University, TCM Center in Luxembourg,

3 "北京东城区举办 '一带一路 非遗风情'展示活动–-中国文明网," accessed October 18, 2021, http://www.wenming.cn/syjj/dfcz/bj/201606/t20160613_3436753.shtml.

4 "2018 '一带一路 爱上北京'系列活动启动," accessed October 18, 2021, https://baijiahao.baidu.com/s?id=1599521143584140811&wfr=spider&for=pc.

5 "北京大学 '一带一路'书院," accessed October 18, 2021, http://www.bri.pku.edu.cn/.

Brussels, and the Nanjing TCM University, as well as the TCM Center in Australia.[6]

Islamabad, Pakistan

Islamabad, capital city of Pakistan, is located in the northeast of the country, not far away from Kashmir, a region contested between India and Pakistan, contributing to India's withdrawal from the One Belt One Road project. Built in the 1960s to replace Karachi as capital city, it is now the county's ninth largest city. China-Pakistan-built Benezir Bhutto International Airport sees direct flights to and from Beijing.[7] In 2014, a China-Pakistan art exhibition opened, with eight Chinese artists bringing just over 100 artworks to show. Invitations were issued by the National Pakistan News Broadcasting Heritage Bureau, and the Chinese Ministry of Culture sent traditional Chinese painters to Pakistan to engage in dialogue about Chinese ink-wash painting.[8] In 2016, the China Cultural Center leased office space in the building complex of the National Arts Committee of Pakistan.[9] In late 2016, China conducted a *Xinjiang Cultural Week* in Islamabad, with festivals and shows celebrating the daily customs and cultural heritage of people in this Northwestern region of China. In 2018, also held at in the building complex of the National Arts Committee of Pakistan, *Sharing Horizons Now* cultural exchange saw performance troupes from Xi'an bring traditional forms of music, dance, and performance for three categories of programming: *Moon is Born at Sea*, *Pining for Love in the Night*, and *Intoxicating Qin Melodies at Chang'an*. Other programming reflected older cultural exchanges between Chang'an (old Xi'an) and Silk Road regions in Pakistan.[10]

6 "北中医的 '一带一路'_北京中医药大学新闻网," accessed October 18, 2021, https://xww.bucm.edu.cn/ztbd/27243.htm.

7 "[远方的家]亲历 '一带一路' 探访伊斯兰堡新航线_CCTV节目官网-CCTV-4_央视网(Cctv.Com)," accessed October 18, 2021, http://tv.cctv.com/2017/10/20/VIDESaAHTCJRn4y0loNTJIiH171020.shtml.

8 "'牵手2014——中巴两国艺术交流展'在伊斯兰堡开幕-国际频道-新华网," accessed October 18, 2021, http://www.xinhuanet.com/world/2014-05/14/c_126500666.htm.

9 "巴基斯坦中国文化中心 '落户'国家艺术委员会-中国侨网," accessed October 18, 2021, http://www.chinaqw.com/zhwh/2016/05-04/87366.shtml.

10 "'盛世大唐相约千年'文艺演出在巴基斯坦举办," accessed October 18, 2021, https://www.mct.gov.cn/whzx/qgwhxxlb/sx_7740/201804/t20180424_831891.htm.

We see through three years a deepening of cultural ties between Shaanxi Province and Islamabad. In 2018, a three-year anniversary of the China Cultural Center was celebrated, with the Pakistan-China Cultural Center, the Baoji Municipal Bureau of Culture, Radio, Television, Press, and Publication, Shaanxi Foreign Cultural Exchange Promotion Association, and Pakistan's Dawn Newspaper holding an *A Thousand Years Since Chang'an* cultural heritage and exchange celebration throughout Islamabad.[11] Also in that year, the 67th anniversary of diplomatic relations between China and Pakistan was celebrated, supported mainly by the Chinese Consulate in Islamabad, the Pakistan National Cultural Center, China's Ministry of Culture and Tourism, and Pakistan National Art Committee.[12] By 2019, we still see Shaanxi Province as a locus of cultural exchange with Islamabad, and we see an expansion into other cultural and creative industry activity. In this year, the *Chinese Qin Qiang* animation series invested in and produced by Shaanxi Zhongshan Film and Television Culture Media Co., Ltd. screened *Three Drops of Blood* on Pakistan National Television's English International Channel over a six-week period.[13]

Kabul, Afghanistan

Documentary filmmaking is an area China is especially encouraging within its cultural and creative industries sector. In late 2017, opening ceremonies were conducted in Kabul for the screening of the first of five parts of the documentary film *China and Afghanistan: The Story of One Belt One Road*.[14] Before that, Confucius Institutes in Kabul began administering the *Hanyu Shuiping Kaoshi* (HSK), a Chinese language proficiency exam needed to enter Chinese universities, graduate schools,

11 "'天涯共此时'文化交流专场演出在巴基斯坦举行-新华网," accessed October 18, 2021, http://www.xinhuanet.com/world/2018-09/27/c_1123491439.htm.

12 "庆祝中巴建交67周年音乐会在白沙瓦举行," accessed October 18, 2021, https://baijiahao.baidu.com/s?id=1600370777580681750&wfr=spider&for=pc.

13 "[陕西新闻联播]秦腔动漫《三滴血》巴基斯坦播出 '大秦之腔'唱响文明交流互鉴_新闻频道_央视网 (Cctv.Com)," accessed October 18, 2021, http://news.cctv.com/2019/05/18/VIDE5IHBC4bJEI9ixkeeuDN3190518.shtml.

14 "《中国与阿富汗 '一带一路'故事》纪录片在喀布尔举行开播仪式-新华网," accessed October 18, 2021, http://www.xinhuanet.com/politics/2017-12/06/c_1122069338.htm.

and other research institutions. By 2015, Chinese language training was also being offered to non-Chinese majors, and in 2016 and 2017, these programs were introduced throughout Afghanistan's top learning institutions, including Marefat school and Avicenna University, which is working with its Confucius University to implement Chinese language and culture learning from primary school through university.[15]

In recent years, Afghanistan NSR development is being incorporated as an extension of the China-Pakistan Economic Corridor (CPEC). In September, 2019, the China-Afghanistan-Pakistan Trilateral Foreign Ministers Dialogue was held in Islamabad.[16] This connectivity recalls that of the ancient Silk Roads, which connected cites throughout the Eurasian Steppes with regional trade of commodities; as well as through culture, religion, and technology. Important technologies such as paper and gunpowder came in from China heading towards the Mediterranean; while weaving, glazing, and vine cultivation went the other way.[17] The history of religions throughout Asia, despite Afghanistan's systematic destruction of its Buddhist, Zoroastrian, Manichaean and other non-Islamic cultural heritage; continues to surface in literature on both ancient and New Silk Roads. While Afghanistan is less stable than other countries in the region; it is seeking ultimately to diversify its economy through New Silk Road People-to-People Connectivity. China's programs in the country are helping to cultivate these aspirations, while both Afghanistan and China draw upon the former's long history as a connective hub within the greater Central Asian regions; trying to deescalate the role of this region as a center of conflict exacerbated by world superpowers such as the U.S. and Soviet Union.[18]

Afghanistan has turned to overcoming the obstacles of cultural loss due to iconoclasm and other political and military conflict in the region. With the country's traditional arts industry ravaged in years of conflict, many skills and traditions were disrupted because of difficulties in sourcing materials, lack of continuity in handing down skills, and inability to access international supply chains as well as markets. There are two street

[15] "Long Steps towards Sagacity – Avicenna University," accessed October 18, 2021, https://avicenna.edu.af/reports/long-steps-towards-sagacity/.

[16] "最新丨中巴经济走廊项目将向阿富汗延伸," accessed October 18, 2021, https://baijiahao.baidu.com/s?id=1644192708996270587&wfr=spider&for=pc.

[17] Tim Winter, *Geocultural Power*, 28.

[18] Tim Winter, 111–12.

markets which help artisans to make a living, allowing rare access to cultural export channels. One in Kabul is called Chicken Street, known by vendors and merchants for its jewelry, antiques and other hand-made arts and crafts; and another known as the Pakistani market. In the last fifteen years, some non-government organizations, such as Turquoise Mountain, have seen collaborations between Kabul and the UK seeking to rebuild the traditional arts sector, helping vitalize cultural organizations and build international trade, even nurturing urban renewal projects, such as with Murad Khane, an old Kabul city center. India has also embarked on cultural exchange of skills, techniques and technologies with Afghanistan, sending artisans from Jaipur to lecture and train Kabul artisans.[19] As for non-traditional arts, such as painting, film and theatre, these were heavily censored for periods in Afghanistan's contemporary history. Steps are being taken to undo the damage this did. One example is the Copenhagen-based Creative Business Network partnered in 2018 with Kabul-based ASARA Consultancy to grow the city's creative sector, seeing this area of industry as transformative and stabilizing. Start-ups rely mostly on donations and face many challenges, not least of which are technological and human resources.[20] These private-sector grassroots People-to-People programs would do well in supplementing China's own efforts in Afghanistan.

Ankara, Turkey

Ankara, the capital of Turkey, has an ancient history and a large urban population. Ankara features cultural heritage sites of Hattian, Hittite, Lydian, Phrygian, Galatian, Greek, Persian, Roman, Byzantine, and Ottoman archaeology. It was the Ottomans who gave the city something close to its contemporary name, Anatolia Eyalet (1393–fifteenth century), with its closest analogue, Angora Vilayet (1867–1922). Ankara's role in the New Silk Roads is an important one, laying at the cross roads of Central Asia into Eastern and Central Europe. Pre-COVID flight

[19] "Rebuilding Afghanistan's Creative Industries | British Council," accessed October 18, 2021, https://www.britishcouncil.org/voices-magazine/rebuilding-afghanistans-creative-industries.

[20] "An Encouraging Movement in Afghanistan - Creative Business Network," accessed October 18, 2021, https://cbnet.com/2018/12/14/an-encouraging-movement-in-afghanistan/.

schedules saw seven weekly flights between China and Turkey connect this capital city to Beijing, Shanghai and Guangzhou for business and tourism. A train from Xi'an to Prague sees Ankara as an important station along the route, celebrating the opening of its operations in late-2019.[21] A five-hundred Megawatt Photovoltaic Industrial Park established in Ankara has continued through the COVID crisis to consolidate China's efforts to develop solar powered industrial sectors in the region.[22] The Baku-Tbilisi-Kars railway connects Azerbaijan via Georgia to Turkey, also helping China to connect with Europe, while at the same time isolating Armenia and Russia.[23] Turkey's cultural industries are working to diversify the national economy, although there is much work to do in this area. The museum sector is robust, while focusing on cultural heritage, contemporary art, as well as ethnography.[24]

Istanbul, Turkey

As listed in a UNESCO database developed and maintained with the support of China, Germany, Azerbaijan, Kazakhstan, and Oman; Istanbul is rich in cultural heritage sites protected or in the process of being approved for funding under the rubric of the Silk Roads Program.[25] Formerly named Byzantium and Constantinople, this city is the economic, cultural and historic center of Turkey, straddling both Europe and Asia. In 2015, the Shanghai Municipal Government Information Office and the Shanghai International Cultural Exchange Association sponsored the *Charming Shanghai* city image promotion event in Istanbul. An auxiliary event, the *Window of Shanghai*, saw 500 books

21 "'一带一路'对接'中间走廊' 中欧班列'长安号'抵达安卡拉," accessed October 18, 2021, https://baijiahao.baidu.com/s?id=1649507481830992968&wfr=spider&for=pc.

22 "土耳其总统祝贺'一带一路'示范性工程安卡拉光产业园全线贯通_新浪科技_新浪网," accessed October 18, 2021, https://tech.sina.com.cn/roll/2020-08-21/doc-iivhuipn9920297.shtml.

23 "10 Things to Know about Baku-Tbilisi-Kars Railway Project – Rail Turkey En," accessed October 18, 2021, https://railturkey.org/2014/10/20/baku-tblisi-kars-railway/.

24 "Republic of Turkey Ministry of Culture and Tourism," accessed October 18, 2021, https://www.ktb.gov.tr/?_Dil=2.

25 "土耳其 | 丝绸之路项目," accessed October 18, 2021, https://zh.unesco.org/silkroad/countries-alongside-silk-road-routes/tuerqi.

donated by the Shanghai Library to the Atatürk Library in Istanbul.[26] That same year saw a Turkish Edition of the China Daily begin publication. Content is provided by China, with topic selection, editing and printing arranged by Turkey, with all funding and distribution of 10,000 copies arranged by the Turkuvac Media Group.[27]

In 2017, a culinary festival *Colorful Food Culture Festival* was hosted by Ayydin University in Istanbul, presenting foods from throughout China's various regions. At the end of 2019, Sichuan cultural heritage, branding, and customs were brought to Istanbul, hosted by the Information Office of the Sichuan Provincial People's Government. Zhou Qing, Deputy Minister of the Propaganda Department of the Sichuan Provincial Party Committee and Director of the Press and Publication Bureau, said in a speech that he believed intangible culture could bring peoples of Turkey and China together across language, nationality, culture, and regional divides.[28]

Riyadh, Saudi Arabia

Riyadh, capital of Saudi Arabia, is a populous urban center which, before COVID, was enjoying a thriving tourist industry. Saudi Vision 2030 is probably the most important transformation in Saudi Arabia's political economy as regards the New Silk Roads. NSR's other four pillars (Policy Coordination, Facilities Connectivity, Unimpeded Trade, and Financial Integration) will surely revolve around the appropriation of as much energy as possible from the older Saudi economic political economy. NSR's fifth pillar of People-to-People Connectivity will provide opportunities for more culturally based connections with China in the region. By way of illustration, Saudi Arabia's old political economic model was divided into six main bodies; Ministries of: Commerce and Industry; Petroleum and Mineral Resources; Water and Electricity; Agriculture; Hajj; and the Education Evaluation Committee. Recently, the Ministry of Education and Commerce/Industry has diversified into the Council

26 "伊斯坦布尔迎来'魅力上海' 促进中土文化交流-中国侨网," accessed October 18, 2021, http://www.chinaqw.com/zhwh/2015/06-16/53496.shtml.

27 "Turkuvaz Media Group," accessed October 18, 2021, https://www.tslproducts.com/tech-insight-hub-resources/case-studies/studios-networks/turkuvaz-media-group/.

28 "腾讯内容开放平台," accessed October 18, 2021, https://page.om.qq.com/page/Ol2Zp_CXCwim-8I_zI_M0_KQ0.

of Economic and Development Affairs, National Center for Performance Management, General Authority for Culture, General Authority for Entertainment, Strategic Management Committee and Strategic Management office, as well as the Ministry of Commerce and Investment, and the Ministry of Labor and Social Affairs. The other five ministries have remained structurally the same, as single entities with slightly different names: Ministry of Environment, Water, and Agriculture; Ministry of Hajj and Umrah, and the Public Education Evaluation Commission.

China's interactions with Riyadh have been stepping up in the name of Saudi Vision 2030, such as with the construction of Jazan Industrial Cluster, along with other projects in energy and infrastructure, including Yanbu Refinery, Rabigh Power Plant, and a railway project known as the Continent Bridge. High-tech cooperation is also stepping up with multiple satellite launches and the Arab World's first exploration of the Moon, all made possible with Chinese funding and technology.[29] China is encouraging Saudi Arabia's transition from tribal rule of public sectors, reporting a greater commitment from Riyadh to invest in the private sector. This will encourage most of the skillful labor to transition from the public to the private sector, where cultural and creative industry development is taking place at present with largely expat labor. A commitment to mutual exchange of intellectual and research resources has seen a branch of the Saudi King Library opened at Beijing University.[30] In late 2016, the China National Museum opened the exhibition *The Arabian Road: Cultural Relics Unearthed in Saudi Arabia*, displaying objects from the pre-Islamic period through the birth of the Saudi Kingdom. These objects, coming from a number of Saudi museums, were unearthed along spice and pilgrimage routes, meant to contribute to a narrative of connectivity between regions east and west of the Arabian Peninsula.[31] It's not only the overland Silk Road Economic Belt which celebrates a shared history between Saudi Arabia and China. The 21st Century Maritime Silk Road narrative also points to the Salin Port as an important

29 "'一带一路'对接'2030愿景' 中沙务实合作掀起新高潮 - 产业要闻 - 中国卫星导航定位协会," accessed October 18, 2021, http://www.glac.org.cn/index.php?m=content&c=index&a=show&catid=2&id=5188.

30 "首页," 国王公共图书馆北京大学分馆, accessed October 18, 2021, http://kapl.pku.edu.cn/zh-hans/node.

31 "'阿拉伯之路——沙特出土文物'展览在我馆开幕," accessed October 18, 2021, http://www.chnmuseum.cn/zx/gbxw/201612/t20161221_1861.shtml.

node of the ancient maritime route. Jiang Bo, director of the Institute of Underwater Archaeology of the Underwater Cultural Heritage Bureau, highlights copper weights, lapis lazuli, agate, ivory products, coins, Arabic stone tools, Persian glazed potter, Song and Yuan dynasty Longquan and Jingdezhen celadon, as well as Ming and Qing blue and white Chinese porcelain as part of the rich material culture shared by China and Saudi Arabia.[32]

Damascus, Syria

Damascus, capital city of Syria, has a population of just two million. Information on cultural relations between China and Damascus is not as readily available as information on many other Silk Road cities. Infrastructure, energy, industry and port development take precedence more so than in other Silk Road nodes. Chinese news does report on Syria's efforts to rebuild Aleppo, with a Silk Road Market featuring just under three hundred vendors, portraying this as an attempt to revive cultural products and markets after years of armed conflict.[33] In 2019, the Syria Studies Institute at Northwest University in China collaborated with the Social Sciences Press to publish the Syria Bluebook Development Report. These bluebook reports are released in China yearly on usually national and provincial levels regarding various market sector developments. This bluebook reports on political, economic, diplomatic and refugee conditions; as well as development and cultural trajectories, including humanitarian aid, education, and cultural heritage in the region. The report conveys the message that Syria is an important city in New Silk Roads development and its post-war reconstruction should be a priority in lieu of continuing historical ties; but that present risk factors, uncertainty, and unpredictability require caution as to how to proceed.[34] While pre-conflict saw cultural sector inroads made into Syria, for example with Chinese screening films about the Silk Road in Syria's *Silk Road Festival*

32 "沙特塞林港考古为海丝研究提供珍贵实物资料–文化–人民网," accessed October 18, 2021, http://culture.people.com.cn/n1/2019/1224/c1013-31520692.html.

33 "叙利亚'丝绸之路市场'在阿勒颇开始运营," accessed October 18, 2021, https://world.huanqiu.com/article/9CaKrnK1PDe.

34 "一带一路与叙战后重建对接是两国互联互通的历史机遇," accessed October 18, 2021, https://baijiahao.baidu.com/s?id=1665118337825277886&wfr=spider&for=pc.

of 2010, these types of exchanges are difficult to invest in or arrange visas for in recent unstable political conditions.

Once China's private sector gets more involved with helping develop the cultural and creative industries of nations, we may see efforts such as that of Ettijahat-Independent Culture organization which supports and connects exiled Syrian artists and researchers in Lebanon. In September of 2020, this organization published *Creative Industries in Syria: Changes and Adaptation*, edited by Ettijahat—Independent Culture (ibidem Press). Ettijahat's focus is on independent culture in Syria and the Arab region and is an example of grassroots People-to-People Connectivity along the New Silk Roads which would be worth paying attention to while following cultural and social change in these regions.[35]

Jerusalem

Jerusalem, with claim laid to it by three major religions: Christianity, Judaism, and Islam, could easily be misunderstood by an atheist nation such as China. Be that as it may, in 2019, the first stop of the Israeli Ministry of Tourism's 2019 China Roadshow officially opened in Beijing. Thirty-two local tourism bureaus, local agencies, diamond dealers, hotels, cosmetics companies and other institutions and enterprises from Israel attended the roadshow and met with Chinese tourism industry experts.[36] In 2017, at an Israel Tourism Promotion Conference held in Jerusalem, *Out-of-print Zhangjiajie: Stunning New Silk Road*, saw an announcement that all Israeli citizens holding passports would be sponsored for free travel to Zhangjiajie in Hunan province, a tourist destination known as 'China's Grand Canyon.' Zhangjiajie has entered into similar agreements with other Belt and Road countries.[37] Thus we see that tourism prior to COVID-19 was already one well-paved cultural avenue for China-Israeli Belt and Road collaboration. Another strong cultural arena of cooperation for the two countries is in technology. While technology is not considered by all countries to be a cultural and creative industry; in China it is seen

[35] Ettijahat-Independent Culture, ed., *Creative Industries in Syria: Changes and Adaptations* (Stuttgart, Germany: ibidem Press, 2020).

[36] "以色列国家旅游部 2019 中国路演在京拉开帷幕_游客," accessed October 18, 2021, https://www.sohu.com/a/315478628_169814.

[37] "张家界和以色列携手旅游合作–旅游–人民网," accessed October 18, 2021, http://travel.people.com.cn/n1/2017/0728/c41570-29433736.html.

as such. In March 2017, China and Israel announced the establishment of an Innovative Comprehensive Partnership as a joint mechanism for innovation. Thus, Israeli technology companies have received substantial investment from China. In 2016, Huawei acquired HexaTier, an Isreali cloud database security company, for US $42 million.[38] Another grey area of cultural and creative industries is that of the agriculture sector. China does include agriculture, and domestically encourages the development of farm entertainment centers, for urban tourists to enjoy pastoral life for an afternoon or a weekend. Even automation in agricultural management is included in the Chinese rubric of culture. Therefore, a test site in the name of China-Israel cooperation was established in Fujian as an illustration of agricultural automation in irrigation, serving as a creative and cultural exchange for both its technological as well as agricultural sectors.[39]

Astana, Kazakhstan

Recently renamed Nur-Sultan, Astana is the capital of Kazakhstan. Its urban population is just over a million souls, second in the country only to Almaty. This is a planned capital city designed by Japanese architect Kisho Kurokawa with a futuristic cityscape. It is where on September 7, 2013, Chinese President Xi Jinping announced for the first time his vision for the overland Silk Road Economic Belt in a speech titled, *Promote People-to-People Friendship and Create a Better Future*, delivered at Nazarbayev University. Each year since, there has been a Silk Road Tianshan Forum held in Astana. The fourth such forum also commemorated the 40th anniversary of Reform and Opening Up and celebrated the fifth birthday of the Economic Belt. Forums are held by the Cultural Center in Astana, the Chinese Embassy in Kazakhstan, the CITIC Reform and Development Research Foundation, the Belt and Road Research Center of the Chinese Academy of Social Sciences (CASS), the Xinjiang International Economic and Cultural Development Center, as well as at the Kazakhstan China Studies Center.[40]

38 "中以创新合作联委会联合工作组第一次会议在以色列召开," accessed October 18, 2021, http://il.china-embassy.org/chn/gdxw/t1307219.htm.

39 "福建'中以'示范农场建成自动化农业样板-中新网," accessed October 18, 2021, http://www.chinanews.com/tp/2013/11-26/5549972.shtml.

40 "中国国际文化交流中心," accessed October 18, 2021, https://www.cicec.org.cn/.

In 2017, for the 17th meeting of the Shanghai Cooperation Organization (SCO), which coincided with the opening ceremony of the Astana Special Expo; cultural events were coordinated by State Administration of Press, Publication, Radio, Film and Television as well as China Radio International in tandem with Kazakh cultural institutions. Among major agreements and documents signed throughout this initiation of the *Silk Road Theater* was a *Cooperation Agreement on Interchange and Broadcasting of Film and TV Programs*. During this period of time, the Kazakh documentary *Da Huang Mountain*, and the Chinese *Silk Road, a Journey Started Again* were broadcast publicly on Kazakhstan Habar TV.[41] China has made other inroads into Kazakhstan's film industry, making great efforts to introduce contemporary Chinese ink-wash painting and calligraphy as well as photography to Kazakh audiences.[42] While Chinese and Kazakh institutions are creating arts infrastructure in Kazakhstan in a top-down manner, creative industries in Kazakh are receiving support from other countries as well, as in the case of the British Council working with the Astana Convention Bureau of the City Administration to create a network of leaders who are equipped to develop the city's cultural economy.[43]

Moscow, Russia

Moscow, the largest and capital city in Russia, has one of the world's coldest and largest urban economies. With a complicated relationship throughout the twentieth century, China and Russia are forging ahead with cultural ties, and 2019 marked the 70th anniversary of the establishment of their diplomatic relations. To celebrate this event, cultural displays of China's traditional culture in Moscow included the *One Belt One Road Martial Arts Tour*, which focused on the sports sector of the creative economy. This event was held at the Moscow Central Cultural Center and brought forty-six *taichi* masters from throughout China to

[41] "东方网," accessed October 18, 2021, http://www.eastday.com/.

[42] "哈萨克斯坦 2017 中国电影展举办–新闻–中国作家网," accessed October 18, 2021, http://www.chinawriter.com.cn/n1/2017/0612/c403992-29334081.html.

[43] "Developing Kazakhstan's Creative Industries Will Boost Economy, Say Creative Central Asia Participants - The Astana Times," accessed October 18, 2021, https://astanatimes.com/2018/11/developing-kazakhstans-creative-industries-will-boost-economy-say-creative-central-asia-participants/.

demonstrate the Yang and Chen styles of *taichi* as well as *fan*-style and *taichi* boxing.[44] The previous year, also at the Moscow Cultural Center, Chinese cultural authorities featured Chinese painting with a stop in the *One Belt One Road Overseas Tour Exhibition of Famous Chinese Painting in Pen and Ink*. This exhibition was organized by the Shandong Art Museum in an effort to follow President Xi's directive to strengthen cultural ties, advocate for cultural equality, protect cultural heritage, promote cultural innovation, and to place cultural cooperation with other nations at the core of China's cultural narrative.[45] China is also spending a great deal of money making great efforts to bring together Central Asian nations to discuss regional musical and ceramic traditions, placing China's own traditions at the center of these discussions.[46] China's tea culture is also making inroads into Moscow, with events introducing the arts of tea cultivation, collecting, and serving.[47]

Bishkek, Kyrgyzstan

Bishkek is the largest and capital city of Kyrgyzstan (also known as the Kyrgyz Republic). The city has a tribal and Russian past and does so for the centrality of its location along trade and caravan routes. China has allocated a good deal of funding for developing cultural power in Kyrgyzstan. *Perceive China: Kyrgyz Journey* in mid-2019 was a large-scale China-themed event produced by the China State Council Information Office of China Overseas. This involved several events targeting traditional Chinese culture, with *Kunqu* opera and face changing; as well as contemporary youth-oriented Chinese culture, such as with the *Silk Road Youth: Belt and Road Youth Video Exhibition* and the *Charming Beijing Video Exhibition*. The latter utilised new technologies to display intangible cultural heritage including paper-cutting and medicinal incense

44 "'一带一路·文武中国世界行'太极文化交流活动在莫斯科举行," accessed October 18, 2021, https://baijiahao.baidu.com/s?id=1632146610224479112&wfr=spider&for=pc.

45 "'一带一路——笔墨意象中国画名家海外巡展'将在莫斯科中国文化中心举办_交流," accessed October 18, 2021, https://www.sohu.com/a/260357289_99909345.

46 "'一带一路'音乐会奏响莫斯科: '一带一路'为文化艺术互联互通创造便利条件_新闻频道_央视网 (Cctv.Com)," accessed October 18, 2021, http://news.cctv.com/2017/05/14/ARTIwxyZiKNIZVz0MvrDFI0l170514.shtml.

47 "'一带一路'中国茶文化展览会在莫斯科开幕," accessed October 18, 2021, https://baijiahao.baidu.com/s?id=1650976723992552448&wfr=spider&for=pc.

making.[48] In as early as 2017, the Middle East's first China-themed bookstore was opened. The Shangsi Bookstore is operated by Russia's Shangsi International Publishing Group, a private cultural enterprise originating, strangely enough, in China, which operates through seven independent publishing institutions and distribution channels in Russia, Kyrgyzstan, and Kazakhstan. The group already has over 300 Chinese titles that have been translated and published on the genre of literature, art, cultural relics, architecture, and history.[49] The Confucius Institute based at Kyrgyz National University since 2007 also plays a role in reporting cultural events which mark the successful development of People-to-People Connectivity in Kyrgyzstan. The creative economic sector already accounts for 7% of national GDP, as of 2020. Advertising, architecture, art, interior design, fashion industry, film and video production, entertainment computer programs and games, music, and stage all appeal to not only public top-down arts infrastructure investment from China, but also private sector investors seeking to supplement arts infrastructure.[50]

Dubai, United Arab Emirates

Dubai is the capital of the Emirate of Dubai and has the largest population of the United Arab Emirates (UAE). The story of UAE as an economic hub in West Asia is an old one, and now the main thrust of the plot is to diversify its economy, reducing reliance on its vast carbon resources; as well as transitioning away from a labor-intensive economy. The plan is to develop a knowledge economy rich in technology and skilled labor. While federal and separate Emirate policies encourage investment to develop material resources other than oil, such as aluminum, a longer term transition emphasises moves towards tertiary economic sectors such as tourism, re-export commerce, and telecommunications.

48 "吉尔吉斯斯坦: '感知中国'系列活动促进中吉交流," accessed October 18, 2021, https://baijiahao.baidu.com/s?id=1636130970220672132&wfr=spider&for=pc.

49 "中亚第一家中文书店在比什凯克开业_新闻中心_北京尚斯国际文化交流有限责任公司," accessed October 18, 2021, http://www.bjss010.com/index.php?m=&c=chuban&a=show&id=39.

50 "Kyrgyzstan Starts Developing Concept of Creative Economy," accessed October 18, 2021, http://en.kabar.kg/news/kyrgyzstan-starts-developing-concept-of-creative-economy/.

Abu Dhabi's Economic Vision 2030 and the Strategic Plan 2015, as well as Saudi Vision 2030 are leading these transformations. UAE's own 2021 Vision seeks to meet targets much sooner than may be realistic. As tourism and aviation are both a large part of meeting these vision plan targets, COVID-19 has taken a big chunk out of anticipated outcomes. Conferences, regional and international exhibitions, major global sporting events, such as the Dubai Desert Classic Golf Tournament, Dubai World Cup, Abu Dhabi Formula One Grand Prix, and the FIFA Club World Cup are all on hold as of 2021. Film festivals in Dubai and Abu Dhabi also serve as industry magnets and tastemakers both regionally and internationally. The 2020 World Expo for which the UAE won the bid is another COVID casualty, originally scheduled for October 20, 2020–April 10, 2021. Due to the ongoing COVID-19 pandemic, the new dates are October 1, 2021–March 31, 2022. The China Pavilion at this World Expo will be titled, *Building a Common Destiny—Innovation and Opportunity*, dedicated to developing awareness of and investment in the New Silk Roads.[51] Travel agent expedia.co.uk awarded Abu Dhabi as a top 10 travel destination bases upon the region's cultural heritage and links with the old Silk Road. Held in Dubai in 2019, the *Hala Embracing the Cultural Exchange Exhibition in China* was an effort to win the hearts and minds of Dubai leaders. 2018 saw Chinese President Xi travel for an official visit to UAE commemorating 29 years since the first such official visit between China and the UAE, the first since the conclusion of the 19th National Congress of the Chinese Communist Party (CCP) in 2017.[52] Many events dealing with tourism and the development of travel services were a part of the Hala-China event, insuring that Chinese tourists would have the packages they sought, complete with the accommodations, shopping, restaurants, entertainment, sight-seeing, health, safety and protocol they are accustomed to in domestic travel as well as in travel to Europe and America.[53] Events to celebrate China-UAE events were also held in China, such as in December of 2019, when the Rosamonde Soong Foundation and the Everbright Corporation hosted

[51] "迪拜世博会将成 '一带一路'大舞台," accessed October 18, 2021, https://baijiahao.baidu.com/s?id=1643524010210098937&wfr=spider&for=pc.

[52] "Hala拥抱中国一带一路迪拜文化交流展》即将拉开帷幕_丝绸之路," accessed October 18, 2021, https://www.sohu.com/a/328676169_120176874.

[53] "迪拜 '拥抱中国 Hala China' 计划启动 众信旅游集团成首批战略合作企业," accessed October 18, 2021, https://www.sohu.com/a/241889250_100071.

the *Perceiving China China-UAE Youth Cultural Exchange Week* with the UAE ambassador and his family; exchanging lessons and workshops on Chinese porcelain and *qin* zither with lessons on Arabic language and culture.[54] These cultural exchanges are finding bi-lateral funding. For example, in 2019, the *Second Dubai-China Film Week* had sponsors ranging from China's banking sector (Union Pay, Bank of China) to Dubai Parks and Resorts.[55]

Kuala Lumpur, Malaysia

Kuala Lumpur is the capital city of Malaysia, with a population of under two million, although the Greater Kuala Lumpur, or Klang Valley, is an urban area with a population of over seven million people. A rapidly developing city, both in terms of economy and population, Kuala Lumpur and China's cultural relationship receives a great deal of attention due to the former city's status as the fastest growing city in Southeast Asia. Malaysia set up the first One Belt One Road Center, directly under the China Affairs Committee of the Malaysian Chinese Association (MCA). It is mainly responsible for conducting research related to the Belt and Road Initiative, providing consulting services for companies, assisting companies in opening up markets, and conducting business connections between the government and private companies.[56] In 2020, China held a number of events, including the online media event *The Writer's Writer*, wherein Malaysia-born Chinese writers were invited to recommend their favorite Chinese writers to Malaysian reading audiences. 2020 was also the *China–Malaysia Cultural Year*, with events both online and offline, cultural events, and culture weeks, featuring virtual reality tours of Chinese villages and famous sites.[57] Celebrating 45 years of cultural

54 "'感知中国·美美与共'中国·阿联酋青少年文化交流周在京举办," accessed October 18, 2021, https://baijiahao.baidu.com/s?id=1653127376223814907&wfr=spider&for=pc.

55 "第二届迪拜中国电影周开幕-新华网," accessed October 18, 2021, http://www.xinhuanet.com/world/2019-09/30/c_1125060294.htm.

56 "马来西亚成立首个'一带一路'中心-新华网," accessed October 18, 2021, http://www.xinhuanet.com/world/2016-12/12/c_1120103761.htm.

57 "吉隆坡中国文化中心：用文化温暖后疫情时代 - 文化交流 - 中国—马来西亚钦州产业园区管理委员会网站 - Zmqzcyyq.Gxzf.Gov.Cn," accessed October 18, 2021, http://zmqzcyyq.gxzf.gov.cn/zmhz/whjl/t6074452.shtml.

diplomacy between the two nations, 2020 was a culmination of ongoing events involving multiple creative and cultural sectors.

Djibouti, Djibouti

Djibouti is a coastal location in northeast Africa, on the Red Sea and the Gulf of Aden. It is bordered by Eritrea in the north, Ethiopia to the south and west, and Somalia to the south. Connecting Africa with Asia and Europe, the Doraleh Multi-Purpose Port and the Chinese-built Djibouti International Free Trade Zone (DIFTZ) link the 21st Maritime Silk Road with overland networks in China. The Doraleh Multi-Purpose Port was built by the China State Construction Engineering Corporation (CSCEC) between 2014 and 2017. The Addis Ababa-Djibouti Standard Gauge Railway (Ethiopia-Djibouti Railway) is a 725 kilometer fully electrified transnational railway which has been in operation since 2018. Djibouti also hosts the US-Africa Command (USAFRICOM) base in Africa, Camp Lemonnier, as part of the Operation Enduring Freedom—Horn of Africa (OEF-HOA). It is conjectured that as Djibouti struggles to repay its debt for Chinese-built infrastructure projects, handing over control of these rail and port projects will limit US control over its own military operations in the region.[58] It is unclear how much access the US has to this new port. The strategic location of the Horn of Africa increases the geo-political focus on the countries along Africa's eastern seaboard, including Kenya, Uganda, Ethiopia, and Egypt along with Djibouti. The Belt and Road Initiative focuses its projects in this region as the commencement of its African leg of the New Silk Roads, pivoting through the Red Sea and Suez Canal into the Mediterranean, and towards Chinese-owned Piraeus Port in Greece.[59] Djibouti hosts not only USA's only military base in Africa, but also Japan's one base world-wide, in addition to bases belonging to China, France, Britain, Italy, and Germany. 2017 saw the China's People Liberation Army (PLA) open its first overseas base in Djibouti. The base sits next to one of Djibouti's main ports only fifteen minutes

[58] Sarwar A. Kashmeri, *China's Grand Strategy: Weaving a New Silk Road to Global Primacy* (Santa Barbara: Praeger, 2019), 74–79.

[59] Sarwar A. Kashmeri, 72.

away by vehicle from the US military's Camp Lemonnier. China's military presence in the country is seen as having inevitable influence upon the country's foreign policy.[60]

While three massive infrastructure projects have greatly increased China's opportunities in the region, as well as opportunities for economic development in countries in and around the Horn of Africa; it remains to be seen how these infrastructure projects have linked up with People-to-People development projects. Ever practical, China prioritizes job creation for citizens of the region, stating that not only are jobs being created; but vocational training is also being provided. In a Chinese report dated January of 2020, 61,000 jobs were created in Ethiopia and more than 5000 have been created in Djibouti in the construction of the Ethiopia-Djibouti railway. Since commencement of passenger and freight operations in 2018; 3,900 jobs have been created between Ethiopia and Djibouti, with indirect employment estimated between 25,000 and 30,000. The Chinese-built free-trade zone is expected to create manufacturing, warehousing, logistics, export and service jobs.

China cites knowledge transfer assistance as a key element of its vocational training, imparting "much-needed practical and theoretical knowledge and skills" to Djibouti's youth."[61] Development of African human resources is enacted through programs such as the Luban Workshops, the first of which happened in March 2020. On site for that first of ten workshops throughout the African continent were Djibouti President Ismail Omar Guellleh, China ambassador to Djibouti, Zhou Ruisheng and the President of the China Civil Engineering Construction Corporation (CCECC), Yuan Li. The CCECC works with academic support from various higher learning institutions from China. In this case it was the Tianjin First College of Commerce and the Tianjin Railway Technical and Vocational College providing academic support for the workshop.[62] While Djibouti has little industry or natural resources; its port and rail

[60] "China and the United States Face off in Djibouti | CNN," accessed October 18, 2021, https://www.cnn.com/2019/05/26/africa/china-belt-road-initiative-djibouti-intl/index.html.

[61] "Chinese Engagement in Djibouti's Economic Transformation in a Nutshell-Belt and Road Portal," accessed October 18, 2021, https://eng.yidaiyilu.gov.cn/qwyw/rdxw/115204.htm.

[62] "Africa's First Luban Workshop Launched in Djibouti-Belt and Road Portal," accessed October 18, 2021, https://eng.yidaiyilu.gov.cn/qwyw/rdxw/84216.htm.

operations, which are heavily Chinese-invested and controlled, are considered a key element of People-to-People connectivity between China and Djibouti, if not all of Africa. With further development of digital, energy and transportation sectors; these infrastructure projects will also fit into the category of this fifth pillar development of the New Silk Roads.

Cultural exchanges between China and Djibouti have coincided with BRI infrastructure development, with hundreds of students travelling from Djibouti to China on Chinese government scholarships for training and other higher learning programs. Study in China Application Services (SICAS) was working as early as 2013 with Djibouti's Cultural Exchange Association Chairman, Ibrahim Abdourahman, to facilitate Djibouti students learning abroad in China.[63] Medical diplomacy is also a component of People-to-People Connectivity. China's Peace Ark hospital ship and medical teams constituted important medical aid diplomatic efforts in the region, even before COVID-19. Speaking more directly to cultural development in the region, there is a Chinese New Year gala held annually in Djibouti. China is also involved in archival and dissemination efforts of Djibouti culture and history, giving aid to Djibouti's National Library and Archives, Djibouti City's largest museum.[64] Interaction with Djibouti's historical narrative helps to coordinate an understanding of the region's role in early Ming dynasty maritime trade with China as part of Zheng He's efforts. Djibouti has served as a crucial geographical passageway for civilizations as early as the Egyptians, Phoenicians, Ptolemaists, Romans, Greeks, Byzantine, Arabs and then European merchants.[65]

Duisburg, Germany

Our last urban cultural center to discuss is Duisburg, Germany. Duisburg is the Western most terminus of the Silk Road Economic Belt. It links up not only Central China to Europe overland, but also China's

63 "Meeting Between Chairman of China and Djibouti Cultural Exchange Association and CEO of SICAS," accessed October 18, 2021, https://www.sicas.cn/Students/Info/Content_131101145359263.shtml.

64 "A Century-Old Dream Finally Comes True - Chinadaily.Com.Cn," accessed October 18, 2021, http://www.chinadaily.com.cn/global/2019-11/13/content_37522575.htm.

65 Sarwar A. Kashmeri, *China's Grand Strategy: Weaving a New Silk Road to Global Primacy*, 74–79.

north-eastern coastline in Yantai of Shandong Province northward via the north Ice Silk Road. Duisburg is also a terminus of the 21st Century Maritime Silk Road via the Port of Piraeus in Greece which then links over land through Europe to Germany.[66] Ralf Meurer, managing director of the Agency for Business Promotion Duisburg, describes how cargo trains also arrive from southwestern China cities of Chongqing and Chengdu, in addition to the more central cities of Xi'an and Wuhan, the latter of which enjoys sister-city status with Duisburg.[67] The German city has the world's largest inland port, with over 40 kilometres of wharf. It is in the north-western state of North Rhine-Westphalia, a very modern city which was rebuilt after being levelled in the Second World War. Duisburg suffered such devastation for much the same reason that it is enjoying such prominence in the New Silk Roads, in that it has always been an important center of iron, steel, and chemicals industry as well as an important logistics hub.

Sino-German relations as a whole have been thriving for sometime, until just recently, as Germany is stiffening its back in regards to China as it gets closer to the US and its allies. Previously, however, Germany spearheaded the favorable trade conditions fostering the European Union as China's number one trade partner. China-Germany bilateral trade is so voluminous that it grants Germany status as China's number one trading partner within the EU, at USD $183 billion in 2018, growing yearly at 9.4%, according to a 2019 China Daily article.[68] A timeline of political ties establishes diplomatic ties in 1972, annual prime-minster level meetings as early as 2004, a government consultation mechanism in 2010, and full strategic partnership in 2014, followed more recently by bilateral high-level meetings in 2019.[69]

[66] "New Freight Train Route Links Yantai, Duisburg - Xinhua | English.News.Cn," accessed October 18, 2021, http://www.xinhuanet.com/english/europe/2019-07/27/c_138262912.htm.

[67] "BRI Brings Fresh Opportunities to Germany's Duisburg: City Official - Xinhua | English.News.Cn," accessed October 18, 2021, http://www.xinhuanet.com/english/2019-04/25/c_138009768.htm.

[68] "China-Germany Ties at a Glance | Nation | China Daily," accessed October 18, 2021, https://www.chinadailyhk.com/articles/226/89/21/1567763895346.html.

[69] Peter Frankopan, *The New Silk Roads: The New Asia and the Remaking of the World Order* (New York: Vintage Books, 2020), 134–36.

Main Western media organs such as The Guardian diminish the role of Chinese cultural influence in the region, looking only at Duisburg-Essen University's hosting of a Confucius Institute and a few Chinese restaurants as indicative of the low number of Chinese citizens living in the area.[70] This Western media spin is as questionable as some articles we read in Chinese media organs such as China Daily. Scratching beneath the surface, we see that various cultural channels have indeed been opening up between the two regions. Panda diplomacy has been a key element of China-German cultural exchange, with Meng Meng and male partner Jiao Qing sent to Germany in 2017, where they gave birth to the first German-born pandas. German Chancellor Angela Merkel and Chinese President Xi Jinping opened the Berlin Zoo's Panda Garden during a state visit in 2017. In 2018, there was a Germany-China Hubei Cultural Festival held in Beijing, continuing the Agreement on Cultural Exchange signed in 1979, just seven years into official diplomat relations. With the Berlin-based Chinese Culture Center opening in 2008, activities were held in more than 40 cities throughout Germany between 2012 and 2013 alone. 2013 was the Language Year and 2016 was known as the China-German Youth Exchange Year.

In addition to the Confucius Institute mentioned by The Guardian in Duisburg-Essen, there were 18 other such institutes by the mid-June 2019. Another key player in China-Germany cultural exchange is the Goethe-Institute, Germany's worldwide cultural institute. When the Institute set up office in 1988, it was the first overseas cultural institute in China. Education constitutes a long and already well-developed channel of People-to-People relationship building between Germany and China, with the two countries signing a mutual recognition agreement on higher education qualifications as early as 2002. This was the first such document signed by China and a developed nation.

Conclusion

This chapter has attempted to fill a void created by overemphasis in the world media as well as in scholarship upon the first four pillars of

[70] Philip Oltermann, "Germany's 'China City': How Duisburg Became Xi Jinping's Gateway to Europe," *The Guardian*, August 1, 2018, sec. Cities, https://www.theguardian.com/cities/2018/aug/01/germanys-china-city-duisburg-became-xi-jinping-gateway-europe.

China's New Silk Roads. We have done this by tracking China's fifth pillar People-to-People Connectivity in major urban cultural centers along the New Silk Roads, including: Beijing, China, Islamabad, Pakistan, Ankara and Istanbul, Turkey, Riyadh, Saudi Arabia, Damascus, Syria, Jerusalem, Astana, Kazakhstan, Moscow, Russia, Bishkek, Kyrgyzstan, Dubai, United Arab Emirates, Kuala Lumpur, Malaysia, Djibouti, Djibouti, and Duisburg, Germany. While this covers Central and Western Asia, as well as the Middle East quite well, this analysis only touches upon Africa and Central Europe, as well as Southeast Asia. We wanted to touch upon the most central hubs of connectivity while also including Duisburg for its importance as a linking point to Europe, and Kuala Lumpur for its centrality in the 21st Century Maritime Road. Further analysis should include Latin America and Eastern Europe as well as more thorough mapping of additional African and South Asian cultural nodes.

When looking at urban centers of the New Silk Roads, we have explored what China is contributing to their cultural vibrancy today in connection with not just cultural heritage and tourism, but other creative and cultural sectors as well. China's cultural diplomacy and discourse on People-to-People Connectivity throughout New Silk Regions contribute to the country's strategy of developing cultural power, helping China to develop influence and diplomacy by strengthening diplomacy and contributing to economic diversification in regions which had otherwise limited resources to contribute to international markets. These ties also contribute to China's image as a benevolent initiator of new win–win global governance.[71]

[71] Dahlia Patricia Sterling, "A New Era in Cultural Diplomacy: Promoting the Image of China's 'Belt and Road' Initiative in Asia," *Open Journal of Social Sciences* 06, no. 02 (2018): 102–16.

CHAPTER 8

China's Creative Class and the New Silk Roads

This chapter examines how China's new creative class is contributing to social transformation in China, considering China's international development, especially along the New Silk Roads. In Chapters 5 and 6, we developed an understanding of contemporary art as an exceptional cultural indicator. That is to say, the cultural messaging of many artworks clearly reveal artists that do not agree with top-down Chinese cultural policy and ideology; and collectors that buy the work (both domestically and abroad) are hungry to consume these cultural expressions as a commodity. Then in Chapter 6, we dove deep into a field study of Southwest China's museum sector, also looking at the broader field of arts management in that region. We found that, indeed, there has been an uptick in government involvement in the region's arts management, and that this level of funding and consequent enrichment of arts infrastructure did not extend directly towards the experimental and avant-garde niches of the creative sector. We did suggest, however, that enrichment of cultural and arts infrastructure can trickle down or, if you will, out towards cultural and artistic margins. One example of this is in the use of funds earned through full-time employment or gig economy earning in design sectors to subsidise an artist's practise. While that artist will still face difficulties in finding a venue in which to display or disseminate his or

S. Kidd, *Culture Paves The New Silk Roads*, Contemporary East Asian Visual Cultures, Societies and Politics, https://doi.org/10.1007/978-981-16-8574-3_8

her work, he or she will have the means to buy materials and enjoy a standard of living that affords enough leisure time to produce artwork. This artwork will then be created without needing to conform to art market pressures that a full time artist would answer to. Art produced outside of art market demand cycles, then, will tend to be more experimental and idiosyncratic. Thus, while an increase of New Silk Road cultural policy funding into China's Southwest does not directly benefit artists who are working on the margins of creative practise, these funds do create creative sector jobs which can otherwise subsidise these artists' practise.

We also discussed how domestic and international actors are arriving in the region looking to mine the cultural resources of the Southwest. While this works against local ecologies in some cases, as with the Pompidou's Cosmopolis exhibition, where resources are great enough to support the creation of narratives which overwrite local histories; a little footwork provides access to a rich history of uniquely embedded artistic ecologies which changes and develops with the times, with or without resources. Wealth being created in this region creates conditions where entrepreneurs are opening private museums, keen to mine creative resources unique to the Southwest of China. Similar trends may develop in other New Silk Regions, as wealth is created in those regions as part of the push for infrastructure development, enrichment of trade, and People-to-People Connectivity. Here in Chapter 8, we deepen and extend the discussion of how China's creative economy may operate within the greater milieu of New Silk Roads development.

In Chapter 5, we discussed 'cultural discount' and 'cultural trade deficit' as an endemic problem in China when it comes to cultural export, where the value of cultural products is immediately lowered upon crossing China's borders into other territories. This problem is both a result of and a contributing factor to Sinophobia, 'yellow peril,' 'China threat,' and saber rattling in some of the regions China is working to collaborate with. In this chapter, we further develop a central argument for this book, that fifth People-to-People pillar development of the Belt and Road is paramount for the success of the other four pillars. Unless both government and peoples of New Silk Road regions understand more about Chinese culture, economy, politics and society, old fears will not dissipate. As misunderstandings or challenges arise in the implementation of the other four pillar projects; these fears will grow exponentially, resulting in social unrest. Once we have explored both the benefits and contestations of China's political economy of culture, we will look at how this model can utilize an emphasis upon culture and People-to-People bonds to strengthen New Silk Road development. We look at how, as China invests in a more concentrated and systematic manner in educational exchange, cultural programming, personnel exchanges and training, media cooperation, as well as youth, women, and volunteer services; greater support can be won for deepening bilateral and multilateral cooperation with countries and regions along the New Silk Roads.

Need for Creative Solutions and the 'spatial Fix' of the New Silk Roads

China's past four plus decades of economic growth has turned out to pose huge challenges. This hyper development was triggered by several engines including industry, agriculture, and services; and now these very triggers are challenging China's economic stability.[1] Problems exacerbated by this economic growth include a huge gap between classes, uneven development throughout regions, inability to sustain the current economic model, environmental problems, increasing energy demands, and plateauing domestic consumption rates. Chinese people are seeking employment opportunities, small business and entrepreneurship support, and training for technological innovation. These impulses see flows of human capital leaving the countryside for better schooling in the cities, and then staying in the cities to take advantage of a better job market. Thus we see the cities building up massive amounts of human resources, especially in areas of creativity, technological innovation, entrepreneurship, and innovation. This flow of human capital exacerbates an already existing disparity between urban and rural education and employment opportunities. This problem is being addressed in two main ways thus far. The first is in urban sprawl, which seeks to incorporate and renovate rural outskirts as the cities expand. Satellite cities are established and nurtured with support for small businesses that want to build their headquarters in these satellite areas, such as tax breaks, low cost of housing for employees, and as well for commercial real estate. The second way

[1] Nalbantoglu, "One Belt One Road Initiative."

in which the urban-rural divide is being addressed is through philanthropic and poverty alleviation programs.[2] A key issue is the need to address internal economic and social inequality by offering opportunities for Mainland Chinese to engage in rapid economic developments. This requires creating greater employment opportunities, supporting entrepreneurship, and seeding technological innovation. Non-profit organizations, such as the China Foundation for Poverty Alleviation (*zhongguo fuping jijing hui* 中国扶贫基金会) are a major component of the drive to alleviate poverty by 2030 in building of what policy terms a *xiaokang shehui* 小康社会 (literally, "small healthy society").'

There is a bottleneck in consumption in China, however, for which the New Silk Roads provide a 'spatial fix,' creating, nurturing, and diversifying markets throughout international New Silk Road regions. We introduced this idea of a 'spatial fix' in Chapter 4, in our discussion of political economies. A spatial fix allows for consumer goods and services to flow outside of China's borders, alleviating the bottleneck, and strengthening the overall economy of China. As some of these regions for China's planned market expansion have heretofore been nurtured as export markets for the United States, the United Kingdom, Australia, Japan, South Korea and other Quad and G7 nations, competition for these markets creates conflict. This destabilization of supply chains triggers anti-China sentiment in first world nations. Those who are relatively objective in their view of the New Silk Roads see China as a strategic competitor rather than as a civilisational threat.

Just as there is an inequality divide between urban and rural in China, so there is also a demographic inequality divide, with the inner and particularly Western regions of China suffering from much lower population density than North-eastern and South-eastern Seaboard areas. China is approaching this problem with massive development programs in both the Northwest, and also the Southwest, as discussed in Chapter 6. There we highlighted flows of capital enriching the creative sectors in Chengdu especially. Urban renewal and urbanisation of rural areas see cities being rebuilt section by section, and urban centers built out which elevates the standard of living for populations throughout rural outskirts. These trends of urbanisation (*chengshi hua* 城市化) and seeding of satellite

[2] Khun Eng Kuah, "China's Soft Power: Culturalisation Along the Belt Road Corridors," in *Silk Road to Belt Road: Reinventing the Past and Shaping the Future*, ed. Md. Nazrul Islam (Singapore: Springer, 2019), 127.

townships in rhizomatic fashion (*qiaoxiang* 侨乡) create nodules of development through infrastructure and capital flows. New Silk Roads function as a 'spatial fix' in this case of demographic unevenness, as it does with urban-rural inequality issue. It does this by redistributing capital and human capital flows over a much larger territory. New Silk Road regions are seeded with urban cultural centers, as we have discussed in Chapter 7, which lead out of and back into China's Western regions via the overland Silk Road Economic Belt and also the 21st Century Maritime Silk Road. It also helps to alleviate the precarity of urban youths along China's South-eastern seaboard, by providing employment opportunities, entrepreneurship and small business opportunities, and training throughout New Silk Regions for tech-savvy youths who would otherwise be left to ferment in their dissatisfaction with a bottlenecked consumer economy. In his article outlining these domestic social problems seeking alleviation in New Silk Road development, Khun Eng Kuah terms these cultural centers in which Chinese millennial creatives could develop their skills through international career paths the scholar terms 'collaborative territorial spaces.'

> Along with this is the Belt and Road strategy in creating socio-economic and cultural spaces that straddle across geopolitical boundaries where its population could legitimately utilize such spaces for their own use and self-actualisation. I term such spaces as 'collaborative territorial' spaces. In the twenty-first century, unlike in the early centuries, political conquest and annexation through military forces is non-feasible. Creating nodes of connectivity in the form of collaborative territorial basins to provide opportunities for the Chinese population to engage in socio-economic activities is one strategy. The Belt-Road speaks to this.[3]

As Chinese financial and human capital flows into NSR regions as part of China's 'spatial fix,' Chinese populations will be integrating into, influencing and being influenced by a greater socio-cultural milieu. There is an inevitable fear of how native populations will react to these flows of human capital into their labor market, and also to cultural fluctuations that arise in an increasingly diverse cultural demographic. If NSR's fifth pillar of People-to-People Connectivity is not brought out well ahead of

[3] Kuah, 128.

time, in step with Policy Coordination, Facilities Connectivity, Unimpeded Trade, and Financial Integration; then there will be pushback and additional challenges. China's attempt to fix its own socio-economic problems by spatially expanding the economic geography as a system could lead to the superimposition of these tensions between private and civil life across a much larger playing board. That is to say, the nature of the system may not change, although impoverished classes would then be located outside of China's borders, rather than within them. Profit and rent-seeking behaviours created by market forces in state-mobilised capitalism may merely find new, non-Chinese, subjects. These are the fears of writers on the subject who are critically examining various New Silk Road futures.

For China's promise of a 'win–win' to truly work or resonate for publics dealing with possible negative New Silk Road futures, there must be, as economic geographer David Harvey suggests, a "transcendence of a duality between public and private life."[4] This duality bifurcates the individual existence into a schism in the duality Rousseau fixed as 'homme' and 'citoyen.' An 'homme,' or man, has individual needs and the 'citoyen,' or citizen, has social requirements. When these two parts of the individual person in society fails to integrate, then happiness and well-being suffer. Looked at on a larger level, of the nation-state, we see how social requirements are simplified to a singular set of top-down policies within a given region which reflect and simultaneously reinforce a communally created set of social norms. However, when the spatial fix enters the equation, and expands the equation to include bilateral and multilateral relations with over a hundred nations; the roles of 'homme' and 'citoyen' grow much more complex. When Chinese policies interact with those of Iran, for example, as political and economic bonds continue to strengthen; cultural forces will also come into a state of confluence in these 'collaborative territories.' Thus, the sensibilities cultivated within the private Iranian sphere and as well as within the public will continue to integrate Chinese values which format aesthetic tastes and consumer decisions. Hegel saw that the only way to integrate Rousseau's duality

[4] David Harvey, *Spaces of Capital. Towards a Critical Geography*, 285.

of 'homme' and 'citoyen' into a holistic individual entity was through a 'universalistic consciousness.'[5]

We suggest that it is this universalistic consciousness that Chinese President Xi Jinping is evoking in his iteration of a Community of Common Destiny (*Gongtong mingyun* 共同命运体). These notions of both Hegel's 'universalistic consciousness' and Xi's Community of Common Destiny are so highly theoretical that it proves difficult to understand how they could play out along the New Silk Roads. While most would ask how a Common Destiny can be cultivated through policy, infrastructure, trade, and Financial Integration; we assert that it is first and last through NSR's fifth pillar of People-to-People Connectivity that such a Common Destiny can begin to be visualized or mapped out. Connectivity must be established along both top-down and bottom-up grassroots trajectories. These trajectories could provide the information and feedback needed to conduct thorough feasibility studies in order to anticipate and manage risk along other pillar developments in NSR regions.

An excellent modality for these top-down and bottom-up trajectories to meet is through the development of cultural and creative industries, which often comprise public/private partnerships. Looking back at our discussion in Chapter 5 of creative industries, we recall that the UNCTAD "Classification of Creative Industries" lays out the following types of Creative Industry in the four areas of heritage, arts, media, and functional creations. Heritage includes traditional cultural expressions as well as cultural sites.[6] Arts include both visual as well as performing arts. Media ranges from audiovisual media such as film, TV, radio, and publishing platforms. Publishing overlaps with UNCTAD's last creative industry category, that of functional creations, which includes the vast domain of new media (everything from gaming to digital creative content), as well as the expansive domains of design and creative services (which means everything from architecture to tourism). It is in these realms that People-to-People Connectivities can simultaneously strengthen economies and cultural communication.

[5] Georg Wilhelm Fredrich Hegel, *The Phenomenology of Spirit*, ed. Terry Pinkard and Michael Baur, 1st ed. (Cambridge University Press, 2018), 415–21.

[6] "Creative Economy Report 2010."

Cultural Components of the 'Spatial Fix'

Let's now go back to Chapter 3, where we laid out the basic structures for the New Silk Road's fifth pillar of People-to-People Connectivity (P2P). We learned there that China has been building out its P2P through six major channels: health assistance (Health Silk Road), humanitarian assistance (aid diplomacy), academic exchange, professional exchange, cultural exchange, and creative sector development (both domestic and international). In Chapter 3 we discussed the top down and bottom-up mechanics of People-to-People Connectivity. In our earlier discussion we focused on P2P in top-down, bottom-up complementary, and bottom-up supplementary formats. The first sees culture being produced at the policy level, while the latter see culture arising organically at the popular or grassroots level. The difference, then, between complementary and supplementary organic P2P is that the former produces cultural products and messaging that is in alignment with official cultural policy, while the latter may be or may not be in alignment, as its motivational driver and chief influence is independent to some extent from top-down influence. It may be market-driven, speaking to aesthetic tastes divorced from values of goodness or truth, such as we find in 'art for art's sake,' or it may be even antagonistic to official values and cultural messaging, as we find in the contemporary Chinese art of artists such as Ai Weiwei.

Of the six primary P2P channels just mentioned, health assistance, humanitarian assistance, and academic exchange are almost exclusively top-down government directed channels in China. Whereas in the United States, non-government organizations may provide a good deal of health assistance to developing nations; China's political economic model exerts such a high degree of control over its non-government organizations that the same independence from top-down cultural policy cannot be asserted. Academic exchange in China sees a primarily public sector interacting with academic institutions of other nations which are also primarily public sector. There may be some instances where a public Chinese academic institution is conducting academic exchange with a small private college in the US, for example, but this would generally be frowned upon, as Chinese organisations prefer to have lateral relations with other institutions, and would see a private sector educational organization as a liability in terms of certification and recognition. Professional exchange, on the other hand, may see advantages to private sector interaction in developing bottom-up grassroots People-to-People Connectivity.

Cultural exchange and creative industry development, then, have great potential as bottom-up P2P channels. Both can operate equally well along the axes of complementary P2P and supplementary P2P, with public sector being aligned with the former, and private with the latter. China's top-down cultural policies express clear cultural priorities, such that there is little cultural ambiguity or diversity, unlike in other regions such as the US, where government funding is often made available for anti-authoritarian public artworks, for example. There are situations where Chinese cultural policy makers appear to 'not see' some of the artworks on display in some of their public institutions, as with many of the exhibitions in China mentioned in Chapter 5 on Chinese contemporary art in the past four decades. These are often situations where the envelope is being pushed, and much of this is a result of bottom-up grassroots cultural upheaval being spurred in some cases by international influences, as is also seen in Chapter 5 with its many mentions of cultural exchange. Much of this was subsidised by the expanding private sector, but some of it was funded by public bodies which consist, after all, of human beings who have their own ideas about how to interpret and implement public cultural policy.

We have discussed throughout this book the importance of P2P development in paving the way for NSR's other four pillars. In this chapter, in particular, we have focused on various channels and typologies of P2P. While each of these channels and typologies are important, we will focus now upon the cultural and creative industries as extremely effective in paving the New Silk Roads. We emphasize the unique cultural conditions and messaging that accompany innovation and creative production. This uniqueness can be attributed to greater private sector involvement as well as to the openness and tolerance factors closely linked with these sectors. True, there is much debate about China's uniqueness factors when it comes to studying cultural and creative industries. Richard Florida has pointed out that, "Members of the creative class are mainly attracted by 'soft' rather than 'hard' factors, especially the 'bohemian component,' an 'openness index,' a high level of amenities, and an entrepreneurial context,"[7] China's 'openness index' is influenced by its political economy which leans towards protection of local markets; and its 'bohemian component' is unique in that China is a culture of convergent thinking,

[7] Richard L Florida, *The Rise of the Creative Class: And How It's Transforming Work, Leisure, Community, and Everyday Life* (New York: Basic Books, n.d.), 19.

mimeses and measured innovation, as opposed to one which encourages divergent thinking above all, as in the West. We will orient our discussion of 'openness index' and 'bohemian components' around a discussion of how younger generations of Chinese millennials are populating China's creative classes. We will ask how millennials are influenced by and influencing not only complementary and supplementary bottom-up grassroots P2P, but also top-down government P2P.

China's Creative Millennials and the New Silk Roads

Preparing to discuss the effects of People-to-People Connectivity on possible New Silk Road futures, we focus on China's younger generations, specifically millennial creatives. They are known as ***jiulinghou*** 九零后 (born after 1990) and ***linglinghou*** 零零后 (born after 2000) generations. These creative professionals live lives of vastly improved comfort, education, and opportunities as compared to their parents and grandparents. Their participation in the creative and cultural sectors at New Silk Road cultural centers could vastly improve China's understanding of the needs of these societies, contributing to more sustainable New Silk Road futures. Many of these millennial creatives have been educated in top-tier arts management, digital marketing, human-based engineering and entrepreneurship programs within China, while others have been educated throughout the Global North, returning to China in a recent trend away from China's former 'brain-drain' problem.

China's newer generations could exert an important influence upon New Silk Road development, bringing their academic and professional training to bear upon markets, which would then integrate with policy and trade flows along the New Silk Roads. Recall that the New Silk Roads are being built not just outside of China, but just as importantly within China, originating in Xi'an (Overland Silk Road Economic Belt) and Quanzhou (21st Century Maritime Silk Road). China's domestic New Silk Roads also consist substantially in a redistribution of population, manufacturing, and logistics, with a general restructuring of the domestic economy. The inner and Western provinces are now growing to be as significant to China's economic, political, and cultural makeup as are the coastal Eastern provinces. Second-tier cities such as Chengdu and Chongqing are being upgraded to first-tier cities, serving as cultural, economic and political hubs along the New Silk Roads as China prepares to pivot Westward overland into Central and South Asia.

Chengdu, without Beijing's strong political atmosphere, and as well without Shanghai's developed commercialism, breeds a diverse cultural and fine art ecology, proving to be increasingly attractive to China's creative classes, especially as funding for cultural and arts infrastructure arrives into the region. However, if we are looking to establish which cities would prepare Chinese millennial creatives most readily for transnational employment, i.e. employment in "collaborative territories" or cultural urban centers along the New Silk Roads, then Shanghai and Beijing still top the list. With relatively early *hukou* reform (a system which traditionally confined workers to a single city in which to find employment), as well as talent schemes to attract educated migrants, Shanghai has been a leader in creating a diverse cultural and fine art ecosystem drawing from all over the country. At the same time, since the 2010 Shanghai International Expo, the city has been relatively open for Foreign Direct Investment, creating greater flows of international capital, as well as human and intellectual resources.

Young Shanghai creatives live lifestyles comparable to that of expatriates living in Shanghai, although the pinnacle of urban creative class aspiration in China is no longer so much to emulate how foreigners live, but to feel comfortable living upper-class Chinese lives. As transnationals, themselves, Chinese millennials returning from study abroad have the option to head out to urban centers in "collaborative territories" along the New Silk Roads. In his book *Young China: How the Restless Generation Will Change Their Country and the World*, Zak Dychtwald gives the example of what he calls China's "coming out party" when China hosted the 2008 Olympics.

> It was China's coming-out party as a modern nation, and it began with 2008 Chinese drummers lined up on the floor of one of the world's most impressive stadiums, engineered to look like an enormous bird's nest of steel and iron. All were dressed in identical pale yellow Chinese silk ensembles. In front of each was the same ornate iron drum. Suspended cameras panned across the rows of drummers, a sweep of hard, neat lines. In perfect unison, the drummers began to pound their complex rhythm.

> People moving in such hive-minded coordination was both beautiful and chilling.[8]

Dychtwald develops this image of total synchronicity pictured at the opening of the 2008 Beijing Olympics as an affirmation of the image of China held by publics across the world, as a "unified, homogenous, tightly choreographed glide into the future," where individuals are "blurred" into the whole population. He then goes on to assert that the "reality is different," and points to what he sees as a "fragmented" China in many overlapping phases of development which can be loosely grouped into decades of development over the past one hundred and twenty years. Arriving in 2011, he points to half of a nearly billion and a half population living in urban centers, and half of China's GDP consisting in services rather than manufacturing.

> The generation-naming system isn't perfect, but it is how China understands itself and why its generations are so different. The young people I describe here were born into a country brimming with ambition and aspiration. Now, the post-90 and post-2000 generations are part of the world's middle class, the first modern Chinese generations less preoccupied with needs and more involved with wants, in particular, "Who do we want to be?" Their generations will define what being Chinese in the modern world means.[9]

In my own experience teaching undergraduates at Sichuan University, I have observed how a growing middle-class in China has provided students not only with better learning tools, such as tablets, computers, and other note-taking tools; but overall material wealth as can be observed in their health, hygiene and wardrobe. Fashions range from exactly as they were twenty years ago, with poorer students coming in on scholarships from the countryside, to gothic and cosplay for wealthier students able to afford both imported and increasingly famous domestic clothing designer brands. Students appear well-rested and relaxed, with air conditioning

[8] *Young China: How the Restless Generation Will Change Their Country and the World* (New York: St. Martins Publishing Group, 2018), 7.

[9] *Young China: How the Restless Generation Will Change Their Country and the World*, 10–11.

in their dormitories as well as spaces provided for study, reading, and preparing foods. There was none of this just five years ago. Without the struggles of poverty and absolute conformity demanded in the classroom, students are able to embark upon questions of identity, realizing that this question of 'who do we want to be,' as Dychtwald articulates, is a primary one over which individuals now have an unprecedented amount of control.

Chinese Millennial Views of the New Silk Roads

Younger generations of the US tend to be unaware of the activities of US businesses abroad, but they are aware that there are international opportunities awaiting them, should they wish to expand their geographical horizons. With ample cultural capital and no real need to learn a second language in order to communicate and conduct business abroad, Americans grow up without a sense of limitation on their mobility, sometimes taking for granted their ability to move across international borders. Chinese youth on the other hand, grow up with the assumption that they will stay in the city they were born in, as that is where their *hukou* is issued for, allowing them legal employment and public goods in that city alone. If they manage to rise above their peers through intense competition, which usually requires private resources for tutoring and tuition, they may test into one of the city's better schools, and then into a university in a first-tier city. If the student's aptitude and private resources place them in the highest and rarest of echelons, they may then have the ability to study abroad in a first-world nation. Up to this point, only the brightest and wealthiest students show up in any one of the G7 nations, something their new peers rarely understand about their new classmates from China.

All of this is changing. Although COVID's disastrous effects have temporarily limited China's academic and professional exchange throughout NSR regions, as well as both public and private small and medium-sized enterprise development on the international level; trends have been seeing US schools eager to absorb growing numbers of Chinese students with resources. Small and medium-sized enterprise development has expanded outside of the Global North, more prominent in the Global South, in Africa, South and Southeast Asia, as well as in the Middle East. Trade with Central and Eastern Europe, as well, provide more opportunities for Chinese students and business people of all ages to participate in the international economy in unprecedented ways. Before COVID hit, the NSR 'spatial fix' was steadily changing the future for Chinese millennials, presenting them with an expansive and diverse future.

It remains to be seen moving forward, then, in what ways millennial Chinese will influence New Silk Road development. Presently, this development is being driven, conceived and implemented by older generations of Chinese policy makers, business people, and cultural engineers. As researcher and lecturer in a Chinese university, I was given the opportunity to explore this question. In teaching Chinese Culture, a core curriculum course, to large groups of undergraduate Chinese students in both 2019 and 2020, I was encouraged by my colleagues to teach Chinese culture from the perspective of an American, rather than trying to emulate the curriculum usually consisting of Chinese classics normally known as *guoxue* 国学. I decided to do both, to teach the Chinese classics and also to teach contemporary Chinese culture from a comparative cultural perspective.

Thus I incorporated into the curriculum an ongoing inquiry into the New Silk Roads. This way, I would be able to guide the students through a survey of China's political, economic and primarily cultural inroads into New Silk Road nations. While doing so I could observe their own willingness to self-reflect upon their views of other cultures, and upon the real actions and consequences of these international developments. While the United States is not a Belt and Road nation, I did include a unit on Chinese-US cultural exchange; if only as a control group, for so much of American culture's actions and influences upon China has shaped these student's views of their own culture's place in the world. Indeed, it is the overturning of China's heretofore passive role in regards to the US, which sees China in the role of active cultural agent, defining this moment in the history of US-China relations. Also discussing Chinese classics helped to focus the students on cultural heritage, helping them to avoid the disconnect that has been cultivated in contemporary Chinese culture when discussing foreign cultures. That is to say, rather than discussion of foreign cultures existing in a vacuum, as isolated cultural forces that translate immediately into a pop Chinese culture divorced from tradition; we were able to forge a connection between the old and the new in Chinese culture.

Importance of Language Services and Dissemination

We began the New Silk Road units by focusing on the issue of translation in relation to cultural production. Through lectures, readings, and group project presentations, students were brought to understand that in order for cultures to interact and relate to one another, they have to be able to do so in words, both written and spoken.[10] The issue of what Chinese texts to translate for foreign export, along with best translation practices, is of paramount importance. A great deal of Chinese funding has been wasted on miscalculations in this regard, leading to some Chinese to English translations failing to find distribution abroad, returning to be re-marketed for domestic consumption by English-language learners amongst the Chinese population.[11] This, of course, defeats the cultural aims and goals of programs and funding designed to promote Chinese cultural literacy outside of China. The dissemination of the Chinese language, as well as the propagation of language services for both Chinese and partner business people and policy makers relies on multicultural cultural sharing and education. As places open up for cultural 'newness,' many realisations about Chinese culture will be harvested. As my students researched foreign lands in this way, in a spirit of collaboration, they questioned own cultural confidence. Saudi Arabia and Djibouti were no longer just words with vague images attached to them, having nothing at all to do with their own lives. Now they were countries with regional histories, multiple dialects, and local economies which were now inextricably bound up with the Chinese economy. Languages and spaces came alive as students recognised that "places are not inert containers."[12]

One group of students gave a presentation in our course based upon comprehensive study of how language and communication effect all five

[10] 黄友义, "一带一路_和中国翻译_变革指向应用的方向," *Shanghai Journal of Translators 上海翻译* 3 (2017): 1–3.

[11] 贾文波, "一带一路_名下的汉语典籍外译_难以_合拍_的舞者," *Shanghai Journal of Translators 上海翻译* 2 (2018): 58–63.

[12] Margaret C. Rodman, "Empowering Place: Multilocality and Multivocality," *American Anthropologist, New Series* 94, no. 3 (1992): 640–56, http://www.jstor.org/stable/680566.

pillars of the Belt and Road Initiative.[13] When it came to Policy Coordination, this group of ten students came to the consensus that it was important to guard against the loss of certain languages by creating laws which controlled the dissemination of textual materials in a foreign language. An example was given of France instituting laws against the dissemination of English textual materials at a time when English was growing into the language of cultural hegemony. It is possible that the students were suggesting that the Chinese language, like French, had been under similar threat of being passed over as not only lingua franca within China, but also in the greater Asian region. Their presentation then turned to the discussion of 'language service' as an economic phenomenon, as part of the tertiary service sector, providing not just translation service, but also language training, the key being that producers and consumers need to be able to communicate in a common language. The central thrust to this discussion was the need to increase the volition and cultural power of the Chinese language by providing more language service that geared towards translating Chinese texts and other cultural products into the foreign languages of New Silk Road nations. This was to counterbalance the past trend of translating foreign cultural products such as books and movies into Chinese. These young Chinese students were excited to elaborate the need for China to shift focus from importing foreign cultural influence to exporting China's cultural influence.

Xi Jinping's Community of Common Destiny relies on language in three important ways. First is the ability of Chinese NSR policy makers, businesspeople, workers, and cultural organizations to grasp over 200 languages needed to handle the intricacies of international development. Then world-wide discourse systems, or conversations, must be reworked for China to gain international discursive power. In China, this is known as *huayuquan* 话语权, which translates as the right to speak and be heard. Lastly the work of constructing the New Silk Roads requires what Chinese scholars are calling 'language intelligence' (*yuyan zhineng* 语言智能) and 'global governance of language resources' (*yuyan ziyuan*

13 卢俊霖, "一带一路_建设背景下_语言互通_的层级_定位与规划," *Applied Linguistics* *语言文字应用*, no. 2 (May 2017).

de quanqiu gongjian gongxiang 语言资源的全球共建共享). The problems this will resolve include: language conflicts, language endangerment, linguistic imperialism, and information marginalisation.[14]

My students were very interested in this discussion, for two reasons. Firstly, they are very sensitive to the suppression of Chinese culture worldwide, and the marginalisation of Chinese information and discourses. Secondly, in an activity I opened the course with, we divided the student body of 242 students into regions, according to where in China they were born and raised. They were then asked to discuss what it was that made their own region unique within the meta-narrative of Chinese culture (*Zhonghua wenhua* 中华文化). Representatives were selected to share their findings with the rest of the class. Later, on as we moved through NSR sub-units on language, soft and geocultural power, and international relations with various NSR and non-NSR regions such as the US; there was much discussion on how Chinese culture could be disseminated world-wide, what was going too far, and how to respect indigenous languages and cultural forms while conducting cultural exchange and integrating economies as well as policies in the formation of the New Silk Roads. Sometimes these discussions grew intensely heated, with one student advocating that China had no right to interfere with other cultures, just as the US and other developed countries also had no right to do so, although they had, to the detriment of many traditional cultural forms and languages.

Lastly the group discussed the paramount importance of language in NSR development when it came to its fifth pillar, that of People-to-People Connectivity. Here the students stressed the importance of the cultural—economic connection, stating that the New Silk Roads constituted first and foremost a large-scale cultural economy which allowed Western and Eastern, or Global North and Global South to communicate with one another in the formation of a Community of Common Destiny. We see here that Xi's vision of a Common Destiny for mankind is a living reality for young millennial Chinese people. Is it possible that their reality today will be the world's reality tomorrow?

Another group chose to present on the topic of Chinese soft power in the development of the Silk Road. They chose to discuss this using Chinese martial arts as a central example. After giving a brief overview of

14 李宁明, "语言在全球治理的重要作用," 外语界, no. 188 (2018): 2–10.

the historical Silk Road with a focus on China's role in that history, they stated their central thesis that the key component of Silk Road history is the geocultural flows that fed into and grow out of its development, focusing on the flows between East and West. They also stressed the importance of flows of technical and scientific knowledge as part of the larger project of geocultural exchange. When arriving at the present, the students asserted that while the project of multiculturalism is a thread spun through both ancient Silk Road and today's Belt and Road, as stated by Xi Jinping in 2013 in Kazakhstan and Indonesia; the New Silk Roads are not, in fact, an updated version of the ancient Silk Roads. What the New Silk Roads are, rather, is a framework for a new age altogether, which borrows the ancient Silk Roads as a historical and symbolic reference point. This new age would be one where a number of smaller regional networks would be connected through regional economic cooperation. In order for the whole to be composed of these many parts, it was essential that China's 'soft power' serve as the cohesive, in order to insure the smooth implementation and sustainability of Policy Coordination, Facilities Connectivity, Unimpeded Trade, and Financial Integration. They then made the assertion that the New Silk Roads are not an economic engine alone, but a cultural one; once again consolidating the sense of a cultural economy of the New Silk Roads. Their definition of 'soft power' then turned to Joseph Nye's development of the term, involving the attractiveness of a culture, its ideology, values, cultural diplomacy, and international agility. China is challenged to develop systems and institutions that have international appeal outside of Asia. The group of students then returned to their use of Chinese martial arts (*wushu* 武术) as their central example of Chinese soft power. Tracing the etymology of the word to its constituent parts, *wu* and *shu*, they explained that the ideogram *wu* is composed of two simpler ideograms, '*zhi*' and '*ge*,' which mean, respectively, 'stop' and 'weapons.' '*Shu*' then means 'methodology.' Thus, in the students' analysis, Chinese martial arts consist in the very art of avoiding war. Citing the first textual appearances of the word in the *Book of Odes* and the *Book of Rites*, both compiled and edited by Confucius and his disciples, my students explained how the earliest forms of *wushu* consisted in a kind of martial dance, as well as in ritualistic archery. The connection between archery and ritual, then, embeds in the practice of martial arts a moral code and a normative ethics; this then serving as the conceptual kernel of what my students understood as Chinese soft power. In archery, for example, measured movements accompanied by ritualistic music encoded each movement of the archer with meaning and intention to reflect inner righteousness and outward propriety of the archer. The students then went on to clarify the notion of *wushu* to be one liberated from any notion of metaphysical or supernatural ability, distilling it down to the scientific and material realities of practiced ability and trained acumen rooted in moral development. This, no doubt, was meant to address the popular depictions of Daoist and Buddhist masters popular in Hollywood, Hong Kong and even recent Mainland Chinese martial arts movies and television shows. Such spectacular depictions failed to render the seriousness of martial art's relationship to ritual ethics. After making this point, the students then gave examples of martial arts being officially recognised and promoted as part of the Chinese 'going out' (*zou chuqu* 走出去) and Belt and Road cultural development programs. They cited a speech given in April, 2014 when Liu Yandong, Vice Premier of the State Council visited Shaolin Temple made a public proclamation that:

> In recent years, Shaolin Temple has made many contributions to Chinese culture, as the progenitor of Chan Buddhism, in the 'going out' of Chinese culture, increasing the influence of Chinese culture, and facilitating cultural diplomacy with other nations. Shaolin Temple has been very helpful in these ways.

The students then turned in their presentation, by way of making a comparison, to US and EU soft power practices. Here they presented images of the Hollywood sign, Talyor Swift, the NBA logo, as well as both 20th Century Fox and Columbia Pictures logos, along with various social media logos. US and EU soft power sought, the students maintained, to homogenize cultural differences into a 'melting pot,' consolidating a centralised power which controlled, engineered, and manufactured cultural forces and products which they then utilised cultural diplomacy to disseminate. Once again, it's important to realize that this is how younger Chinese generations view Western cultural forces, as a homogenising force which they now, finally, have the chance to protect themselves from. There is much work to be done, for younger Chinese people to grow more aware of the role their country, government, economy, and culture will be playing abroad. Right now it's a very new idea, as the Chinese national 'self' is only barely just individuating in context with the international 'other.' The biggest development at the moment is the release of this 'self' from what Slavoj Zizek terms the 'big other.'[15]

However, if Chinese people are to continue shifting focus away from the 'big other' which will not desist from bullying them; they must do so by focusing whole-heartedly on the new world they are building. They must do this by intelligently understanding New Silk Road nations not merely as a conglomerate 'other,' but as "a new international space of discontinuous historical realities." As H. Babbha explains, this new international space must be mapped, and this will be a "problem of signifying the interstitial passages and processes of cultural difference that are inscribed in the 'in-between,' in the temporal break-up that weaves the 'global text.'"[16] China must continue guiding cultural, economic, and political conversations about China's involvement in the Belt and Road Initiative by beginning with markets already open to it, such as greater Asia, Africa, and Latin America; and by opening up its cultural export to include more popular and celebrity culture, updating its traditional culture and especially classical textual tradition.[17] Again, the key will be asking China's younger generation to engage in critical thinking about the diversity of cultural forces not only within China, but importantly, in each of the New Silk Road's collaborating nations. Within China, the geocultural narrative of the ancient Silk Roads feeds into the New Silk Roads under the umbrella of a harmonious Han civilization; while emboldening many Chinese people to accept their own culture as playing an important role in the world's destiny.

Conclusion

In this chapter, we have continued building out the space created in Chapter 3; where private sector and public–private partnerships are operating on grassroots levels to foster indigenous voices and creative practices. This happens in some cases because of and in others, despite arts and cultural infrastructure put in place by top-down New Silk Road

[15] Sophie Fiennes, "The Pervert's Guide to Ideology," 2006, https://www.youtube.com/watch?v=A3d5y2j28yE.

[16] Homi K. Bhabba, *The Location of Culture* (New York: Routledge, 1994), 217.

[17] Linda Jaivin, "SOFT POWER, HARD TIMES," ed. Jane Golley, Linda Jaivin, and Paul J. Farrelly (Canberra: ANU Press, 2019), 237–42.

P2P policy. We revisit the notion of the 'spatial fix' as best conceptual framework for understanding the New Silk Roads, discussing the cultural components of this spatial fix. With an emphasis upon private-sector creative and cultural industry development as the best modality, especially when working in conjunction with public sector cultural programming, we turn our attention towards younger generations of China's population. Presentations by students on Chinese soft power as well as on language service and dissemination as parts of fifth pillar development demonstrate younger generations of China growing increasingly aware of their role as global citizens, and as future participants in global governance.

My research aims for this chapter were initially to demonstrate the role that Chinese millennials are playing in urban cultural nodes along the New Silk Roads. Through a series of interviews of millennial creatives in the city of Chengdu, I discovered that my subjects had little knowledge of the New Silk Roads, and even less knowledge of their cultural component. They had rarely if ever thought of these international trade and cultural networks as being built for them as well as for future generations. With the advent of COVID-19 in early 2020, even the millennial-run creative and cultural organizations I spoke with that were geared towards international cultural exchanges were now turned inwards, with focus turned now upon the re-shaping of imported international cultural programming. Additionally, due to COVID-19 travel restrictions, I was also unable to retrieve primary data from New Silk Road cities outside of China. Thus, I focus upon primary data I could analyse provided by my students in their own research into and presentations on China's fifth pillar development throughout the New Silk Roads.

CHAPTER 9

New Silk Road Futures

Just as the ancient Silk Roads were all about connectivity, so the New Silk Roads are about rhizomatic networks of power, capital and culture. These networks can be loosely configured around six corridors that travel over land as well as routes that travel overseas. Recall from Chapter 3 that, in its original 2013 version, the Belt and Road Initiative was divided primarily into a belt and road, as the name suggests in its Chinese Form, Yi Dai一带 (One Belt) and Yi Lu一路 (One Road). Since then, we have seen other projects bloom throughout Latin America, Arctic regions, and throughout Africa, in addition to the proliferation of Digital Silk Roads, constituting a network of extensive under-sea, below-ground, and outer-space digital infrastructure. Let us first assess how things look now, 8 years on, as compared with the original framework of the overland Belt and overseas Road.

Original proposed overland Belt routes	*Overland Belt routes now, as consensus consolidates and development shapes up*
New Eurasia Land Bridge Corridor	North Belt (China-Central Asia-Russia-Europe)
China-Mongolia-Russia Economic Corridor	Central Belt (China-Central Asia-West Asia-Persian Gulf-Mediterranean)
China-Central Asia-West Asia Economic Corridor	South Belt (China-Southeast Asia-South Asia-Pakistan-Indian Ocean)

(continued)

S. Kidd, *Culture Paves The New Silk Roads*,
Contemporary East Asian Visual Cultures, Societies and Politics,
https://doi.org/10.1007/978-981-16-8574-3_9

(continued)

Original proposed overland Belt routes	*Overland Belt routes now, as consensus consolidates and development shapes up*
China-Pakistan Economic Corridor Bangladesh-China-India-Myanmar Economic Corridor China-Indochina Peninsula Economic Corridor	

Silk Road Economic Belt, Then and Now

Original Six Corridors

The New Eurasian Land Bridge goes from Western China through Kazakhstan to Western Russia, moving onward to Belarus, Poland and Germany. The China-Mongolia-Russia Corridor originates in Northeastern China towards the far eastern regions of Russia, while the China-Central Asia-West Asia Corridor provides service from Western China to Turkey. The China-Indochina Peninsula Corridor originates in China and runs through to Singapore; and the China-Pakistan Economic Corridor sees several routes crossing from northern to southern Pakistan, gravitating towards the terminus of Pakistan's Gwadar Port, where shipments can then be sent onward to Africa and Western Asia. There are also additional corridors being planned and implemented, such as the Second Eurasian Bridge, which as of 2017 began development on an as-the-crow-flies straight shot from Xi'an, China to Moscow, Russia.

Northern & Central Belt

In the more recently consolidating geographies of the Overland Economic Belt, Kazakhstan features as a nodal key to the Northern (China-Central Asia-Russia-Europe), Central (China-Central Asia-West Asia-Persian Gulf-Mediterranean), and Southern (China-Southeast Asia-South Asia-Pakistan-Indian Ocean) routes. Kazakhstan's Nurly Zhol state infrastructure proposes between 2020 and 2025 to repair 27,000 km of local roads, repair and reconstruct 21,000 km of national roads, and electrify over a thousand km of railway tracks, raising the 2019 figure of 40%

of tracks thus far electrified an additional 7%.[1] Other projects in Kazakhstan include an oil pipeline co-owned by China National Petroleum Corporation (CNPC) and KazMunaiGas.[2] In 2007 Turkmenistan was included in the China-Kazakhstan oil pipeline project. A high-speed railway line between Astana and Almaty also orients Westward towards Western Europe via development through Western Kazakhstan which began in 2010, and Eastward towards China. The Ekibustuz Power Plant in Kazakhstan saw China and Russia combine funding for expansion in 2014. Two nuclear power plants were built in Iran in 2015. Belarus railway electrification was completed between 2013 and 2015, and a Budapest-Belgrade railway upgrade was agreed upon in 2013. High-speed railway links have also been nurtured with Turkey as of 2003, with the first section of 533 km begun in 2009, linking Istanbul with Ankara, and the Marmaray Project and Tunnel connecting railway lines between the European and Asian-oriented areas of Istanbul.

Southern Belt

The Southern Route includes the China-Pakistan Economic Corridor (CPEC), which is one of the most developed areas of the New Silk Roads. Its main objective was always to connect Kashgar in Xinjiang with the Gwadar Port in the southwest of Pakistan, connecting China with the Indian Ocean. This is true especially now that Myanmar has undergone its recent military coup, and India has pulled out of the Belt and Road Initiative, at-least in name, to develop its own center of commerce connecting overland with overseas import and export. CPEC has become an extremely important strategic political, economic, and military nodal point in New Silk Road development. Its Gwardar port became fully operational in November 2016, with Chinese goods travelling via the port northward into Central Asia and Eastward via sea to Africa.

[1] "Kazakhstan Will Electrify over 1,000 kilometres of Tracks | RailTech.Com," accessed October 19, 2021, https://www.railtech.com/infrastructure/2019/08/30/kazakhstan-will-electrify-over-1000-kilometres-of-tracks/.

[2] The CNPC is part of the State-owned Assets Supervision and Administration Commission. In May, 2021, together with the Sinopec Group (SINOPEC) and the China National Offshore Oil Corporation (CNOOC), the CNPC co-hosted the inauguration of the China Oil and Gas Methane Alliance (OGCI). The OGCI Alliance includes seven members: CNPC, SINOPEC, CNOOC, PipeChina, Beijing Gas, CR Gas, and ENN Energy. CNPC serves as first president of the alliance.

Strategic Hubs for 21st Century Maritime Silk Road Futures

Fujian

Fujian is a coastal province in eastern China seeing rapid and sizeable increase in trade volume. 2019 saw an 11% increase in its trade volume with countries and regions along the 21st Century Maritime Silk Road. China News Service reported the opening in Fujian of an additional 16 shipping routes running the trade route receiving goods from Taiwan, bringing them from a container port in Kaohsiung, Taiwan to Fujian, and then sending the goods overland to Europe via cargo trains to 30 cities in Europe and Asia. Fujian constitutes a core area of 21st-Century Maritime Silk Road construction.[3] The additional development of airports as well as expansion of fisheries and cultural tourism adds to the economic, infrastructural and cultural dimensions of this core. The Digital Silk Road is also taking rhizomatic root in this core area, as China seeks to develop stronger ties with the Association of Southeast Asian Nations (ASEAN) nations (Brunei, Cambodia, Indonesia, Laos, Malaysia, Myanmar, the Philippines, Singapore, Thailand, and Vietnam). Digital Silk Roads mainly consist in satellite data service centers, standard data products, value-added products, and satellite remote sensing application systems.

Vietnam

Leaving Fujian, sailing along the 21st Century Maritime Silk Road, then, we head towards the Strait of Malacca. A major first stop is Vietnam, which is an interesting study, as when it comes to soft or geocultural power, Vietnam has been in a period of transition since 2014, when public uproar sounded in 2014 over China deploying an oil tanker in what Vietnam perceived as their own territorial waters. These territorial disputes in the South China Seas lead to a great deal of tension between China and its ASEAN partners, such as Brunei, Malaysia, Indonesia, Philippines, and Vietnam. Western media reports the people of Vietnam as having joined forces with India, Pakistan, Myanmar,

[3] "Fujian to Speed up Building of Core Area of 21st-Century Maritime Silk Road - People's Daily Online".

Bangladesh and other South and Southeast Asian nations in public protest against Chinese-led infrastructure projects. These conflicts provide valuable insights for Vietnamese and Chinese business people, as merchants seek to link Vietnam up to the rest of the 21st Maritime Silk Roads.

For China's part, it has sought out further development of connectivity. By 2017, China had long-term leased ownership of ports in Gwadar (Pakistan, 40 years), Kyaukpyu (Myanmar, 50 years), Kuantan (Malaysia, 60 years), Obock (Djibouti, 10 years), Malacca Gateway (99 years), Hambantota (Sri Lanka, 99 years), Muara (Brunei, 60 years), and Feydhoo Finolhu (Maldives, 50 years). Ownership of these ports goes a long way in securing logistical movement along the Maritime Silk Road. Despite the problems in 2014, Vietnam is now developing industrial parks within which to incubate national brands in partnership with foreign direct investments, considerably so with Chinese investors. On the Chinese language website, China Border Economic and Trade Cooperation Zone Network (*Zhongguo jin jingmao hezuo qu wang* 中国境经贸合作区网) as recently as June 17, 2021, we see Chinese investors focusing on Longjiang Industrial Park in Qianjiang, Vietnam. This industrial park specialises in textiles, paper making, pharmaceuticals, rubber and plastic manufacturing, computing, as well as computer and other digital equipment manufacturing. Tax incentives as well as customs export tariff exemptions are offered for 15 years and 9 years, respectively, revealing that this project, if not entirely public sector, at least has government support. While the number of 36 is given for the companies who have invested thus far, the countries of origin and names of investors are not listed. The degree of Chinese investment is not made clear in this article, which has been reposted to China's official *Belt and Road Portal*; but two contact phone numbers are made available, one with a Vietnam country code and the other with a Chinese country code.[4] On June 4, 2021, Chinese Premier Li Keqiang spoke on the telephone with Vietnam's Prime Minister, the former urging the later that strengthened cooperation on Belt and Road development could help to economically strengthen the South Asia greater region, increasing the rate of economic recovery from the COVID-19 pandemic. The Chinese Premier spoke of not only the Belt and Road as vehicle for the two countries' mutual cooperation, but also a project known as the Two Corridors One Circle

[4] "越南龙江工业园 - 中国一带一路网," accessed October 19, 2021, https://www.yidaiyilu.gov.cn/xwzx/swxx/hwwg/177367.htm.

project (*Liang lang yi quan* 两廊一圈). This project strengthens the building of cross-border economic collaboration and infrastructure industrial value chains, COVID safety measures, as well as vaccination research and development. The Premier promised to provide aid in recovery from COVID, and also sought to further develop the goals of a November, 2020 Regional Comprehensive Economic Partnership (RCEP) agreement.[5] The possibility for such unlikely cooperation could be due to the fact that RCEP was initiated not by China, but by Indonesia, and according to a statement by World Bank Managing Director, Mari Elka, RCEP was created precisely in order to balance relations with the cultural, economic and political behemoths of Asia, such as China.[6] Phạm Minh Chính responded by congratulating the Chinese Communist Party on its 100th year anniversary, stating that the traditional ties of friendship between the nations deserves to be protected and further developed. In a recent article in the Diplomat discussing the competition between China and US for Vietnam's attention, a recent survey conducted by the Vietnam Barometer Survey polled members of the Vietnamese public as indicating that the majority of Vietnamese see China as the most influential power in Asia, with just under 15% of the public seeing the US as the most powerful presence in Asia. This is up for China from only 43% seeing them as the most powerful, and also up for the US, which in 2010 saw only 10% of Vietnamese people feeling the US to influence power relations in Asia more than any other nation, Asian or not. While both nations are seeing an uptick in their reach with the Vietnamese public, this gap is widening. This could be due to development in China's Belt and Road Initiative, with 50% of survey respondents indicating that economic prosperity is their number one priority.

As we can see with Fujian, there has been heavy domestic investment into the Fujian region by Belt and Road public and private partners, especially as regards Fujian's future as both a logistics hub for the Belt and the Road and a node for the Digital Silk Roads. In Vietnam, we see a region where the US has been heavily invested militarily as well as in soft power

[5] The free-trade agreement includes Australia, Brunei, Cambodia, Indonesia, Japan, Laos, Malaysia, Myanmar, New Zealand, the Philippines, Singapore, South Korea, Thailand, and Vietnam.

[6] "World Bank: Inisiator RCEP Adalah Indonesia, Bukan China," accessed October 19, 2021, https://www.cnbcindonesia.com/news/20201130110944-4-205621/world-bank-inisiator-rcep-adalah-indonesia-bukan-china.

development throughout recent history, as this is a place where China can be moved against, confining its Maritime influence. Vietnam, with the right amount of development across all BRI's pillars, could increase regional prosperity while cultivating public opinion of China's role in the region.

Myanmar

Myanmar's recent military coup and consequent political and economic instability forced Chinese workers, companies, and investors to rethink and in some cases to abandon operations in Myanmar. Recall, also, that China has a long-term lease on Kyaukpyu port in the country, an important part of the New Silk Road's connectivity in the region's waters as well as overland strategies, connecting a Special Economic Zone in Kyaukpyu to the container port. A South China Morning Post story dated April 15th, 2021 breaks the silence on this subject which permeates both Chinese and non-Chinese media spheres since the onset of the Myanmar coup, with the situation so difficult to grasp that few dare to report on anything but the most superficial information.[7] The *Opinion* section story suggests that Myanmar will remain a crucial part of Beijing's plan, especially in terms of infrastructure and energy, but that the problems which have already surfaced early on between Myanmar's people and the Initiative will continue to be a concern. These problems involve environmental, social, and political risks that come with large infrastructure and energy projects. While these suggestions make the sub-headlines of the article, promising some insight into the darkened Myanmar-China media sphere, the text then turns to very general discussion of the Belt and Road Initiative as being set back by COVID-19 in some respects (slowing down of projects, border-flow issues, downtick in tourism), but more generally underscoring the needs of ASEAN countries which are not being met by Western nations, stating that, "post-Covid-19 economic pressures and the demand for infrastructure investment will drive member states of the Association of Southeast Asian Nations to work more closely with China." The World Bank (WB) and Asia Development Bank (ADB) have

[7] "How Will Covid-19 and the Coup Affect China's Belt and Road Investments in Myanmar and Southeast Asia? | South China Morning Post," accessed October 19, 2021, https://www.scmp.com/week-asia/economics/article/3129590/how-will-covid-19-and-coup-affect-chinas-belt-and-road.

not been able to provide the infrastructure needed for developing nations to capitalize from free-trade agreements traditionally designed around their region. Without roads, bridges, airports, seaports, dry ports, digital connectivity and capital as well as labor flows, economically disadvantaged nations and regions only fall further behind. The article refers to a Brookings Institute report citing reasons for a gap in Western investment shying away from infrastructure in the region. These reasons mostly involve environmental challenges, social complexity and political instability. According to the article, domestic challenges being faced by China at the moment outweigh risks of investing not only in Myanmar, but throughout South East Asia. This is especially the case considering connectivities with other NSR regions.

These connectivities pulse along five pillars, as we have discussed, and they deploy not only in material flows, but also intangible flows throughout cultural and digital spheres. While this connectivity works as an economic strengthening agent most of the time, China's management of so many large-scale container ports are a burden on the nation's administrative responsibilities. On June 18, 2021, the South China Morning Post reported on China's largest port, the Yantian International Container Terminal, accounting for 10.5 of its foreign trade, being hard hit by a COVID-19 outbreak in China's Pearl River Delta region.[8] There had been a 300% percent increase in 'blank sailings,' when a vessel is not allowed to dock and thus skips a port, failing to unload its cargo and reload new cargo. 298 vessels in just 15 days sailed thus blankly. The damages, according to logistics giants such as Maersk, already exceed that of the Suez Canal debacle earlier in 2021 which was caused by negligence in handling strong winds, rather than to COVID, as with the Yantian port.

[8] "China Shipping: Yantian Port Delays Already Worse than Those Caused by Suez Canal Debacle in March | South China Morning Post," accessed October 19, 2021, https://www.scmp.com/economy/china-economy/article/3137920/china-shipping-yantian-port-delays-already-worse-those-caused.

Strategic Regions for Silk Road Economic Belt

Central Asia

There are issues with terrorism in this region, issues which trouble the security and sustainability of the Belt and Road Initiative. Bishkek, Kyrgyzstan saw three wounded in a suicide bomber attack at the Chinese embassy. An article in The Diplomat ties this bombing to the East Turkestan Islamic Movement (ETIM), now rebranded as the Turkestan Islamic Part (TIP), which is associated with core activities in the Syrian civil war.[9] Issues such as terrorism call upon an increased Chinese military presence in the Central Asian region, such as in Tajikistan where on the border with Afghanistan, China has been charged with building and improving dozens of border posts. While military development is not one of the five pillars of the Belt and Road Initiative, it is essential to protecting the interests and sustainability of Policy Coordination, Facilities Connectivity, Unimpeded Trade, and Financial Integration. While the hard power of military presence is a fact of geopolitical development, the soft and geocultural power of the BRI's fifth pillar of People-to-People Connectivity could be effective in developing sustainability goals for the initiative.

Recall in Chapter 7, where we listed P2P development in Islamabad, Pakistan, Kabul, Afghanistan, Ankara, Turkey, Riyadh, Saudi Arabia, Istanbul, Turkey, Damascus, Syria, Jerusalem, Astana, Kazakhstan, Bishkek, Kyrgyzstan, Dubai, and United Arab Emirates, among other urban centers along the Silk Road Economic Belt. While most books discussing Belt and Road development will focus on the hard infrastructure and trade routes of BRI, they tend to veer towards China's authoritarian need for military force in order to protect their interests. We suggest that fifth pillar development is already seen as an alternative to authoritarian and military control over BRI regions, or if not an alternative, at least a healthy supplement.

Development of People-to-People Connectivity occurs along the Health Silk Road, not just in terms of COVID-19 relief, sometimes known as face-mask and vaccine diplomacy, but also in terms of Chinese medicines and traditional healing techniques such as Acupuncture and

[9] Catherine Putz, "3 Convicted for Chinese Embassy Attack in Bishkek," accessed October 19, 2021, https://thediplomat.com/2017/06/3-convicted-for-chinese-embassy-attack-in-bishkek/.

Chinese herbology, as well as educational exchange programs bringing doctors to Central Asian and Middle Eastern countries, while also bringing students and doctors to China for training. These top-down government-designed and often government-implemented P2P programs are most visible in NSR development, but they might not be the most effective. Rather, grassroots private sector cultural and creative development may see entrepreneurs making the most sustainable and hearty inroads into these regions. Tea and coffee trade between the nations, now that China is making the transition from tea to coffee as a popular source of caffeine, also has the potential to revive ancient trade routes and cultural trajectories of exchange. Additionally, new technologies and social media apps are making great inroads for China into Central Asian and Middle Eastern regions. In 2018, of the top 20 video-sharing app downloads in the Middle East, half of them were Chinese, with Tik Tok, Bigo Live, Xiaoying, and Kuai taking up the top four spots. Tencent PUBG Mobile Star Challenge recently saw a group of young Chinese entrepreneurs hold an e-gaming festival in Riyadh, Saudi Arabia, where the government just two months earlier lifted the dress code and opened visa channels for merchants and tourists from 39 countries. These entertainment ventures will hold great attraction for Saudi Arabia, where 70% of the country is under 30 years old. The entrepreneurs helped Tencent to coordinate the large scale gaming event in a region that previously did not have the bandwidth, technology or infrastructural knowledge of how to hold such an event. The team led the local government in building a smart stadium specifically for this event and others like it in the future.[10]

Russia

The future of the New Silk Roads will undoubtedly be tied to Russia's own role in the this initiative. As balance of power shifts in the wake of Biden-US administration's willingness to partner with the EU, Britain, Japan, Australia, Canada, and the UK; Russia and China may grow closer. Russia's past in the Central Asian region, coupled with China's thickening present in this region may add up to a future where the two nations can look out for mutual interests. On the other hand, Russia is not at present a part of the official Belt and Road, although some of the projects

[10] BK 短纪录片，"中东妹子超爱PUBGM 中国电竞算不算文化输出 2020-01-03," https://www.bilibili.com/video/av81864503/.

that were commenced under the rubric of Belt and Road are being now continued under other monikers. Russia is also a wild card for China, and the disengagement between the two communist countries in the latter part of the twentieth century is testament to how volatile the relationship is. If Western powers were to be more amenable to Russia's interests, then alliances could shift. However, while policy and media trends have seen the West stiffen considerably towards China and its BRI, President Putin has spoken positively of the China-Russia cooperation after the 2019s Belt and Road Forum on International Cooperation in Beijing, and also at a BRICS Summit year in Brasilia, in November of the same year.[11] Phone call transcripts between Chinese President Xi and Russian President Putin record "mutual support in protecting sovereignty, preventing any interference in internal affairs from outside and ensuring the supremacy of international law."[12] Put succinctly:

> The Russia-China relationship is likely to remain characterised by long-term uncertainty for some time to come as their interests converge when it comes to limiting Western influence in Central Asia and Belarus but diverge where Western and Chinese interests are more closely aligned. This is the case when it comes to stability in the Western Balkans, and potentially in the South Caucasus, Ukraine, and Moldova, if the so-called Middle Corridor ever takes on greater significance for China as a potential economic corridor.[13]

Central and Eastern Europe

China's footprint in Central Asia, the South Caucasus, the Western Balkans, and Eastern Europe is making an increasingly greater impression in geopolitics and geoeconomics across all of these subregions. Is it, however, making a greater impression on geocultural dynamics?

[11] Stefan Wolff, "China's Belt and Road Initiative: Implications for the Orgnaization for Security and Co-Operation in Europe (OSCE)" (OSCE Network of Think Tanks and Academic Institutions, 2021), https://osce-network.net/fileadmin/user_upload/publications/China-BRI-Report-2021-fin.pdf.

[12] Team of the Official Website of the President of Russia, "Telephone Conversation with President of People's Republic of China Xi Jinping," President of Russia, accessed October 19, 2021, http://en.kremlin.ru/events/president/news/63621.

[13] Stefan Wolff, "OSCE Network of Think Tanks and Academic Institutions," 2021, 13.

Table 9.1 Numbers and types of China's BRI and bilateral projects in Central Asia[15]

Sectors	*Total number by sector*	*Kazakhstan*	*Kyrgyzstan*	*Tajikistan*	*Uzbekistan*	*Turkmenistan*
Total by country	261	102	46	44	43	26
Trade and industrial development	131	61	17	17	24	12
Rail and road connectivity	51	14	11	16	5	5
Energy connectivity	48	20	5	7	12	4
People-to-people projects	31	7	13	4	2	5

Greater numbers of Confucius Institutes in these regions are only the tip of the iceberg. The greater strength of China's soft power projection lies in its influence upon local and regional media, as well in cultural programming in both public and private sectors. The 17 + 1 mechanism, composed of 17 Central and Eastern European Countries along with China, is an integral part of the Belt and Road Initiative and increases trade between partner nations. In 2019, China was the top trading partner with Albania, Armenia, Belarus, Kazakhstan, the Kyrgyz Republic, Montenegro, North Macedonia, Tajikistan, Ukraine, and Uzbekistan. However, in some Central Asian countries, there is data indicating negative perceptions of Chinese foreign direct investment. This general trend of anti-Chinese sentiment amongst publics in these regions, as with all regions of the world, can be addressed by strengthening of cultural ties and fifth pillar development. People-to-People projects are still often outnumbered by developments in the other four pillars of the Belt and Road Initiative[14] (Table 9.1).

The Need for Fifth Pillar Strengthening

As of 2019, a study conducted by the Central Asia Data-Gathering and Analysis Team (CADGAT) measures the number of China's BRI and bilateral projects in Central Asia. There are 261 total projects listed throughout Kazakhstan (102), Kyrgystan (46), Tajikistan (44), Uzbekistan (43) and Turkmenistan (26). Trade and industrial developments top the list with 131 projects, comprising over half of all projects. Rail and road connectivity come next, with 51 projects, followed by 48 energy connectivity and only 31 People-to-People Connectivity projects. P2P projects constitute just over ten percent of total projects. Looking at the US dollar amounts allocated to each category, we see that over 55 billion USD have been poured into mineral and petroleum exploration and processing, while only 44 million have been spent on BRI's P2P pillar. Returns on resource exploration and processing are more quickly recoverable than are moneys spent on P2P programs, This should, however, be weighed against considerable costs incurred by negative perceptions of China's activities in the region, a trend which we propose will increase with a lack of People-to-People programming (Table 9.2).

When there are external criticisms of BRI projects, these criticisms must be dealt with by local partners as a measure of branding 'damage control.' Local partners can either ignore these issues, or they can provide counter-arguments to these criticisms. When this happens, the official assessments of BRI can continue to brand their activities as win-win and both peaceful and economic in nature. If this fails to happen, then military presence needs to be increased in order to protect BRI projects. When external criticisms cannot be ignored or countered in official assessments, and undeniable problems must be acknowledged, then the situation has to be improved. An Organization for Security and Co-operation in Europe (OSCE) report cites a 2017 Chinese Academy of Social Sciences annual

[14] Wolff, "China's Belt and Road Initiative: Implications for the Orgnaization for Security and Co-Operation in Europe (OSCE)," 20.

[15] Farkhod Aminjonov et al., "BRI in Central Asia: Overview of Chinese Projects," SSRN Scholarly Paper (Rochester, NY: Social Science Research Network, 2019), https://papers.ssrn.com/abstract=3505264.

Table 9.2 Total investment of Chinese projects in Central Asia (USD mln)

	Total by country	*Rail and road connectivity*	*Energy connect! vity*	*Industry*	*Agriculture and food*	*Mineral and petroleum exploration and processing*	*Finance and IT*	*People-to-people projects*
Total by sector	136,251.06	23,499.74	35,693.8	12,299.55	1451.88	55,159.65	8100	46.44
Kazakhstan	90,862.43	14,539.3	18,849.5	10,545.5	1049.63	37,778.5	8100	NA
Turkmenistan	24,842.5	1402.5	9410	NA	NA	1403	NA	NA
Tajikistan	10,518.7	4515.9	4516	679.8	342	465	NA	NA
Kyrgyzstan	5391.68	1773.04	2713	150.8	31.55	676.85	NA	46.44
Uzbekistan	4635.75	1269	205.3	923.45	28.7	2209.3	NA	NA

report which states that 65% of Chinese foreign direct investments make a loss in areas of socio-political instability.[16] Politics, culture, law, morality and business ethics as well as business culture are all areas in which People-to-People programs seek to facilitate conversation and communication. Without proper proportions of P2P spending, these huge losses will continue to be incurred.

Development of creative and cultural industries such as film, television, publishing, digital media and technologies can help to shape local, regional, and international narratives while increasing understanding about the project. Many reports speak of this as soft power and measure these efforts in terms of 'penetration.' These flows of geocultural power meet with other flows of such geocultural power. Meeting points of these flows can either create turbulences or confluences. When they do the latter, these confluences of geocultural power can change world-systems. Efforts by Western media to insure these meeting points remain turbulent are efforts to insure that world-systems will not change, that the axis of world power will remain in the Global North, insuring that value and supply chains as well as resources are geared towards the Global North.

In the South Caucasus and in Central and Eastern Europe, BRI has seen great investment on the part of China. These regions are of crucial importance as they help to contain Central Asia by, paradoxically, providing connectivity in and out of the region. Flows of labor, tourism, capital, and commodities into the Caucasus, Balkan region, and Central Europe provide stability and security for Central Asia, serving as core areas for the New Silk Roads, both overland and by sea, with many ports and roads leading to ports. All of this is threatened by security challenges, stability concerns, governance problems, and geopolitical competition in the region, all of which can be countered by increased People-to-People connectivity.

We argue that while Policy Coordination buttressed by increased military presence both in Central Asia and connecting regions, as well as throughout Africa and Latin America, can help to deal with these challenges, the development of top down and grassroots-based People-to-People Connectivity may be more effective. These forms of P2P serve as tools of soft power and generators of geocultural power. There is steep geopolitical competition in Central Asia from Russia, the US, and

[16] Wolff, "OSCE Network of Think Tanks and Academic Institutions," 20.

the EU, as everybody wants access to resources and supply chains in the region. China is carefully negotiating good relations with Russia and Belarus which, again, help to negotiate throughout Central Asia, while providing access to EU markets. The OSCE report focuses also on China's "increased investment in soft power tools" in the Western Balkan Bosnia, Herzegovina, Croatia, Montenegro, North Macedonia, Serbia, and Slovenia. These tools include stronger P2P exchanges, stronger penetration of media in the region to disseminate positive messaging about BRI, as well as reliance on Confucius Institutes while focusing on cultural integration in cultural centers. Such activities have resulted, it is reported, in less Sinophobia in the Western Balkans. The OSCE report mentions that while a similar disparity between elite support and public skepticism does occur; it happens in a milieu of great civil liberties and political freedom. This is in contrast to other areas we mentioned above, such as Central Asia and South Caucasus. There have been instances of popular resistance at the local level to BRI infrastructure projects for environmental reasons, as well as withdrawals from some projects which are now being taken over by European banks. In all, these are tricky regions for China to be dealing with.

Top-Down P2P Developments to Strengthen NSR Futures

NSR Futures anticipated by sustained top-down P2P would see Chinese policy makers and state-owned enterprises leading fifth pillar cultural programming and implementation. As we discussed in Chapters 3 and 7, there have been very good developments in top-down P2P, especially in the education sector with academic exchange students coming to China. This could be improved by increasing the flow of Chinese intellectual capital to New Silk Road nations. There have also been challenges brought about by lack of responsiveness and sensitivity to local publics' social and cultural needs and parameters. Confucius Institutes are an example of an extremely effective tool of soft power being quickly recognised and problematised as such on a global scale. With over half of the US Confucius institutes closing down since 2018, it will take other kinds of P2P to win over publics across the Global North. Until then, the development of Belt and Road will be a source of contention that bristles Sinophobe 'dragon-slayers', at times alarming even Sinophile 'panda-huggers.' Then, in New Silk Road nations, if publics are not 'on the same page' with Chinese infrastructure, trade, finance, and cultural exchange in their country, development will fail to be sustainable, and economic risk and loss will increase.

Looking once again at Vietnam, we can see that additional development of People-to-People Connectivity could serve to counterbalance and even adjust public reactions to Chinese actions such as occurred in 2014. Negative Vietnamese perceptions of China have been cultivated in Vietnam's educational system, where text books in Vietnam contribute to the sensitivity of Vietnamese people's to Chinese aggression and influence.[17] How these texts books came to focus on one ideological stance towards China may have something to do with US People-to-People, or soft power, development in Vietnam. We see China now making more concentrated fifth pillar efforts in Vietnam region, attempting to change impressions of China amongst young Vietnamese people. On April 17, 2021, Vietnamese youth gathered in Hanoi to celebrate both their own as well as China's folk traditions of song and dance. Experts on folk culture studies also gave lectures on the subjects. The event was held by the Hanoi Confucius Institute with students and teachers of the Vietnam National Music Conservatory as well as the Hanoi University Chinese Studies Department. The event was part of a series 'Tale of Two Rivers' celebrating the river cultures of the Lancang and Mekong Rivers. The former constitutes the upper reaches of the Mekong River, located in Qinghai and Yunnan, both Southwest provinces of China.[18]

If development continues as it is post-Covid between ASEAN nations, the Belt and Road will enjoy a prosperous future, forging stronger bonds between nations based upon economic prosperity and medical aid; with hiccups in forging cross-border policy, trade, and labor cooperation. As of 2018, the Xinhua-Baltic Shipping Centre Development Index Report indicated an overall strengthening of Asia-Europe trade.[19] With medical aid such as Covid relief and vaccine diplomacy working well in China's favor, this balances the loss of cultural tourism, which was originally meant to be the main thrust of NSR fifth pillar development. As these regions

[17] "China and the US: Who Has More Influence in Vietnam? – The Diplomat," accessed October 19, 2021, https://thediplomat.com/2021/05/china-and-the-us-who-has-more-influence-in-vietnam/.

[18] "越南-中国青年民歌文化交流活动在河内举行-新华网," accessed October 19, 2021, http://www.xinhuanet.com/2021-04/17/c_1127342543.htm.

[19] "Baltic-Exhchange-International Shipping Centre Development Index Report" (Xinhua-Baltic International Shipping Centre Development Index Report, 2018).

recover from Covid, new bonds along the Health Silk Roads will be augmented by the initial plans for cultural exchange based on a shared Silk Road heritage. These bonds may serve to be stronger, possibly, than originally anticipated. 21st Century Maritime Silk Road will continue to develop with the major ports serving as logistical hubs and centers for overland development inland towards overland corridors. The Silk Road Economic Belt, then, will find itself reworking around regions which are politically unstable, such as Myanmar, with public and private Chinese ventures continuing to probe market feasibility in that country, planting seeds, cultivating relationships until that time when the situation stabilises and seeds can be harvested, linking up then with the routes which were designed around Myanmar.

Conclusion

Given the amount of development that has already been achieved across the five pillars of the New Silk Roads, we have determined that the future of the world is one with the New Silk Roads in it. Five years ago, first world nations and the leaders that speak on behalf of them could have made moves to counteract China's bid for global governance. However, with the isolationism of the US and UK up until recently, and with the trend of Western media not taking the New Silk Roads quite seriously enough, this massive international infrastructural rerouting of world supply chains is here to stay. While the US-Biden administration is rallying to bring allies together with it in counteracting the effects of the Belt and Road, and the G7 have proposed an allegedly greener more sustainable plan of its own with the Build Back Better World (B3W) program, these efforts will have to be expedited with great care and coordination in order to make a dent in China's New Silk Roads. In the meantime, the number one dent that can be made in the New Silk Roads is the same dent China has been banging out since its Century of Humiliation ended after World War II—the dent of 'China-threat' and Asian-hate. This last chapter of our book has outlined some key nodal areas of the 21st Century Maritime Silk Road and strategic areas of the overland Silk Road Economic Belt that can be developed culturally through NSR's fifth pillar People-to-People development. Through geocultural development stemming in these nodal and strategic areas, China will be able to illuminate its aims and objectives, readjust to public feedback, and explain more clearly on its own discursive terms what it means by a Community of Common Destiny, and what role the New Silk Roads play in this destiny.

CHAPTER 10

Conclusion

Guo Pu's fourth century 'River *Fu*' mapped out *Tianxia*, or all under Heaven, tying together disparate cultural regions and embedding the northern Chinese mytho-poetic into a community of common destiny populated by previously culturally segregated northern and southern Chinese people. In a similar way, Xi Jinping's New Silk Roads are building a contemporary Community of Common Destiny, weaving the Chinese spirit and culture into a global paradigm. The Chinese Communist Party's effort to rehabilitate China from its Century of Humiliation at the hands of Western Powers has succeeded over the past century in effecting a phenomenal political and economic recovery. Having gathered enough wealth and stability domestically, Xi Jinping has triggered the next phase in making China great again. The New Silk Roads are instrumental in China taking its place once again not only as Asia's greatest economy, but also possibly as the strongest power in the world. Naturally, Western powers are resistant to this development, and are seeking ways, with its Build Back Better World plans for the Indo-Pacific. A disproportional part of these plans, however, are based largely on the need to delegitimise China's own New Silk Roads and bid for global governance. The push-back on China can be seen in Asian-hate crimes throughout the US and UK, and rising anti-China sentiment at all levels of government and policy. Thus, China will have to step up its geocultural power in order

S. Kidd, *Culture Paves The New Silk Roads*,
Contemporary East Asian Visual Cultures, Societies and Politics,
https://doi.org/10.1007/978-981-16-8574-3_10

to control the narrative well enough to maintain the wins it has gained, while also winning further support for its policy, infrastructure, trade, and financial developments throughout New Silk Road regions.

The New Silk Roads developed out of the Western Development Project and China Goes Global programs, programs which had each already been in motion for a couple of decades. In Chapter 2, we mapped out the five pillars of New Silk Road development, before going on to describe its geography along the six planned corridors of the Silk Road Economic Belt as well as the 21st Century Maritime Silk Road. We then touched upon recent expansions of the project, namely the Polar Silk Roads, the Pacific Maritime Silk Road, Digital Silk Road, and Health Silk Road. Lastly we discussed the financing of the New Silk Roads, leaving discussion to make a strong connection between China's powerlessness in global financial institutions, and the need to develop its geocultural power on the world stage.

Our next step, then, was to identify NSR's fifth pillar of People-to-People Connectivities as the single most powerful instrument of geocultural power generation available to Xi Jinping and China's ruling CCP party. After first contextualising NSR's five pillars within a much older Chinese system of thinking in fives, we then began our discussion of the problems of intercultural communication that arise from linguistic and cultural translation. The five pillars (*wu tong* 五通) are not structural pillars, but rather flowing channels of interconnections. The English translation of *wutong* into pillars is an unfortunate mistranslation, the native contextual systems type of thinking that China brings to the table of global governance. Transitioning, then, into a discussion of soft power, cultural diplomacy, and *minxin xiangtong* (People-to-People Connectivity (P2P)); we first outline an established typology of P2P before describing a more specialised P2P typology adjusted for Chinese use along the New Silk Roads. This Chinese NSR typology, then, focuses on two trajectories (top-down and bottom-up) of the original typology. What is essentially at work in the distinction between top-down and bottom-up P2P is a differentiation between public-sector and private-sector cultural programming. We conclude that the ideal P2P model is one most effectively bringing publics along the New Silk Roads closer to understanding and practising acceptance of the 'otherness' of Chinese culture, are public–private partnership P2P programs. These are ideal because they draw upon the resources of both public and private sectors, which are considerably different. While the public sector has authority and large institutions at its disposal, the private sector has greater flexibility with an ability to adjust to conditions changing quickly through time and space. Public–private partnership People-to-People programs can most effectively provide feedback loops which have the ability to change and regroup according to both market demand and public opinion. For these reasons, they have the ability to generate the most effective geocultural power.

In Chapter 4, we explored the multi-valency of politics, economics, and culture, especially in China. This complexity of cultural narrative is difficult to grasp without adopting the 'world-view' of Chinese people, which maps out China's political-economy today as 'special socialism with Chinese characteristics.' This liberalized economy opened to extensive global trade routes is anything but liberal politically. Thus, when predicting actions of China's political economy of culture today, it is hard to tell whether we should pay more attention to its economic liberalization, or to its political conservatism. Until we examine and fully analyse China's political economy from a cultural perspective, we will not be able to grasp or anticipate cultural policy along the New Silk Roads. Thus this book sets out an (albeit rough) rudimentary discussion of political economy theory, sketching cultural milieus from which these theories arose. We briefly touch upon historical roots of both Western political economy in the fifteenth through nineteenth centuries, as well as Chinese political economic theory in the Ming through late Qing periods. We then focus on the notion of the 'spatial fix,' as a political economic theory set forth by both Chinese and Western political economists. We then identify the New Silk Roads as just this spatial fix, and discuss what this means for Chinese culture and the cultures China will confront and integrate along the New Silk Roads.

Thus far we have developed an understanding of how Chinese cultural ideals have been crafted into a narrative which always suits the Chinese Communist Party. This model of shaping a narrative is the anticipated and even natural result of a political economy of culture which sees culture as an instrument of ideology, a vessel into which cultural messages are poured and then served domestically and internationally. We have also discussed how publics, especially in the Global North, struggle with this cultural messaging, due to the differing value systems embedded within them. It is possible that as China raises the attractiveness of its profile internationally in regions along the New Silk Roads by coming to the economic aid of these people, especially in other regions of the Global

South, a greater degree of openness towards Chinese cultural values may ensue. However, this kind of economic 'hard power' is expensive and will not take root without a complementary cultural 'soft power.' However, the question remains, is Chinese culture as homogenous as the CCP would have us believe? Might Chinese geocultural power be comprised of diverse confluences of cultural messaging that may even collide with and contradict one another?

Contemporary Chinese artists have pushed the margins of what is true, good, and beautiful in China's cultural narrative. By cultivating this diversity in China's cultural narrative, these artists have created a financially and culturally successful niche for China's cultural export. Much of this artwork has been created and marketed outside of China, by political dissidents and other Chinese diaspora; but this is changing. In our sixth chapter, we dove deep into the fine art museum sector in Southwest China to explore how artists and arts administrators along the cultural margins of China's national borders have spent the past few decades cultivating these diverse cultural narratives in a dearth of arts infrastructure funding. This chapter on contemporary art and the museum sector in Southwest China is the heart of this book. Here we have continued the conversation developed in Chapter 5 about China's problem of 'cultural discount,' and 'cultural trade deficit.' We have also looked within China's borders at one of its frontier New Silk Road regions to see how top-down government cultural policy in regards to NSR influences artists and arts professionals, particularly as regards the museum sector in the Southwest of China. We have also seen ways in which the public arts sector interacts with the private in the curation, exhibition, promotion, and preservation of contemporary art. In order to contextualize this discussion of Southwest China's arts ecology, we also discussed how cultural implants, such as the Cosmopolis #1.5 exhibition put on by the Centre Pompidou in collaboration with extra-regional as well as local government actors, fail to serve local arts ecologies in the long term. The export of arts funding to foreign and extra-regional actors fails to build sustainable arts and culture infrastructure within the Southwest regions. On the other hand, the notoriety of artists exhibited is promoted and organizational networks develop surrounding such a large scale exhibition do indeed build value for Southwest China art markets. Thus, local artists and arts professionals do benefit, albeit in an indirect manner. It remains to be seen how much or to what extent local actors benefit from this added value. Perhaps a hint lies within the vocational training that interns working for Cosmopolis organizers received whilst working with foreign actors in the experience of facilitating the large-scale exhibition. Perhaps some of these interns will go on to the fine arts sector of Chengdu. The 2019 Cosmopolis #1.5 Biennale contrasts with more recent developments which see the Chengdu Municipal government fully funding *Superfusion*, 2021 Chengdu International Biennale, working in conjunction with nearly a dozen other museums and galleries in the city to highlight and showcase regional as well as national and international artists.

In examining three main areas of data derived from my 2018 research residency at Luxehills Museum, we saw that the answers concerning NSR influence upon the Southwest China museum and fine art sector are not cut and dry. Experiences of NSR cultural policy vary according to the role various actors play, i.e., artists, critics, museum professionals. There has been such a dearth of arts and culture infrastructure for so long, and the museum and fine art sector is still in its nascency. Thus, it will take some time to determine the real results of this funding. One thing that we can observe, however, is that some funding is better than no funding. As it is, the avant-garde have always been under the radar, and will remain there for some time to come. We conclude that this will be much the same in regions outside of China, as NSR cultural policy creates more extensive inroads into international regions along the Belt and Road. Local arts ecologies will be mostly left alone, unsupported as they have been, while actors will compete to benefit from top-down government People-to-People cultural programming. Be they local or not, they will benefit because of their language ability, international networks, and ambition to do so. There is a danger in these areas, as there is in Chengdu and Chongqing, that history will exclude the local heroes, so to speak, as narratives of contemporary art as well as cultural heritage evolve under the umbrage of the New Silk Roads. This trend is quite normal in the histories of contemporary art throughout the world, and would not be unique to China.

After diving deep into the local arts ecology of China's Southwestern New Silk Road region, we then pull back out for a long shot of several urban cultural centers outside of China. This chapter attempts to fill a void created by overemphasis in the world media as well as in scholarship upon the first four pillars of China's New Silk Roads. We did this by tracking China's fifth pillar People-to-People development in major urban cultural centers along the New Silk Roads, including: Beijing, China, Islamabad, Pakistan, Ankara and Istanbul, Turkey, Riyadh, Saudi

Arabia, Damascus, Syria, Jerusalem, Astana, Kazakhstan, Moscow, Russia, Bishkek, Kyrgyzstan, Dubai, United Arab Emirates, Kuala Lumpur, Malaysia, Djibouti, Djibouti, and Duisburg, Germany. While this covered Central and Western Asia, as well as the Middle East quite well, this analysis only touched upon Africa and Central Europe, as well as Southeast Asia. We wanted to touch upon the most central hubs of connectivity while also including Duisburg for its importance as a linking point to Europe, and Kuala Lumpur for its centrality in the 21st Century Maritime Road. Further analysis should include Latin America and Eastern Europe as well as more thorough mapping of additional African and South Asian cultural nodes.

When looking at urban centers of the New Silk Roads, we looked at what China is contributing to their cultural vibrancy today in connection with not just cultural heritage and tourism, but other creative and cultural industries as well. China's cultural diplomacy and discourse on People-to-People Connectivity throughout New Silk Regions contribute to the country's strategy of developing cultural power, helping China to develop influence and diplomacy by strengthening diplomacy and contributing to economic diversification in regions which had otherwise limited resources to contribute to international markets. These ties based upon developing these regions' cultural vibrancy also contribute to China's image as a benevolent initiator of a new win–win global governance.[1] Information on private-sector cultivation of the creative and cultural sector has proven difficult to come by. Further analysis should include field research in New Silk Road urban cultural centers to generate primary data on bottom-up grassroots People-to-People Connectivities. This primary data would look like what we discussed in Chapter 5, on China's Southwest artistic and exhibition practices, where we discovered how NSR policy acts upon local arts ecologies.

In Chapter 8, we revisited the notion of the 'spatial fix' as an ideal conceptual framework for understanding the New Silk Roads, and discussed the cultural components of this spatial fix. With an emphasis upon private-sector creative and cultural industry development as the best modality, especially when working in conjunction with public sector cultural programming, we turn our attention towards the younger generations of China's population. This chapter relied, as with most chapters

[1] Sterling, "A New Era in Cultural Diplomacy."

in this book, upon desk research and analysis of secondary sources. However, we also worked with primary data again in this chapter, bringing forth research I have done teaching a course on the role of culture in the New Silk Roads to large groups of university undergraduates. Presentations by students on Chinese soft power as well as on language service and dissemination as parts of fifth pillar development were highlighted in this chapter.

My research aims for this chapter were initially to demonstrate the role that Chinese millennials are playing in urban cultural nodes along the New Silk Roads. I conducted a series of interviews of millennial creatives in the city of Chengdu. These interviews, as with all such primary data presented in this book, were conducted in Chinese, allowing for the greatest amount of comfort in my subject so as to encourage openness and honesty. Most of my subjects revealed little knowledge of the New Silk Roads. They had rarely if ever thought of these international trade and cultural networks as being built for them as well as for future Chinese generations. With the advent of COVID-19 in early 2020, even the millennial-run creative and cultural organizations I spoke with that were geared towards international cultural exchanges were now turned inwards, with focus turned now upon importing international cultural programs. Additionally, due to COVID-19 travel restrictions, I was also unable to retrieve primary data from New Silk Road cities outside of China. Thus, I focused upon primary data I could analyse provided by my students in their own research into and presentations on China's fifth pillar development throughout the New Silk Roads.

Our ninth chapter discussed how New Silk Road futures could be optimised. Given the amount of development that has already been achieved across the five pillars of the New Silk Roads, we have determined that the future of the world is one with the New Silk Roads in it. Five years ago, first world nations and the leaders that speak on behalf of them could have made moves to counteract China's bid for global governance. However, with the isolationism in this period on the part of the US and UK up until quite recently, and with the trend of Western media not taking the New Silk Roads quite seriously enough, this massive international infrastructural rerouting of world supply chains has crept up on the Global North. While the US-Biden administration is rallying to bring allies together to counteract the effects of the Belt and Road, and the G7 have proposed an allegedly greener more sustainable plan of its own with the Build Back Better World (B3W) program, these efforts will have to be expedited with great care and coordination in order to make a dent China's New Silk Roads.

In the meantime, the number one dent that can be made in the New Silk Roads is the same dent China has been banging out since its Century of Humiliation ended after World War II—the dent of 'China-threat' and Asian-hate. This last chapter of our book has outlined some key nodal areas of the 21st Century Maritime Silk Road and strategic areas of the overland Silk Road Economic Belt that can be developed by China culturally through NSR's fifth pillar People-to-People development in order to optimise New Silk Road futures. Through geocultural development stemming in these nodal and strategic areas, China will be able to illuminate its aims and objectives, readjust to public feedback, and explain more clearly on its own discursive terms what it means by a Community of Common Destiny, and what role the New Silk Roads play in this destiny. The question we must continue to ask is whether China will be able to engage in cultural conversations that are more than just telling other cultures about itself, but also characterized by curiosity, questioning, learning and sharing.

Works Cited

"10 Things to Know About Baku-Tbilisi-Kars Railway Project—Rail Turkey En." Accessed October 18, 2021. https://railturkey.org/2014/10/20/baku-tbilisi-kars-railway/.

"13th Korea-Central Asia Cooperation Forum Takes Place View|Press ReleasesMinistry of Foreign Affairs, Republic of Korea." Accessed October 7, 2021. https://www.mofa.go.kr/eng/brd/m_5676/view.do?seq=321408.

"2018 '一带一路　爱上北京'系列活动启动." Accessed October 18, 2021. https://baijiahao.baidu.com/s?id=1599521143584140811&wfr=spider&for=pc.

"A Century-Old Dream Finally Comes True—Chinadaily.Com.Cn." Accessed October 18, 2021. http://www.chinadaily.com.cn/global/2019-11/13/content_37522575.htm.

"A Typology of People-to-People Diplomacy | USC Center on Public Diplomacy." Accessed April 12, 2020. https://www.uscpublicdiplomacy.org/blog/typology-people-people-diplomacy.

"A Year After Xi's Landmark Speech on the Arts, Some Things Get Left Out—WSJ." Accessed October 18, 2021. https://www.wsj.com/articles/BL-CJB-27898.

"A4 Art Museum—2019年11月23日，新展「从街头到语言：2008年以来的西南行为艺术」开幕，敬请期待! The New Exhibition——「From Streets to Languages: Performance Art in Southwest Area of China Since 2008」." Accessed October 12, 2021. https://m.facebook.com/666948357073948/posts/772008049901311/#_=_.

S. Kidd, *Culture Paves The New Silk Roads*,
Contemporary East Asian Visual Cultures, Societies and Politics,
https://doi.org/10.1007/978-981-16-8574-3

"Africa's First Luban Workshop Launched in Djibouti-Belt and Road Portal." Accessed October 18, 2021. https://eng.yidaiyilu.gov.cn/qwyw/rdxw/84216.htm.

Aminjonov, Farkhod, Alina Abylkasymova, Anna Aimée, Bahtiyor Eshchanov, Daniyar Moldokanov, Indra Overland, and Roman Vakulchuk. "BRI in Central Asia: Overview of Chinese Projects." SSRN Scholarly Paper. Rochester, NY: Social Science Research Network, 2019. https://papers.ssrn.com/abstract=3505264.

"An Encouraging Movement in Afghanistan—Creative Business Network." Accessed October 18, 2021. https://cbnet.com/2018/12/14/an-encouraging-movement-in-afghanistan/.

Archive, Asia Art. "Introduction of the Annie Wong Art Foundation." Accessed October 18, 2021. https://aaa.org.hk/en/collections/search/archive/zheng-shengtian-archive-reports-admin-documents/object/introduction-of-the-annie-wong-art-foundation.

Assessment of China's Belt and Road Initiative. "Lecture: Liaqat Ali Shah, Centre of Excellence, China-Pakistan Economic Corridor." Accessed October 11, 2021. https://www.uvachinabriproject.com/event/2021/2/18/liaqat-ali-shah-centre-of-excellence-china-pakistan-economic-corridor-date-amp-time-tbd.

Austin, J.L. *How to Do Things with Words*. 2nd ed. Oxford: Clarendon Press, 1962.

"Australia, U.S., India and Japan in Talks to Establish Belt and Road Alternative: Report." *Reuters*, February 18, 2018, sec. Business News. https://www.reuters.com/article/us-china-beltandroad-quad-idUSKCN1G20WG.

Bacon, Francis. *The New Organon (Cambridge Texts in the History of Philosophy)*. Edited by Lisa Jardine and Michael Silverthorne. Cambridge: Cambridge University Press, 2000.

"Baltic-Exhchange-International Shipping Centre Development Index Report." Xinhua-Baltic International Shipping Centre Development Index Report, 2018.

Baoyun, Xiang 向宝运, ed. *Annual Report on Cultural Development of Sichuan 四川文化产业发展报告*. Beijing: Social Sciences Academic Press, n.d.

Baruah, Darshana M. "India's Answer to the Belt and Road: A Road Map for South Asia." Carnegie India. Accessed October 9, 2021. https://carnegieindia.org/2018/08/21/india-s-answer-to-belt-and-road-road-map-for-south-asia-pub-77071.

Bhabba, Homi K. *The Location of Culture*. New York: Routledge, 1994.

Burkhanov, Aziz. "The Impact of Chinese Silk Road Strategy on National Identity Issues in Central Asia: A Media Review." In *China's Belt and Road Initiative and Its Impact in Central Asia*, edited by Marlène Laruelle,

153–61. Washington, DC: Central Asia Program, The George Washington University, 2018.

"'Bizarre' Sanxingdui Ruins: A Tale of Cultural Integration." Accessed October 10, 2021. https://www.prnewswire.com/news-releases/bizarre-sanxingdui-ruins-a-tale-of-cultural-integration-301260276.html.

BK 短纪录片. "中东妹子超爱 PUBGM 中国电竞算不算文化输出 2020-01-03," n.d. https://www.bilibili.com/video/av81864503/.

"Boao Forum for Asia Annual Conference 2021 Holds Opening Ceremony—Xinhua | English.News.Cn." Accessed October 6, 2021. http://www.xinhuanet.com/english/2021-04/20/c_139893192.htm.

"BRI Brings Fresh Opportunities to Germany's Duisburg: City Official—Xinhua | English.News.Cn." Accessed October 18, 2021. http://www.xinhuanet.com/english/2019-04/25/c_138009768.htm.

"BRI-Economic-Corridors-and-Key-Operational-Investments__SIIS.Pdf." Accessed October 9, 2021. http://www.chinainvestmentresearch.org/wp-content/uploads/2018/07/BRI-Economic-Corridors-and-Key-Operational-Investments__SIIS.pdf.

"Can China Build a Community of Common Destiny?—The Diplomat." Accessed October 6, 2021. https://thediplomat.com/2013/11/can-china-build-a-community-of-common-destiny/.

"Central Asia | Fact Sheets on the European Union | European Parliament." Accessed October 13, 2021. https://www.europarl.europa.eu/factsheets/en/sheet/178/central-asia.

"China and the United States Face off in Djibouti | CNN." Accessed October 18, 2021. https://www.cnn.com/2019/05/26/africa/china-belt-road-initiative-djibouti-intl/index.html.

"China and the US: Who Has More Influence in Vietnam?—The Diplomat." Accessed October 19, 2021. https://thediplomat.com/2021/05/china-and-the-us-who-has-more-influence-in-vietnam/.

China Copyright and Media. "Xi Jinping's Talks at the Beijing Forum on Literature and Art," October 16, 2014. https://chinacopyrightandmedia.wordpress.com/2014/10/16/xi-jinpings-talks-at-the-beijing-forum-on-literature-and-art/.

"China-Germany Ties at a Glance | Nation | China Daily." Accessed October 18, 2021. https://www.chinadailyhk.com/articles/226/89/21/1567763895346.html.

"China Shipping: Yantian Port Delays Already Worse Than Those Caused by Suez Canal Debacle in March | South China Morning Post." Accessed October 19, 2021. https://www.scmp.com/economy/china-economy/article/3137920/china-shipping-yantian-port-delays-already-worse-those-caused.

"China's Traditional Cultural Values and National Identity—Carnegie-Tsinghua Center—Carnegie Endowment for International Peace." Accessed October 18, 2021. https://carnegietsinghua.org/2013/11/21/china-s-traditional-cultural-values-and-national-identity-pub-53613.

"Chinese Engagement in Djibouti's Economic Transformation in a Nutshell-Belt and Road Portal." Accessed October 18, 2021. https://eng.yidaiyilu.gov.cn/qwyw/rdxw/115204.htm.

"Chinese State TV Station Barred From U.K. Airwaves—WSJ." Accessed October 16, 2021. https://www.wsj.com/articles/chinese-state-tv-station-barred-from-u-k-airwaves-11612459277.

Confucius Institute U.S. Center. *2020 CIUS Center Annual Report*, 2021. https://www.youtube.com/watch?v=9vVIwo4oJz4.

"Craving Jobs? Revisiting Labor and Educational Migration from Uzbekistan to Japan and South Korea—Acta Via Serica | Korea Science." Accessed October 7, 2021. https://www.koreascience.or.kr/article/JAKO202005054962763.page.

"Creative Economy Report 2010," 2010, 422.

Cull, Nicholas J. "Public Diplomacy: Taxonomies and Histories." *The ANNALS of the American Academy of Political and Social Science* 616 (2008): 31–54. https://doi.org/10.1177/0002716207311952.

Dave, Bhavna. "Silk Road Economic Belt: Effects of China's Soft Power Diplomacy in Kazakhstan." In *China's Belt and Road Initiative and Its Impact in Central Asia*, edited by Marlène Laruelle, 97–108. Washington, DC: Central Asia Program, The George Washington University, 2018.

"Developing Kazakhstan's Creative Industries Will Boost Economy, Say Creative Central Asia Participants—The Astana Times." Accessed October 18, 2021. https://astanatimes.com/2018/11/developing-kazakhstans-creative-industries-will-boost-economy-say-creative-central-asia-participants/.

Dong, Chung Van, and Hoan Quang Truong. "The Determinants of Creative Goods Exports: Evidence from Vietnam." *Journal of Cultural Economics* 44, no. 2 (June 2020): 281–308. https://doi.org/10.1007/s10824-019-09359-y.

EEAS—European External Action Service—European Commission. "Fact Sheet of the EU-China Comprehensive Agreement on Investment." Text. Accessed October 13, 2021. https://eeas.europa.eu/delegations/china/91230/fact-sheet-eu-china-comprehensive-agreement-investment_en.

Emerson, John. "Yang Chu's Discovery of the Body." *Philosophy East and West* 46, no. 4 (1996): 533–66. https://www.jstor.org/stable/1399495.

Ettijahat-Independent Culture, ed. *Creative Industries in Syria: Changes and Adaptations*. Stuttgart, Germany: ibidem press, 2020.

Eurasia Group. "Digital Silk Road Expanding China Digital," 2020.

European Commission. "Education and Culture: EU and China Launch People-to-People Dialogue." Text. Accessed October 11, 2021. https://ec.europa.eu/commission/presscorner/detail/en/IP_12_381.

Fang, Tony, and Guy Olivier Faure. "Chinese Communication Characteristics: A Yin Yang Perspective." *International Journal of Intercultural Relations* 35, no. 3 (May 2011): 320–33. https://doi.org/10.1016/j.ijintrel.2010.06.005.

Fiennes, Sophie. "The Pervert's Guide to Ideology". https://www.youtube.com/watch?v=A3d5y2j28yE.

Florida, Richard L. *The Rise of the Creative Class: And How It's Transforming Work, Leisure, Community, and Everyday Life*. New York: Basic Books, n.d.

Frankopan, Peter. *The New Silk Roads: The New Asia and the Remaking of the World Order*. New York: Vintage Books, 2020.

"Fujian to Speed up Building of Core Area of 21st-Century Maritime Silk Road—People's Daily Online." Accessed October 7, 2021. http://en.people.cn/business/n3/2019/0122/c90778-9540213.html.

"Full Text: China's International Development Cooperation in the New Era." Accessed October 11, 2021. http://english.www.gov.cn/archive/whitepaper/202101/10/content_WS5ffa6bbbc6d0f72576943922.html.

"Full Text of Chinese President's Speech at Boao Forum for Asia—Xinhua | English.News.Cn." Accessed October 4, 2021. http://www.xinhuanet.com//english/2015-03/29/c_134106145.htm.

Ghiasy, Richard, and Rajeshwari Krishnamurthy. "China's Digital Silk Road." *Institute of Peach and Conflict Studies, Leiden Asia Center*, 2020, 26.

Gladston, Paul. *Contemporary Chinese Art, Aesthetic Modernity and Zhang Peili: Towards a Critical Contemporaneity*. Bloomsbury Methuen Drama, 2019. https://doi.org/10.5040/9781350042001.

Global Affairs and Strategic Studies. "A new Silk Road for the 21st Century." Accessed October 7, 2021. https://www.unav.edu/web/global-affairs/detalle/-/blogs/a-new-silk-road-for-the-21st-century.

"Hala拥抱中国一带一路迪拜文化交流展》即将拉开帷幕_丝绸之路." Accessed October 18, 2021. https://www.sohu.com/a/328676169_120176874.

Hankuk University of Foreign Studies, and Kadir Ayhan. "Branding Korea as My Friend s Country : The Case of VANK s Cyber Public Diplomats." *Korea Observer—Institute of Korean Studies* 49, no. 1 (January 19, 2018): 51–81. https://doi.org/10.29152/KOIKS.2018.49.1.51.

Harvey, David. *Spaces of Capital. Towards a Critical Geography*. New York: Routledge, 2001.

Hegel, Georg Wilhelm Fredrich. *The Phenomenology of Spirit*. Edited by Terry Pinkard and Michael Baur. 1st ed. Cambridge University Press, 2018. https://doi.org/10.1017/9781139050494.

Hesmondhalgh, David. *The Cultural Industries*. 2nd ed. Los Angeles: Sage, 2007.

Howkins, John. *The Creative Economy: How People Make Money from Ideas*. London: Penguin Books, 2001.

"How Many Confucius Institutes Are in the United States? By National Association of Scholars | NAS." Accessed October 12, 2021. https://www.nas.org/blogs/article/how_many_confucius_institutes_are_in_the_united_states.

"How Will Covid-19 and the Coup Affect China's Belt and Road Investments in Myanmar and Southeast Asia? | South China Morning Post." Accessed October 19, 2021. https://www.scmp.com/week-asia/economics/article/3129590/how-will-covid-19-and-coup-affect-chinas-belt-and-road.

Hu, Jichuang. *A Concise History of Chinese Economic Thought*. Beijing: Foreign Languages Press, 1988.

"Hu Jintao's Report at 17th Party Congress." Accessed October 18, 2021. http://www.china.org.cn/english/congress/229611.htm.

Hung, Wu, and Peggy Wang, eds. *Contemporary Chinese Art: Primary Documents (MoMA Primary Documents)*. New York: The Museum of Modern Art, 2010.

Jaivin, Linda. "Soft Power, Hard Times." edited by Jane Golley, Linda Jaivin, and Paul J. Farrelly, 237–42. Canberra: ANU Press, 2019.

Jiang, Xueqing. "Concept of Diplomacy Expands to People-to-People Connections—Business—Chinadaily.Com.Cn." Accessed October 13, 2021. https://www.chinadaily.com.cn/business/2014-04/12/content_17429278.htm.

Kaidor. *Русский: Великий Шёлковый Путь и Другие Караванные Маршруты Евразии в I Веке н.э.* October 27, 2016. Own work based on File:Transasia trade routes 1stC CE gr2.png Map: Natural Earth (public domain) and SRTM3 V2 data (public domain) edited with Mapthematics Geocart and vectorized with Inkscape. Albers equal-area conic projection. Scale 1:50,000,000 (1 cm = 500 km). Projection center = 0°N 68°E. Latitude of origin = 0°. Standard parallels: 29°30′N and 45°30′N. https://commons.wikimedia.org/wiki/File:Silk_Road_in_the_I_century_AD_-_ru.svg.

Kashmeri, Sarwar A. *China's Grand Strategy: Weaving a New Silk Road to Global Primacy*. Santa Barbara: Praeger, 2019.

"Kazakhstan Will Electrify over 1,000 Kilometres of Tracks | RailTech.Com." Accessed October 19, 2021. https://www.railtech.com/infrastructure/2019/08/30/kazakhstan-will-electrify-over-1000-kilometres-of-tracks/.

Keane, Michael. *Creative Industries in China: Art, Design, and Media*. Cambridge: Polity Press, n.d.

———. "Creative Industries in China: Four Perspectives on Social Transformation." *International Journal of Cultural Policy* 15, no. 4 (November 1, 2009): 431–43.

Kidd, Sophia. "Conceptual Archaeology: Performance Art in Southwest China." *Yishu Journal of Contemporary Chinese Art* 10, no. 3 (June 2011).

———. "Poetically Performance Art Dwells: Poetry and Praxis in Southwest China." *Yishu Journal of Contemporary Chinese Art* 12, no. 2 (April 2013): 130–37.

———. "Realism in China's Contemporary Moment: Chen Anjian's Transport Teahouse Oil Painting Series." *Yishu Journal of Contemporary Chinese Art* 17, no. 6 (n.d.): 52–67.

———. "To Be or Not to Be a Biennale: On Art Ecologies, a Review of Centre Pompidou's Chengdu Cosmopolis #1.5: Enlarged Intelligence." *Yishu Journal of Contemporary Chinese Art* 18, no. 4 (2019): 45–56.

Kim, Hwajung. "Bridging the Theoretical Gap Between Public Diplomacy and Cultural Diplomacy." *The Korean Journal of International Studies* 15, no. 2 (August 31, 2017): 293–326. https://doi.org/10.14731/kjis.2017.08.15.2.293.

Kuah, Khun Eng. "China's Soft Power: Culturalisation Along the Belt Road Corridors." In *Silk Road to Belt Road: Reinventing the Past and Shaping the Future*, edited by Md. Nazrul Islam, 121–45. Singapore: Springer, 2019. https://doi.org/10.1007/978-981-13-2998-2_8.

"Kunming Meet Revives BCIM Link Plan—The Economic Times." Accessed October 7, 2021. https://economictimes.indiatimes.com/news/politics-and-nation/kunming-meet-revives-bcim-link-plan/articleshow/69921135.cms.

"Kyrgyzstan Starts Developing Concept of Creative Economy." Accessed October 18, 2021. http://en.kabar.kg/news/kyrgyzstan-starts-developing-concept-of-creative-economy/.

Lai, Hongyi, and Yiyi Lu. "Introduction: The Soft Power Concept and a Rising China." In *China's Soft Power and International Relations*, edited by Lai, Hongyi and Yiyi Lu. London and New York: Routledge, 2012.

Langenkamp, Harm. "Contested Imaginaries of Collective Harmony: The Poetics and Politics of 'Silk Road' Nostalgia in China and the West." In *China and the West: Music, Representation, and Reception*, edited by YangHon-Lun and Michael Saffle. University of Michigan Press, 2017. https://doi.org/10.2307/j.ctt1qv5n9n.

Latour, Bruno. *Reassembling the Social: An Introduction to Actor-Network-Theory*. Oxford: Oxford University Press, 2005. https://www.amazon.com/Reassembling-Social-Introduction-Actor-Network-Theory-Management/dp/0199256055.

"Liang Hong x Daan Heerma van Voss: Complex Relations: People and Peoples, Past and Present—Literary Festival." Accessed October 13, 2021. http://eu-china.literaryfestival.eu/liang-hong-x-daan-heerma-van-voss-complex-relations-people-and-peoples-past-and-present/.

Li, Mingjiang. "Soft Power in Chinese Discourse: Popularity and Prospect." In *Soft Power: China's Emerging Strategy in International Politics*, edited by Mingjiang Li, 21–44. Lanham: Lexington Books, 2009.

Liu, Hong, Kong Yam Tan, and Guanie Lim, eds. *The Political Economy of Regionalism, Trade, and Infrastructure: Southeast Asia and the Belt and Road Initiative in a New Era*. World Scientific Publishing Company, 2021.

Lommes. *English: China in Red, the Members of the Asian Infrastructure Investment Bank in Orange. The Proposed Corridors (*https://www.merics.org/en/merics-analysis/infographicchina-mapping/china-mapping/ *and* http://www.cbbc.org/cbbc/media/cbbc_media/one-belt-one-road-main-body.pdf*) in Black (Land Silk Road), and Blue (Maritime Silk Road).Português : Mapa Com a China Em Vermelho, Membros Do Banco Asiático de Investimento Em Infraestrutura Em Laranja, as Rotas Físicas Em Preto e Azul.Русский : Транспортные Коридоры Проекта "Один Пояс - Один Путь"*. May 14, 2017. Own work. https://commons.wikimedia.org/wiki/File:One-belt-one-road.svg.

"Long Steps towards Sagacity—Avicenna University." Accessed October 18, 2021. https://avicenna.edu.af/reports/long-steps-towards-sagacity/.

Lu Peng. *The Story of Art in China: From Late Qing through Today 美术的故事: 从晚晴到今天*. Guangxi: Guangxi Teachers Normal University Press, 215AD.

"Meeting Between Chairman of China and Djibouti Cultural Exchange Association and CEO of SICAS." Accessed October 18, 2021. https://www.sicas.cn/Students/Info/Content_131101145359263.shtml.

Miller, Tom. *China's Asian Dream: Empire Building along the New Silk Road*. London: Zed Books, 2017.

Mirra, Federica. *Art Theory in Xi Jinping's Policy: M.A. Thesis*. Leiden University, 2016.

Nalbantoglu, Cem. "One Belt One Road Initiative: New Route on China's Change of Course to Growth." *Open Journal of Social Sciences* 5, no. 1 (January 6, 2017): 87–99. http://www.scirp.org/Journal/Paperabs.aspx?paperid=73442.

Negri, Antonio, and Michael Hardt. "Value and Affect." *Boundary 2* 26, no. 2 (1999): 77–88.

"New Freight Train Route Links Yantai, Duisburg—Xinhua | English.News.Cn." Accessed October 18, 2021. http://www.xinhuanet.com/english/europe/2019-07/27/c_138262912.htm.

"New Move to Promote BRI Cooperation in Romania-Belt and Road Portal." Accessed October 11, 2021. https://eng.yidaiyilu.gov.cn/qwyw/rdxw/104467.htm.

Nicolas Zufferey, Phillipe. "Traces of the Silk Road in Han-Dynasty Iconography: Questions and Hypotheses." In *The Journey of Maps and Images on the Silk Road*, edited by Philippe Foret and Andreas Kaplony. Leiden: Brill, 2008.

Nye Jr., Joseph S. *Bound to Lead the Changing Nature of American Power By*. New York: Basic Books, 1990.

———. *Soft Power: The Means to Success in World Politics*. 1st ed. New York: Public Affairs, 2004.

———. "Think Again: Power—Foreign Policy." Accessed October 12, 2021. https://foreignpolicy.com/2009/11/03/think-again-power/.

Olimat, M.S. *China and Central Asia in the Post-Soviet Era: A Bilateral Approach*. Lanham: Lexington Books, 2015.

Oltermann, Philip. "Germany's 'China City': How Duisburg Became Xi Jinping's Gateway to Europe." *The Guardian*, August 1, 2018, sec. Cities. https://www.theguardian.com/cities/2018/aug/01/germanys-china-city-duisburg-became-xi-jinping-gateway-europe.

Öniş, Ziya, and Mustafa Kutlay. "The New Age of Hybridity and Clash of Norms: China, BRICS, and Challenges of Global Governance in a Postliberal International Order." *Alternatives* 45, no. 3 (August 1, 2020): 123–42. https://doi.org/10.1177/0304375420921086.

Owennson. *English: This Is the Map of the Countries Which Signed the Belt and Road Initiative Cooperation Documents中文: 這是簽署一帶一路相關合作文件國家的地圖*. April 27, 2019. Own work. https://commons.wikimedia.org/wiki/File:Belt_and_Road_Initiative_participant_map.svg.

Phillipe Foret, and Andreas Kaplony. "Conclusion." In *The Journey of Maps and Images on the Silk Road*. Leiden: Brill, 2008.

———. "Introduction." In *The Journey of Maps and Images on the Silk Road*. Leiden: Brill, 2008.

"PM Modi Offered Xi Indo-Pacific Connect in Response to BRI Offer—The Economic Times." Accessed October 9, 2021. https://economictimes.indiatimes.com/news/politics-and-nation/pm-modi-offered-xi-indo-pacific-connect-in-response-to-bri-offer/articleshow/71608439.cms.

Pomeranz, Kenneth. *The Great Divergence: China, Europe, and the Making of the Modern World Economy*. The Princeton Economic History of the Western World. Princeton, N.J: Princeton University Press, 2000.

Putz, Catherine. "3 Convicted for Chinese Embassy Attack in Bishkek." Accessed October 19, 2021. https://thediplomat.com/2017/06/3-convicted-for-chinese-embassy-attack-in-bishkek/.

"Rebuilding Afghanistan's Creative Industries | British Council." Accessed October 18, 2021. https://www.britishcouncil.org/voices-magazine/rebuilding-afghanistans-creative-industries.

"Republic of Turkey Ministry of Culture and Tourism." Accessed October 18, 2021. https://www.ktb.gov.tr/?_Dil=2.

Rodman, Margaret C. "Empowering Place: Multilocality and Multivocality." *American Anthropologist, New Series* 94, no. 3 (1992): 640–56. http://www.jstor.org/stable/680566.

Sadovskaya, Yelena, and Leah Utyasheva. "'Human Silk Road': The People-to-People Aspect of the Belt and Road Initiative." In *China's Belt and Road*

Initiative and Its Impact in Central Asia, edited by Marlène Laruelle, 109–25, 2018.
"Silk Road Fund's 1st Investment Makes China's Words into Practice—Business—Chinadaily.Com.Cn." Accessed October 10, 2021. http://www.chinadaily.com.cn/business/2015-04/21/content_20497821.htm.
"Snapshot." Accessed October 9, 2021. https://merics.org/en/short-analysis/chinas-health-silk-road-adapting-bri-pandemic-era-world.
Sterling, Dahlia Patricia. "A New Era in Cultural Diplomacy: Promoting the Image of China's 'Belt and Road' Initiative in Asia." *Open Journal of Social Sciences* 6, no. 2: 102–16. Accessed September 29, 2021. https://doi.org/10.4236/jss.2018.62010.
Strauss, Leo. *Thoughts on Machiavelli*. Glencoe, Illinois: The Free Press, 1958.
Sum, Ngai-Ling, and Bob Jessop. *Towards a Cultural Political Economy*. Edward Elgar Publishing, 2013. http://www.elgaronline.com/view/9781845420369.xml.
"'Super Fusion-2021 Chengdu Biennale' Will Be Unveiled Soon—INEWS." Accessed October 12, 2021. https://inf.news/en/culture/b1e6153915eeb098fb710349d9c186de.html.
"Talks at the Yenan Forum on Literature and Art." Accessed October 18, 2021. https://www.marxists.org/reference/archive/mao/selected-works/volume-3/mswv3_08.htm.
Team of the Official Website of the President of Russia. "Telephone Conversation with President of People's Republic of China Xi Jinping." President of Russia. Accessed October 19, 2021. http://en.kremlin.ru/events/president/news/63621.
"The Bookworm (Bookstore)." In *Wikipedia*, May 16, 2021. https://en.wikipedia.org/w/index.php?title=The_Bookworm_(bookstore)&oldid=1023424147.
"Their Irony, Humor (and Art) Can Save China—The New York Times." Accessed October 18, 2021. https://www.nytimes.com/1993/12/19/magazine/their-irony-humor-and-art-can-save-china.html.
"Turkuvaz Media Group." Accessed October 18, 2021. https://www.tslproducts.com/tech-insight-hub-resources/case-studies/studios-networks/turkuvaz-media-group/.
United Nations High Commissioner for Refugees. "Refworld | World Directory of Minorities and Indigenous Peoples—United Kingdom : Chinese." Refworld. Accessed October 16, 2021. https://www.refworld.org/docid/49749c907.html.
"University Consortium of Maritime Silk Road Launched in Xiamen-Belt and Road Portal." Accessed October 12, 2021. https://eng.yidaiyilu.gov.cn/qwyw/rdxw/69333.htm.

"US, India to Revive 'New Silk Road' Seen as Counter to China's Belt and Road Project." Accessed October 7, 2021. https://www.ndtv.com/india-news/us-india-to-revive-new-silk-road-to-counter-chinas-belt-and-road-obor-project-1697632.

Waller, J. Michael. *Strategic Influence: Public Diplomacy, Counterpropaganda, and Political Warfare*. Revised ed. Washington, DC: Institute of World Politics Press, 2009.

Wang, Shichen. "China's People-to-People Diplomacy and Its Importance to China-EU Relations: A Historical Institutionalism Perspective" 4, no. 1 (2016): 19.

Watson, Matthew. "The Historical Roots of Theoretical Traditions in Global Politial Economy." In *Global Political Economy*, edited by John Ravenhill, 26–51. Oxford: Oxford University Press, 2017.

Winter, Tim. *Geocultural Power: China's Quest to Revive the Silk Roads for the Twenty-First Century*. Chicago: University of Chicago Press, 2019. https://doi.org/10.7208/chicago/9780226658490.001.0001.

Wolff, Stefan. "China's Belt and Road Initiative: Implications for the Organization for Security and Co-Operation in Europe (OSCE)." OSCE Network of Think Tanks and Academic Institutions, 2021. https://osce-network.net/fileadmin/user_upload/publications/China-BRI-Report-2021-fin.pdf.

———. "OSCE Network of Think Tanks and Academic Institutions," 2021., 72.

"World Bank: Initiator RCEP Adalah Indonesia, Bukan China." Accessed October 19, 2021. https://www.cnbcindonesia.com/news/20201130110944-4-205621/world-bank-inisiator-rcep-adalah-indonesia-bukan-china.

World Shipping Council. "Top 50 Ports." Accessed October 7, 2021. https://www.worldshipping.org/top-50-ports.

Xiao, Tong. *Wen Xuan: Or Selections of Refined Literature*. Translated by David Knechtges. Princeton Library of Asian Translations. Princeton University Press. Taipei: SMC Publ, 1990.

Xu, Jay. "Presentation of Chinese Contemporary Art in the United States." Presented at the "Aliens" Exhibition Panel Discussion, Stanford University, 2019.

Yan, Xianlei. "Appendix: Chronology of Main Sichuan Cultural Production Events." In *Annual Report on Cultural Development of Sichuan 四川文化产业发展报告*, edited by Xiang Baoyun 向宝运. Beijing: Social Sciences Academic Press, 2019.

Ye, Min. *The Belt Road and Beyond State-Mobilized Globalization in China 1998–2018*. Cambridge: Cambridge University Press, 2020.

Dychtwald, Zak. *Young China: How the Restless Generation Will Change Their Country and the World*. New York: St. Martins Publishing Group, 2018.

Zhang, Denghua. "The Concept of 'Community of Common Destiny' in China's Diplomacy: Meaning, Motives and Implications: Concept of Community of

Common Destiny." *Asia & the Pacific Policy Studies* 5, no. 2 (May 2018): 196–207. https://doi.org/10.1002/app5.231.

Zhang, Yi, and Zigang Zhang. "Guanxi and Organizational Dynamics in China: A Link between Individual and Organizational Levels." *Journal of Business Ethics* 67, no. 4 (October 5, 2006): 375–92. https://doi.org/10.1007/s10551-006-9031-7.

Zhengzhen, Zheng. "Regional Reports." In *Annual Report on Cultural Development of Sichuan 四川文化产业发展报告*, edited by Xiang Baoyun 向宝运. Beijing: Social Sciences Academic Press, 2019.

Zhou Bin. Unpublished in-Person Interview with Zhou Bin, October 8, 2019.

"一带一路与叙战后重建对接是两国互联互通的历史机遇." Accessed October 18, 2021. https://baijiahao.baidu.com/s?id=1665118337825277886&wfr=spider&for=pc.

"'一带一路'中国茶文化展览会在莫斯科开幕." Accessed October 18, 2021. https://baijiahao.baidu.com/s?id=1650976723992552448&wfr=spider&for=pc.

"一带一路（大型系列旅游节目）_百度百科." Accessed October 18, 2021. https://baike.baidu.com/item/%E4%B8%80%E5%B8%A6%E4%B8%80%E8%B7%AF/19926646.

"'一带一路'对接'2030愿景' 中沙务实合作掀起新高潮 - 产业要闻 - 中国卫星导航定位协会." Accessed October 18, 2021. http://www.glac.org.cn/index.php?m=content&c=index&a=show&catid=2&id=5188.

"'一带一路'对接'中间走廊' 中欧班列'长安号'抵达安卡拉." Accessed October 18, 2021. https://baijiahao.baidu.com/s?id=1649507481830992968&wfr=spider&for=pc.

"'一带一路·文武中国世界行'太极文化交流活动在莫斯科举行." Accessed October 18, 2021. https://baijiahao.baidu.com/s?id=1632146610224479112&wfr=spider&for=pc.

"'一带一路——笔墨意象中国画名家海外巡展'将在莫斯科中国文化中心举办_交流." Accessed October 18, 2021. https://www.sohu.com/a/260357289_99909345.

"'一带一路'音乐会奏响莫斯科：'一带一路'为文化艺术互联互通创造便利条件_新闻频道_央视网(Cctv.Com)." Accessed October 18, 2021. http://news.cctv.com/2017/05/14/ARTIwxyZiKNIZVz0MvrDFI0l170514.shtml.

"东方网." Accessed October 18, 2021. http://www.eastday.com/.

"中亚第一家中文书店在比什凯克开业_新闻中心_北京尚斯国际文化交流有限责任公司." Accessed October 18, 2021. http://www.bjss010.com/index.php?m=&c=chuban&a=show&id=39.

"中以创新合作联委会联合工作组第一次会议在以色列召开." Accessed October 18, 2021. http://il.china-embassy.org/chn/gdxw/t1307219.htm.

"《中国与阿富汗'一带一路'故事》纪录片在喀布尔举行开播仪式-新华网." Accessed October 18, 2021. http://www.xinhuanet.com/politics/2017-12/06/c_1122069338.htm.
"中国共产党领导是中国特色社会主义最本质的特征-新华网." Accessed October 18, 2021. http://www.xinhuanet.com/2020-07/15/c_1126241149.htm.
"中国国际文化交流中心." Accessed October 18, 2021. https://www.cicec.org.cn/.
"中国特色社会主义: 概念演变与内涵升华--理论--人民网." Accessed October 18, 2021. http://theory.people.com.cn/n/2013/0116/c49157-20216946.html.
"以色列国家旅游部2019中国路演在京拉开帷幕_游客." Accessed October 18, 2021. https://www.sohu.com/a/315478628_169814.
"伊斯坦布尔迎来'魅力上海' 促进中土文化交流-中国侨网." Accessed October 18, 2021. http://www.chinaqw.com/zhwh/2015/06-16/53496.shtml.
"最新 | 中巴经济走廊项目将向阿富汗延伸." Accessed October 18, 2021. https://baijiahao.baidu.com/s?id=1644192708996270587&wfr=spider&for=pc.
"北中医的'一带一路'_北京中医药大学新闻网." Accessed October 18, 2021. https://xww.bucm.edu.cn/ztbd/27243.htm.
"北京东城区举办'一带一路 非遗风情'展示活动---中国文明网." Accessed October 18, 2021. http://www.wenming.cn/syjj/dfcz/bj/201606/t20160613_3436753.shtml.
"北京大学'一带一路'书院." Accessed October 18, 2021. http://www.bri.pku.edu.cn/.
卢俊霖. "一带一路_建设背景下_语言互通_的层级_定位与规划." *Applied Linguistics语言文字应用*, no. 2 (May 2017).
"叙利亚'丝绸之路市场'在阿勒颇开始运营." Accessed October 18, 2021. https://world.huanqiu.com/article/9CaKrnK1PDe.
"吉尔吉斯斯坦: '感知中国'系列活动促进中吉交流." Accessed October 18, 2021. https://baijiahao.baidu.com/s?id=1636130970220672132&wfr=spider&for=pc.
"吉隆坡中国文化中心: 用文化温暖后疫情时代 - 文化交流 - 中国—马来西亚钦州产业园区管理委员会网站 - Zmqzcyyq.Gxzf.Gov.Cn." Accessed October 18, 2021. http://zmqzcyyq.gxzf.gov.cn/zmhz/whjl/t6074452.shtml.
"哈萨克斯坦2017中国电影展举办--新闻--中国作家网." Accessed October 18, 2021. http://www.chinawriter.com.cn/n1/2017/0612/c403992-29334081.html.
"土耳其 | 丝绸之路项目." Accessed October 18, 2021. https://zh.unesco.org/silkroad/countries-alongside-silk-road-routes/tuerqi.
"土耳其总统祝贺'一带一路'示范性工程安卡拉光产业园全线贯通_新浪科技_新浪网." Accessed October 18, 2021. https://tech.sina.com.cn/roll/2020-08-21/doc-iivhuipn9920297.shtml.

"'天涯共此时'文化交流专场演出在巴基斯坦举行-新华网." Accessed October 18, 2021. http://www.xinhuanet.com/world/2018-09/27/c_1123491439.htm.
"巴基斯坦中国文化中心'落户'国家艺术委员会-中国侨网." Accessed October 18, 2021. http://www.chinaqw.com/zhwh/2016/05-04/87366.shtml.
"庆祝中巴建交67周年音乐会在白沙瓦举行." Accessed October 18, 2021. https://baijiahao.baidu.com/s?id=1600370777580681750&wfr=spider&for=pc.
"张家界和以色列携手旅游合作--旅游--人民网." Accessed October 18, 2021. http://travel.people.com.cn/n1/2017/0728/c41570-29433736.html.
"'感知中国·美美与共'中国·阿联酋青少年文化交流周在京举办." Accessed October 18, 2021. https://baijiahao.baidu.com/s?id=1653127376223814907&wfr=spider&for=pc.
李宁明. "语言在全球治理的重要作用." 外语界, no. 188 (2018): 2–10.
"沙特塞林港考古为海丝研究提供珍贵实物资料--文化--人民网." Accessed October 18, 2021. http://culture.people.com.cn/n1/2019/1224/c1013-31520692.html.
"'牵手2014——中巴两国艺术交流展'在伊斯兰堡开幕-国际频道-新华网." Accessed October 18, 2021. http://www.xinhuanet.com/world/2014-05/14/c_126500666.htm.
"'盛世大唐 相约千年'文艺演出在巴基斯坦举办." Accessed October 18, 2021. https://www.mct.gov.cn/whzx/qgwhxxlb/sx_7740/201804/t20180424_831891.htm.
"福建'中以'示范农场建成自动化农业样板-中新网." Accessed October 18, 2021. http://www.chinanews.com/tp/2013/11-26/5549972.shtml.
"第二届迪拜中国电影周开幕-新华网." Accessed October 18, 2021. http://www.xinhuanet.com/world/2019-09/30/c_1125060294.htm.
"腾讯内容开放平台." Accessed October 18, 2021. https://page.om.qq.com/page/Ol2Zp_CXCwim-8I_zI_M0_KQ0.
贾文波. "一带一路_名下的汉语典籍外译_难以_合拍_的舞者." *Shanghai Journal of Translators 上海翻译* 2 (2018): 58–63.
"越南-中国青年民歌文化交流活动在河内举行-新华网." Accessed October 19, 2021. http://www.xinhuanet.com/2021-04/17/c_1127342543.htm.
"越南龙江工业园 - 中国一带一路网." Accessed October 19, 2021. https://www.yidaiyilu.gov.cn/xwzx/swxx/hwwg/177367.htm.
车向前 Che Xiangqian, and 郭继荣 Guo Jirong. "跨文化外推视阈下的_一带一路_民心相通提升路径_车向前 Multi-Cultural Extrapolation and the Path to Strengthening Minxin Xiangton in One Belt One Road." *Journal of Xi'an Jiaotong University (Social Sciences)* 37, no. 142 (Summer 2017): 45–53.
"远方的家（中央电视台中文国际频道大型日播旅游栏目）_百度百科." Accessed October 18, 2021. https://baike.baidu.com/item/%E8%BF%9C%E6%96%B9%E7%9A%84%E5%AE%B6/10434512.

"[远方的家]亲历'一带一路' 探访伊斯兰堡新航线_CCTV节目官网-CCTV-4_央视网 (Cctv.Com)." Accessed October 18, 2021. http://tv.cctv.com/2017/10/20/VIDESaAHTCJRn4y0loNTJIiH171020.shtml.

"迪拜世博会将成'一带一路'大舞台." Accessed October 18, 2021. https://baijiahao.baidu.com/s?id=1643524010210098937&wfr=spider&for=pc.

"迪拜'拥抱中国Hala China'计划启动 众信旅游集团成首批战略合作企业." Accessed October 18, 2021. https://www.sohu.com/a/241889250_100071.

"'阿拉伯之路——沙特出土文物'展览在我馆开幕." Accessed October 18, 2021. http://www.chnmuseum.cn/zx/gbxw/201612/t20161221_1861.shtml.

"[陕西新闻联播]秦腔动漫《三滴血》巴基斯坦播出 '大秦之腔'唱响文明交流互鉴_新闻频道_央视网(Cctv.Com)." Accessed October 18, 2021. http://news.cctv.com/2019/05/18/VIDE5IHBC4bJEI9ixkeeuDN3190518.shtml.

国王公共图书馆北京大学分馆. "首页." Accessed October 18, 2021. http://kapl.pku.edu.cn/zh-hans/node.

"马来西亚成立首个'一带一路'中心-新华网." Accessed October 18, 2021. http://www.xinhuanet.com/world/2016-12/12/c_1120103761.htm.

黄友义. "一带一路_和中国翻译_变革指向应用的方向." *Shanghai Journal of Translators 上海翻译* 3 (2017): 1–3.

Index

S. Kidd, *Culture Paves The New Silk Roads*,
Contemporary East Asian Visual Cultures, Societies and Politics,
https://doi.org/10.1007/978-981-16-8574-3

D

U

V

The manufacturer's authorised representative in the EU is Springer Nature Customer Service Centre GmbH, Europaplatz 3, 69115 Heidelberg, Germany. If you have any concerns regarding our products, please contact ProductSafety@springernature.com

Printed and bound by CPI Group (UK) Ltd, Croydon, CR0 4YY

01/10/2026

02226249-0003